BLACK
PRIVILEGE
PUBLISHING

ATRIA

I LIVED TO TELL THE STORY

A MEMOIR OF LOVE, LEGACY, AND RESILIENCE

TAMIKA D. MALLORY

BLACK PRIVILEGE
PUBLISHING

ATRIA
NEW YORK   AMSTERDAM/ANTWERP   LONDON
TORONTO   SYDNEY/MELBOURNE   NEW DELHI

ATRIA

An Imprint of Simon & Schuster, LLC
1230 Avenue of the Americas
New York, NY 10020

Copyright © 2025 by Tamika Mallory

First Black Privilege Publishing/Atria Books hardcover edition February 2025

BLACK PRIVILEGE PUBLISHING / ATRIA BOOKS and colophon are trademarks of Simon & Schuster, LLC

For information about special discounts for bulk purchases, please contact Simon & Schuster Special Sales at 1-866-506-1949 or business@simonandschuster.com.

The Simon & Schuster Speakers Bureau can bring authors to your live event. For more information or to book an event, contact the Simon & Schuster Speakers Bureau at 1-866-248-3049 or visit our website at www.simonspeakers.com.

Interior design by Kyoko Watanabe

Manufactured in the United States of America

1 3 5 7 9 10 8 6 4 2

Library of Congress Cataloging-in-Publication Data has been applied for.

ISBN 978-1-9821-7349-4
ISBN 978-1-9821-7351-7 (ebook)

CONTENTS

*My dearest Blair Hunter, Grandma loves you so much.
I wrote this book as a gift to you. May these pages serve as your
cheat sheet for life, making your days easier. May the wisdom I
share give you strength, confidence, motivation, and inspiration.
Always remember, you are never alone. My love will be with you
every step of the way.*

CHAPTER 1

WHAT'S GOING ON

My childhood room was a melting pot of dolls, games, and trinkets all perfectly matched to my personality, with the exception of the walls, painted pink by my dad. Everything bursting with color and wonder. I collected Cabbage Patch Kids, some white, and of course every one of the Black dolls I could find, in every hue. My Little Pony dolls, random Barbies I rarely thought to play with, stuffed animals oversized and miniature perched atop a pink toy box like a gigantic strawberry ready to be picked. The stars of the show, regal in their own right, were a collection of African dolls standing high atop a shelving unit. Everything else paled in their presence. Deep hues of melanin draped in kente cloth. I wanted to look like them—to become them. Even though my room wasn't what some would have considered to be fit for a princess, it was just right for me.

And for every "girlie" element in the room, I had what back then would be considered tomboyish: Super Mario Brothers in the Nintendo, Sonic on the Sega Genesis, and Pac-Man for when I needed a break from the dolls. Soft and hard. Truth be told, my room was a perfect fit for a little New Yorker.

A little New Yorker with her fist clenched and raised in the air, pumping it back and forth, and forth and back, playacting like the real people I looked up to every day. The living embodiment of the kente-clad dolls on the shelves in the room.

"Power to the people! Power to the people! Power to the people," I'd yell with thunder in my voice just before hopping down and cutting my path across the thick blue-carpeted floors. I knew from an early age that I had no desire to be a princess exactly—maybe a warrior princess like Nefertiti or the other African warriors and queens who were closer to my imagination. But at the time those were just dolls. I had demands, as I

1

repeated the phrase over and over and over again, inspired by the rallies I'd joined with my parents, where we were surrounded by the force of powerful people who seemed big and strong and equipped with voices to be heard. My white socks with ruffled trim were slippery enough on the bottom for me to roam around the apartment as if I were wearing roller skates. And I glided around every corner to every door to every room, bouncing, wiggling, and shaking, doing everything in my power to solicit a reaction from everyone else in the apartment with me.

"Close my door, Tamika."

Sharon, my sister fifteen years my senior, has always been Black girl magic in the flesh. She now has four degrees. She had a job, which meant she had her own money and a dream social life. Her friends were the shit, and she had no time for mine. "I'm trying to get ready for work," she said, sucking her teeth to make sure I knew she was done.

Sharon's friends had the best hairstyles. From buns to the asymmetrical cuts, doobies, and fans. Not only did they look good; they lived well. At night, they painted New York with their presence at the hottest lounges and clubs to just kick it. And when they were not in New York, they spread their magic around the world, traveling abroad, something that was unheard of at the time for people their age. Sharon was a Harlem socialite coming up in a time when Harlem was the place to be, oozing with iconic music, fashion, and reverence for Blackness. Sharon got where she was by not taking easy paths out or accepting disrespect, no matter where it came from. And she wasn't any easier on me than she'd be on anyone else who didn't give her the respect she deserved. She never caused any problems, but she was tough and made sure you knew it. And I made sure she knew to carve out space for my little voice as well. "Power to the people!" I screamed again, pumping my fist back and forth in her face.

I left out grinning, knowing I had gotten under her skin. That day, I made sure I was both seen and heard in our apartment. As I was the smallest and youngest, there were times I felt invisible growing up. More than anything, I wanted to make my presence known. Years later as an adult, I'd research what characteristics and traits the family's youngest typically have: rebellion, creativity, outgoingness, and openness. They were all true. And in the early years of my life, rebellion was what I channeled most.

"Power to the people," I began to repeat once more until my mom's voice stopped me dead in my tracks. Booming and resonant. In our house and certainly with her friends, Mom's voice was the closest thing to God's. She spoke words laced with conviction that left you with no choice other than to stop and listen.

"Tamika, get in here," she said.

I eased Sharon's door closed, and made my way to the kitchen, tip-toeing as I drew closer to where I knew Mom would be standing. Peering only my head around the narrow half wall separating the kitchen from the living room, I waited in suspense.

"You know I can see you, right?"

I swear that woman must have had eyes behind her head. I'm reminded of that time I turned around and shot double birds at a boy named Malcolm Simmons in church one Sunday—she knew. Malcolm was the most awkward, most aggravating boy I had ever met in my entire life. He had big eyes and a little face that I never quite understood, with unkempt hair and an always open hand to ask for whatever snacks my mom had given me for church that morning. There were no assigned seats at church, but Malcolm's mom was determined to sit in the same place every Sunday, putting her son right behind us.

"Tamika, it's ok to share," my mom would say. "Not with him," I said under my breath.

I knew better than to mention it out loud. The first Sunday I met Malcolm and his family I was thrown by his voice. Coming from that little head with those big eyes, his annoying tone was odd to say the least. That Sunday I rolled my eyes and paid him dust. The next week, Malcolm returned with a vengeance.

Anytime our pastor went into his rendition of "I'd Rather Have Jesus," it brought all the women in the church to their feet. My mom swayed and sang next to me, in unison with the pastor and other members of the congregation. It was a beautiful moment of unity and clarity. And like clockwork, Malcolm's voice buzzed in my left ear, hands out again, asking for what he already knew he wasn't going to get. I broke form and jolted my head around like an owl for the meanest death stare a twelve-year-old Tamika could muster.

"Turn around, Tamika."

Even though she had eyes in the back of her head, for me at least, she didn't notice when raggedy-ass Malcolm yanked my ponytails as revenge a few minutes later. I was pissed off, but there was only so much I could do about it without getting in trouble. I knew I should contain myself, but the rage burning up through me and now rushing out like smoke pouring forth from a wildfire was too much. I turned around and shot two birds like daggers, one from each hand. I kept them up, making sure my eyes connected with his. I wanted him to know it was time to leave me alone for good.

The other moms and families in the church who sat behind us started to murmur, taking notice of my message, but that was of no personal concern to me. Before I knew it, I felt a tingling sensation at the top of my knee as Mom popped me to get my attention.

"Tamika, have you lost your damn mind in this church???"

Maybe I had.

Two Sundays later, while at service, I noticed a group of boys crowded around Malcolm in the basement of the sanctuary. At first, it wasn't too alarming because that's where they spent most Sundays. All the boys gathered together to talk smack about girls between debates over which cartoons they liked most, and who had the toughest Transformer. Prior to that day, there were times I heard them pick on Malcolm here and there, but I never thought much about it between all the other commotion they'd get into every weekend. But this Sunday was different.

I heard one of the boys, Lonnie, tell the others, "Watch this," as he pushed Malcolm to the floor and raised his fist to strike him. It shocked me that everyone was ready to stand by and watch, and laugh, as one little boy hurt another. I stepped in.

"Stop it, Lonnie!" I said, as I grabbed his arm. "Leave him alone."

Malcolm was curled up on the floor, scrambling to cover his head with his hands as he began to cry. Lonnie turned towards me, snatching his arm away from my hands.

"And if I don't, what are you going to do about it, Tamika?"

"If you don't leave him alone, I'll knock your ass out."

The wave of "ooooooooh" from all the other kids must have been enough for Lonnie to stand down. He stepped over Malcolm and walked back towards the stairs mumbling something under his breath. The other kids watching dispersed and followed Lonnie while I stayed to help Malcolm up. Malcolm didn't say anything, nor did I. There was no need for words. That time had passed, but from that day onward, we shared a mutual understanding.

Malcolm stopped whispering in my ear to ask for snacks. And he didn't need to, because I always made sure I packed two bags of Teddy Grahams. One for him and one for me.

Malcolm and I never became the best of friends, but he knew that I was not going to let anything happen to him and I knew to expect the same in return.

———

"I heard what you did for Malcolm today," my mom told me that evening. "That's what I'm talking about. Be kind. You never know what others are going through. His mom told me that Malcolm's dad passed recently, just before they joined our church. They moved from Queens to get a fresh start."

Those words stuck with me ever since. At the time I had no idea what it was like to lose someone so close. But I was glad I stood up for Malcolm. It felt good. It felt right. Mom was always watching, always planting seeds of self-awareness within me.

Now, standing outside of the kitchen in our apartment, after yelling "Power to the people" all over the house, I was caught, just like I was that day in church.

"Girl, get in here."

I let out a deep belly laugh as I entered, removing Mom's hands from her hips and placing them around me. When I squeezed, she squeezed back. That was our way of saying "I love you" without anyone else knowing. And my way of bringing down the temperature on whatever was about to come next.

"Tamika Danielle Mallory," she said. She only called me by my full name when I was in trouble. But it was a little different this time. The look on her face was one of curiosity, not anger.

"Yes, Tamika! Power to the people is right! But why are you always running through this house!?"

Dad's record player went on in the background, the soundtrack of my young life that still plays within me. Although I didn't always know the name of the artist or song he'd put on, I recognized this melody—a flute over top of a smooth voice, strong and soulful and righteous. Gil

Scott-Heron's "The Revolution Will Not Be Televised" was poetry in motion and in frequent rotation in our apartment.

Still holding me in her arms, Mom peered out at my dad, who was sitting on the couch in the living room, shaking her head. Waiting for him to back her up, she came up short. Mom always looked for Dad to validate her when she chastised us, and rarely got what she wanted, until I got older, and bolder, with my transgressions.

Instead, he laughed, looked at my mom, and replied, "Huh?" "Huh" came out less as a word than as a sound. Ejected as if he were unaware of what was happening (my dad was always fully aware), playing pretend as a way to avoid conflict. This kind of "Huh" was code for "keep me out of it."

Mom was outnumbered. Everyone in that apartment knew I could do no wrong in my dad's eyes. As she accepted her defeat, Mom's mouth curled up into a smile.

"Go sit down somewhere and read a book."

If I'd had a dollar for every time she told me to go read a book, I would have been rich. She and my father were working to create a powerful family dynamic, but I'd be lying if I didn't tell you it felt more like a prison to me at times. A place no one wanted to escape more than I did. It wasn't even about wanting to leave them; I just wanted things to be different.

"Ma," I said in response, hoping for a different outcome this time. Denied. She gave me the look that every Black mother mastered that confirms you're fighting a losing battle.

"Well then, Mika"—my family liked to call me Mika most times unless I was in trouble—"if you think you're so smart, how come you never remember to put those loose teeth under your pillow at night?"

I remember outlining the new space where the tooth was now missing with my tongue. It seemed like I never had a full mouth of teeth until I was at least twelve years old.

Mom was always one step ahead of everyone else. Rolling my eyes and releasing myself from her grasp, I ran back to my room as fast as I could to check under my pillow for the tooth fairy's gift I must have known wouldn't be there.

"Try again tonight, Mika," Mom called from across the apartment.

"Try again." A small but significant gesture that typified young life for me. Mom and Dad wanted a fighter who held faith in possibility, and they got one. I felt like I could do anything. I was strong, courageous, and maybe even a bit delusional. Life had no limitations. I had no limitations. Still too young to understand the meaning of the phrase "Power to the people," but old enough to recognize there was power in those words when I took them on. That there was inspiration in ideas spoken forcefully and with passion. In my home, doing so was a way of life, woven into my existence. The payoff for bravery was drilled into my head in Manhattanville. The rewards afforded to those willing to make a ruckus when the cause was right and just. It's the place where I became a fighter.

———

Years later I woke up in Los Angeles, that childhood dream put me back into the world with a smile on my face. I don't often remember dreams, but today I did. It's 3:00 a.m., and I'm wide-awake while the rest of the world slumbers. Standing between the massive ivory silk drapes, with my toes touching the baseboards of the wall and my forehead pressed into the floor-to-ceiling window, I'm absorbing the full sweep of downtown Los Angeles before me. So much of my world each day is focused on death, and twinkling lights remind me there is life in the city. The buzzing phone on the nightstand is proof. It never stops. Every day, around the clock, my phone is filled with cries for help. By-products of the unjust world we live in. Families in need of money after their lives have been turned upside down after the death of a loved one, videos of police brutality, and advocates enraged and ready to take action. There is a war going on, and from the moment I answer a first ring each day I am on the battlefield. This morning, I need to catch my breath before the war starts again, and I talk with God. I always feel that besides me, he's the only one keeping office hours at this time of the morning.

Inhale, exhale. Pray. And then it happens. It's time to pick up the phone. Melanie Campbell, president and CEO of the National Coalition of Black Civic Participation, convener of the Black Women's Roundtable and a friend and mentor, was on the other end.

"Tamika."

She called my name, but the silence behind her was evident.

She told me that a very close friend of ours had just lost her son.

My heart plummeted.

LaTosha Brown and I had spent countless hours bonding over raising our Black sons in America. Many times, we prayed over our sons together. As young mothers, we grew up with our sons. And I was about to become a grandmother, an experience she'd already had. To learn of LaTosha's son's death left an empty space in the center of my soul. Frantically pacing the floor, I considered leaving Los Angeles to be with her right at that moment. We both made a commitment to be in LA, for an important court hearing, but as she picked up the pieces of her broken heart, I knew the Black Voters Matter co-founder would want me to handle the business.

For over an hour I stood in front of that window, fighting back tears, thinking about whether or not I could leave, but I knew that was impossible. I knew I couldn't afford to break today, before my plans to go to court to support Megan Thee Stallion at the Tory Lanez trial. But I felt like I was on the verge of losing my mind.

As I mustered up the courage to dial my friend directly, my soul was snatched when she actually picked up.

"Hello?"

"Hi, it's Tamika."

LaTosha repeated my name back to me out loud.

Upon her hearing it was me, the screams let out.

"My baby my baby. He's gone. My baby is dead!"

There was nothing I could offer her worthy of the moment. Her son was gone and the reality of the limits of our control and power to protect even our own was jarring. All I could do was listen as she attempted to center herself and catch her breath.

All I could do was hang up, drop down to my knees, and pray for my son, pray for my friend and my child.

Over the years, I've learned to give thanks to God even amidst the gravest moments of life. The older I get, the more often I have these kinds of mornings, when I need to sit with God and seek his wise counsel through the spirit before beginning my day. In his presence, I am allowed to be myself. Communion with God is the only place where I'm not required to problem solve, to have all the answers, or to even ask the right questions. Instead of pouring from an emptied pitcher, in God my soul is filled.

Traumatic days are best punctuated with simple words. On this one I whisper to God, "Thank you."

Thankful for too many reasons to name. Thankful for health and strength. Thankful to be of service. Thankful for family and friends who I know love me and me them. Thankful for my son and the granddaughter who would soon touch my heart in ways I never knew possible. Thankful just to be alive. Three years ago, I found myself standing before glass in contemplation of a different kind. It was a mirror, surrounded not by curtains but walls white like chalk. Sterile. No fancy comforter on the bed, or fluffy pillows to calm my head. No carpeted floors to soothe my feet. Instead, just hard wood and white tiles that shot frigid cold back up and through my body. The reflection in the mirror wasn't one that reminded me of my power, but instead weakness. Shame. Helplessness, and hopelessness. A Tamika I couldn't recognize at all. An addict on the verge of death.

I made the decision to embark upon a mission to discover peace from the inside out. I'm not proud of my addiction, but it is now a part of my truth, one that I will never be ashamed to speak about ever again. My addiction saved my life. The first time Will Smith spoke out after the infamous Oscars slap, he said words that I could not have articulated better myself:

"Disappointing people is my central trauma. I hate when I let people down."

In retrospect, my addiction was a spiraling journey into the valley on a quest for peaceful rest. From that day forward, I vowed to retrace every inch of my life for a deeper understanding of who I was and what I would become.

Malcolm X once said, "The most disrespected person in America is the Black woman. The most unprotected person in America is the Black woman. The most neglected person in America is the Black woman." I learned to let those words fully come into my life and extract the power I'd earned in my struggle—a woman's struggle. A Black woman's struggle.

I'd felt it all: fear, anger, shame, confusion, uncertainty, isolation, self-doubt, and depression. I suffered a whole host of physical ailments too: insomnia, fatigue, nausea, hypertension, impulsive behavior, and ultimately silence. The disrespect of my day-to-day fight—not just those fought in public—had left me unprotected until I self-silenced for protection. With distance I realized I'd turned to silence because every bit of history I knew had encouraged silence. As a Black woman in America, it is at times hard to remember your voice matters. As I was a Black woman in America who fought for justice, society strived to make me forget. Throughout my life I've watched scores of Black women be unprotected, disrespected, and silenced. I've fought for them and stood beside them because we are one and the same.

But on this day, my only mission in Los Angeles was to show up in court for another Black woman unprotected, silenced, and disrespected. Nevertheless, it was clear to me that no one was coming to save her, but I was damn sure going to support her.

A court of law has never been a place to take for granted. I've been so many times, for so many cases I've lost count. When inside I listen for details spoken and those left unsaid. I watch faces and read lips. I take note of body language and most importantly, I allow my intuition to guide my thoughts. More times than not I'm right about that which goes unsaid in these proceedings. Had I not become a freedom fighter, maybe a career in law would have been in the stars for me.

"All rise. We'll hear from our next witness now," the judge said, peering over the rims of his gold-framed glasses, holding the gavel as if he anticipated potential disorder in the court. There wasn't any.

As she approached the stand, statuesque in a purple suit, her makeup flawlessly framed by a perfectly coiffed jet-black bob, the witness walked fearlessly on her black stilettos. But once she was seated at the witness stand, her face and demeanor told a different story. In a previous time, before the incident she was appearing in court for this day, I sat across from her at dinner, admiring the joy in her eyes and her undeniable youth. That fire had been extinguished by the circumstances of her victimization. It broke my heart that not many showed up for her. Not even people who believed her story of assault in full. Too many were worried that if they stood with her and the case did not go in her favor, their brands would suffer the political consequences of alignment.

For me, the scenario was eerily familiar.

Watching her, I realized there was not much of a difference between us. Although she was a lot younger, the world saw her no differently than it saw me. That day I recognized that even if she walked back out of the courtroom doors, she was not free, nor am I.

All I could think about was how the system intended to silence her by holding her to an unreasonable standard in her personal life. There is not one who walks among us who has not held unsure feelings or even regrets about something in their private life. I am no exception. We have all fallen short at one point or another. There are some lows that I've reached, some friends I hurt, and some realities I wish I could change. This woman was no different. A young legend in the making, fighting to save her credibility. And as I sat in the courtroom battling the emotions of my friend from the loss of her son, in silence, I felt chills as I remembered the moments when I had sat in a seat much like the one I saw this woman seated. Although not in the courtroom, I understood the trial of public persecution. And I was torn up to see and know that the partner who hurt her never gave the impression he was even the least bit remorseful for what he did on the awful night when Megan was shot. I was reminded of those moments when I was left to fight alone. To bear the brunt of the disrespect with no help in sight.

On that day I resolved to be there for her the way I've always wanted someone to be there for me. While it is important for me to recognize that there have always been people in my corner who loved and supported me, the truth is that Black women in this country often feel isolated when we are faced with misogynistic attacks. And since she is not free, I am not free. I was born fighting for freedom and I will die fighting . . . until freedom.

CHAPTER 2

REDEMPTION SONG

The first choice is to do nothing. That is the easy way. The second choice costs everything. It is the choice to adopt agency. To force the response. To take action and do something. For Black people in this country, that something has always come in the form of a fight. Fights for freedom. Fights for rights. Fights for equality and safety from harm.

As a collective, we have remained steadfast in the act of sustaining under the harshest circumstances. We have joined forces and aligned with brothers and sisters who did not look or, at times, believe as we did to fight for the good of humanity. Goodness is who we are. Community building is a directive embedded in our DNA.

Amidst the decade-long Great Depression from 1929 to 1939, half of the country's African-American citizens were unemployed. Compounded with discrimination and false hope ignited by then President Franklin D. Roosevelt's aggressive push to popularize his New Deal economic policies, Black people got sent to the back of the line again. Roosevelt was said to be receptive to the African-American perspective, but there were still steps he would not take. Outside organizations like the NAACP were not brought to the table. The onset of WWII in 1939 called attention to the inequities faced by Black soldiers who would be gravely needed to fight the war. It wasn't until labor leader A. Philip Randolph made threats to organize a march on Washington in response to discrimination in the military that President Roosevelt issued Executive Order 8802 to combat discrimination based on race, creed, color, or national origin against any US citizen.

Around the same time Black Americans were winning their first fights in Washington, my grandmother was giving birth to my mother in Franklin, Alabama. By the time my mom was five years old, the whole family moved to Monroeville, Alabama. As the youngest of fourteen siblings, she was a quick study on survival. She went to school while most of her siblings worked. When she wasn't in school, she was on my grandmother's heels as she cleaned the homes of various white families. As the story goes, my grandmother lived part-time in some of the homes she cleaned. On the occasions when my mother wasn't with my grandmother, she was in the care of my oldest aunt, Ola Mae, who was one of those responsible for raising all of the children. When Mom turned seventeen, she was pregnant with her first child. My brother Milton Barnett. Racial tensions, Jim Crow laws, violence, discrimination, and oppression in the South were too taxing to bear. Black people in search of equality and those hoping to create better opportunities for their families relocated to the northern regions of the United States. Ola Mae led the charge by relocating to New York. After Milton was well established in school around ten, Mom made the decision to follow Aunt Ola up north. Milton would stay in Alabama with the rest of the family while Aunt Ola raised him from a distance.

There are some women who can't survive without a man and others who are fully capable of conquering life on their own but happy to create a legacy with one. Mom was the latter. Witty and quiet, yet intentional in words and deeds. She was the personification of strength and beauty. She didn't say much, but her children were always clean and well-kept. She took life seriously. Her arrival in New York was an opportunity to start a better life. Shortly after, that life was expanded to include a future with my dad.

They tell me it was love at first sight. He picked her out of a crowd from across a New York City street. Boldly, he walked across and asked her for her number. After a brief courtship, they vowed for better or worse. Together, they were on a conscious mission to establish a legacy and a blended family that also included my sister Sharon, and my sister Dana, and my brother Wayne. He would succumb to leukemia around nine years old, and after my parents' loss my birth happened on June 8, 1980, as proof of their will to fight again. As the story goes, Mom labored with me for almost a full day at St. Luke's–Roosevelt Hospital in Harlem and when I did arrive I came out screaming something awful.

Manhattanville Houses was home to thousands of families in West Harlem. We were situated between the hopes and dreams of Broadway and the harsh realities of Amsterdam Avenue. It was a public housing project managed by the New York City Housing Authority. Although my parents almost never let me play in the parks adjacent to Manhattanville unaccompanied or even hang around with the other kids without their supervision, the community was an integral part of who we were. From neighbors borrowing a cup of sugar from one another to extended congregations and conversations outside the building and music blasting from speakers to kids drawing graffiti on the backs of buildings with cans of spray paint and girls playing hopscotch and double Dutch in the park, Manhattanville was filled with the essence of culture. We were bonded like anyone else who lived and loved and grew and strived together. The community center on the first floor of my twenty-story building was the home to talent shows, Christmas giveaways, youth parties, and basketball tournaments. Back then, it felt like the best place on earth. Cackling laughter, random dance contests, and hallway rap battles became the soundtrack to the era.

Behind the smiles, people hid the pain of desperation that accompanies a lack of resources, as so many did. Don't get me wrong, there were many families who did ok for themselves, but the reality is we were all in the projects. The projects had once been seen as a way up and out, a place for middle-class families to get ahead with the help of the government. But over time, as conditions changed, poverty and drugs took their toll. By the time I was in elementary school, crack monopolized almost every community around me. People either used or sold, but my family kept the shield up for us. For the most part we stayed out of trouble with the exception of a cousin whom I called my brother, Derrick. He was my main protector, popular, family oriented, and very loving. But he would spend many of his years imprisoned. Like many young Black boys growing up in Harlem, he succumbed to the streets. And regardless of what Derrick has been to me, the system saw him differently. To the system he was a number. To us, he was loving, and family focused. Like many, Derrick was a product of his immediate environment.

The front and back doors to our building were always broken, and the glass windows were always shattered. The rank smell of crack and heroin could not be ignored. The vision of sons selling crack to their friends' mothers isn't one that's easily forgotten. Rainbow-hued glass fragments in the buildings and out on the streets made sure we all were aware of the monsters all around us. In spite of it all, the fight of the people never wavered. Our housing project wasn't as bad as some others, but as I visited friends in places like Grant or St. Nicholas, I knew the situation was atrocious in the projects. It was unsafe to even be in those buildings alone, but we survived. Today, Derrick is still family focused. He is our protector and jokester. In addition to all these attributes, he is an entrepreneur and an overcomer. Derrick is proof that it is not how you start, but how you finish.

This was life in New York City. We lived in the projects and knew the knife's edge of addiction and the criminal justice system, but my family didn't feel poor. The landscape of New York is peculiar in that a public housing project may be next to or even intermingled with apartments inhabited by people making six figures a year. Immersion in the culture and the establishment of the New York community was priceless.

My folks were movements by themselves but became a force together. They were strategic about how they pooled their financial resources to provide for us. Truth be told, I never felt poor a day in my life. We were what you might call hood rich. My parents were selective about how they spent money. Oftentimes, I mistook their moderation in wardrobe spending for being corny. But I knew we were not poor because there were differences in our lives in comparison to the lives of many of my same-aged peers. We never wanted for the things we needed in life, but I knew others who never left Manhattanville for anything other than to go to the welfare office, school, or church outings with Ms. Charlene.

Everybody knew that if you wanted to get out by going to church, Ms. Charlene was the answer. She was a foster mother who believed in giving kids an opportunity to experience hope. She was a statuesque, churchgoing, Bible-toting woman who never had a smile on her face. She was mean as fuck. Even though Ms. Charlene always wore dresses to show everyone that she was saved and sanctified, even though she was heavily involved in her church, she would curse you out if she felt the need. She held her tongue for no one. On many occasions, I watched Ms. Charlene talk crazy to the neighbor's adult children because she suspected they were involved with illegal drugs. Ms. Charlene believed the unvarnished word of God (and a few words God might not be so fond of) was the only way to get through to the kids around Manhattanville. A necessary beacon of hope for a better tomorrow. Ms. Charlene and the church filled the place I'd learn other neighborhoods' kids might fill with extracurricular activities. Instead, in Manhattanville, the kids seeking out trouble had plenty of idle time in which to do it. They were block kids. They spent most of their time unsupervised.

But the upside was that they had to be creative to survive. They became street-smart. Some knew how to catch a meal at somebody else's house. Others figured out how to make a few bucks here and there on their own. Growing up, I envied their freedom. No matter what might be happening beneath the surface, outside looked like a good time from where I sat.

For the Mallorys, our defense against the ills of the projects was the bond of family. Their tactic was to keep us in the house and out of the streets. Together, we formed a wall of protection for ourselves. My mother, Voncile, commanded her purpose early in life. Family, food, and fellowship were the pillars of our existence. We moved in one accord because of her. And she relentlessly ensured we had all of what we needed and some of what we wanted. By her standards, needs were defined as a consistent roof over our heads, a clean domain to roam, and enough food to nourish our bodies.

Our days were structured and proof of her keen organizational skills. She kept a running list on the refrigerator of things that needed to be done and a daily agenda in her head. From the moment we woke up to the time she served breakfast to her arrival at work. Mom honed her organizational skills by doing clerical work at the Taxi and Limousine Commission. The agency was responsible for overseeing the government entity that licenses and regulates the medallion taxi and for-hire vehicle industries. Today it includes companies like Uber and Lyft.

In the evenings, Mom cooked, plated, and served my dad his dinner when he walked through the door from work. And on most nights, she tried to get us to eat all together, but my picky tastes didn't always let that plan happen. The consistency of our days was like clockwork. She had them all mapped out. And as I look back as a mother myself now, I admire the effort at normalcy under very abnormal circumstances. We learned a lot of hard things too early. Why we couldn't stay outside too long after dark, what the world had in store for us when we got outside our protective bubbles at home and in New York, and even dirtier things like the smell of trouble and dangers of the yellowed broken glass on our streets.

I remember some evenings running towards Mom, offering to help unpack on the occasions she came home from the local department store, great big bags from Conway's (kinda like Target) when she brought the world outside back home for us to see up close. Very occasionally I'd go along with her, but she knew I would want to bring the whole store back home with us. Mom was the spender, and she always had a plan for how she was going to manage our money. I remember one time after hearing the word "layaway" one place or another getting a crash course in the perils of debt and generational consequences of unchecked spending: "We don't do that, little girl."

Her clapbacks were undefeated back then and still are to this day. She challenged me to think before speaking.

But she also gave softer lessons. Ones only she could share. The first time I saw Mom put on makeup, I must have been about seven years old. On Thursday evenings after work and making dinner, she'd stand in front of the mirror getting ready. The four walls of the quaint, rectangular yellow and white tiled bathroom positioned at the front of my parents' bedroom had just enough extra space for me to stand at the doorway while Mom stood at the mirror. I watched as she retrieved a small pink cosmetic bag from the cabinet that I hadn't seen before. From it, she pulled out her foundation, a charcoal-black eyeliner, a thin blue tube of mascara, and a gold tube of lipstick. When she looked into the mirror at me, the corner of her mouth lifted and her eyes lit up. That was her way of saying she loved me. She didn't have to utter the phrase; I felt her admiration in my heart.

"And what are you looking at, little girl?"

"Nothin', Ma. Just watchin'. Maybe I'll put on some eyeliner too."

"And maybe you won't," she replied.

We both laughed. I knew exactly what she meant. That I didn't have her permission to wear any makeup yet and I wasn't ready for what taking that step meant for everything else to come. I gazed as she began tracing the rims of her left eye with the liner. She blinked a few times as her eye watered before going to the right side. Eventually, Dad came up behind me, placing his hand on my shoulder and squeezing slightly. He didn't speak, only observed. There was tension on his face.

"Now, Voncile, why would you go and be putting all that stuff on your face?"

He waited for a response. There wasn't one. And so he continued. "You don't need all of that," he warned.

She lifted her head slightly, looking into the mirror and at Dad square in the eyes, and then at me, raising an eyebrow before continuing to apply her makeup without apology. She didn't bother giving an explanation, nor did she entertain any further conversation. Her silence was the response. I snickered under my breath. Mom was bold as hell. She respected my dad but also had her own mind. She knew that Dad was going to be alright. Modeling moments like those laid the foundation for my steadfastness years later and how I would come to understand the contours of the relationship between Black men and Black women.

Eventually, Dad walked away and was left to take up his grievances alone while sitting on the couch in the living room. When it was time for Mom to leave, she kissed Dad on the forehead as she always did before leaving the house.

"See you when you get back, Voncile," he said as she walked towards the front door.

He knew and she knew that once she made up her mind, she was moving forward. And also that nothing had been meant in disrespect. They both needed space in which to thrive and moments to test boundaries. It was the stability of building a life together that mattered most. Although she looked for validation from my dad, she was certain of her personal choices, and he was respectful of her stance.

Instead of arguing in the hallways and fighting in the streets, like some of the other couples, she loved him with her presence. She demonstrated respect for him. She spoke to him kindly and never disagreed with him in public, never wanted to show any cracks or creases in their bond, even if she had a difference of opinion.

Don't get it twisted; my mom was vocal about her concerns and needs. But she showed up for Dad in and outside of our home and she maintained order in his world. All I ever witnessed in their relationship was mutual respect. They rarely fought beyond an occasional argument and I never saw anything rise above that.

But the stories I *heard* from before my birth were a little different. There were moments I overheard exchanges between my mom and aunts as they recalled times when all the Mallory boys were young, and what the kids today would call *outside*.

Several of my dad's brothers were scattered in nearby parts of New York, New Jersey, and Long Island, which meant they could easily spend time together.

Dad spent a good amount of time with his brothers, and as the story goes, the ladies loved them all. By the time I was old enough to keep up with my dad's coming and going, those pursuits had been put to sleep by my mother.

I remember him and me sitting up one night, watching reruns of *A Different World*. Even back then, I was a sucker for love, so this show always got me with its portrayal of young love between Whitley and Dwayne Wayne. It brought joy to my face and my dad got a kick out of it too. But this night, the show wasn't about love. It was about sexual assault. One of Dwayne's friends gets taken on a date where she's about to be raped when Dwayne Wayne manages to show up there just in time to save her. He'd been uneasy about the new guy and followed his intuition to intervene.

He protected her from a world determined to do her harm, not controllingly but with care and a sense of mutual need to look out for each other. For me, Dad epitomized that ethic. I knew he would do anything to protect me, and that he'd spent his life doing the same for his community.

That night, when I got up to go to the kitchen for a snack, my dad met me in the hallway. "Come here, boo," he said.

He was noticeably upset. He knelt down and grabbed me and held me. Rubbing my forehead, I wanted to protect him, but I was too little.

Looking up at him, I waited for him to say something.

"I love you. You know that, right?"

There was so much uncertainty at that moment. Dazed and confused, I wrapped my arms around him, hugging him back, squeezing as hard as I could. The intensity in his eyes was confirmation that whatever happened, it couldn't easily be fixed. Was he in trouble? Were we in trouble?

He broke free of my grasp and left the hallway without explanation. I followed behind him, yelling for him to come back until I got to the living room. Standing in the center of the room, I heard what seemed to be an intense conversation on the other side of my parents' closed bedroom door. My sister Sharon must have been in the room with my mother based on how the conversation was going. Easing towards their room, I could hear more clearly. By the time they saw me standing at the door, the conversation ceased.

My mother looked over towards me and said, "Your dad may not be here with us anymore." I can't remember if she gave me a hug or not, but I do remember that I was in shock.

Easing my back down the wall, my parents' wall, until I was sitting with my legs closed, I felt afraid. I went to my room and sat in disbelief, hoping it was all a bad dream. The sound of my mother's voice of torment of the moment was proof that it was all real. I didn't cry myself to sleep, but I did toss and turn all night. The feeling of helplessness consumed me. Knowing that I could not fix it for any of us troubled me the most. The next morning, when I woke up, my father was in the kitchen like normal. Mom was cooking breakfast like normal. She served us kids each a bowl of cereal as we watched cartoons like normal. I didn't care enough to ask questions. All that mattered was that my protector, our protector, was home.

After that night, all traces of a quest for anything outside of our home were nonexistent, once my mother put her foot down.

I would be remiss if I did not acknowledge that my first example of manhood was in my home. My father was not living with the absence of fault, yet he made decisions at the right time in consideration of the value he placed on his family. He recognized that the establishment of presence and legacy was far greater than anything else. Today I recognize that even if my dad had walked away and still been consistent in our lives, he was a man. The measure of a man is deciding that something is important to you and doing what is necessary to preserve the respect of the relationship or bond. My dad chose to stay and I am glad that he did.

Regardless of the past, my mom and dad managed to do what many couples could not—stay together. They were committed at all costs to building a legacy together.

My dad was a corrections officer, and a rule-abiding man at heart. He believed in systems and honorable character.

Born in Roanoke Rapids, North Carolina, he was raised with his six brothers and four sisters. His father worked in a factory. By the time my dad was a teen, sharecropping was the only opportunity available for advancement. He wanted more from life. Therefore, he and his brothers embarked on a journey north that led them to New York and would lead him to my mom.

Love. Respect. Acceptance. This was the nature of my parents' relationship. Dad was a well-decorated general and she was his lieutenant. Dad was smart enough to recognize Mom's skill set as a great organizer who brought special attention and care to everything she did. As long as she ran the show, Dad was happy and she was happy. And if they weren't, they didn't let me know.

Some nights, I stayed up past my bedtime sitting against the door in my room, immersing myself in what they referred to as grown folks' business to hear the late-night exchanges between Mom and Dad. They were more like strategy sessions and Mom was always thinking of a master plan.

"You know we can't stay here, right? This isn't the type of life we should be exposing the kids to. You know it."

"Come on now, Voncile. Look around. We're giving these kids a better life than most people around here. Besides, we need to make sure they see folks that look like them. They need to know who they are."

"Yeah, but we need a change. I don't think Tamika should grow up here anymore."

My father loved Harlem, and I'm sure he never wanted to leave. The Manhattanville my parents moved into was different. The environment went from clean and family first to something else entirely right under our feet. Addicts wandering the hallways all times of day and night, more gunshots in the community, and robberies becoming grimly routine.

"This ain't no place for us to raise kids anymore and you know it."

"Well, what do you suggest we do?"

My mother recognized that a potential move was on the horizon, and my sister Sharon, who had seen more of the world, immediately began helping her scout new places to live.

Dad was being his usual accommodating self but drew a line at buying a home for the family. My dad loved to travel, to drive his new car back and forth down south to North Carolina and Alabama, and he loved to have money on hand to help his nieces and nephews. He believed that cash was king, and buying a home would be a major responsibility that would prevent him from doing the things that he loved and maintaining a safety net for a rainy day.

"There's a place called Co-op City. Sharon has been doing some re-search and I think it would be the perfect place for us to give ourselves and the kids a fresh start."

"You really think we need a fresh start, Voncile?"

"Yes."

CHAPTER 3

FIGHT THE POWER

Annunciation School at 461 West 131st Street in Manhattanville was a never-ending wall of white marble, broken only by the massive green double doors that led inside. There were also stained glass windows everywhere. Early mornings, we stood outside of the building, waiting for Sister Rose to set our faces alight with her presence. "All are welcome," she'd yell, always in sync with the bell as teachers escorted us to our classrooms. Sister Rose's white hair and buoyant demeanor gave her an air of purity and power. The unfamiliar would say it was as if God himself whispered in Sister Rose's ear to whisper in ours each morning.

But once we were out of the public's sight, Sister Rose's halo turned into horns—at least for certain students, me being one of them. The calm that covered her face outside faded once inside. Instead of her floating through the halls with open arms to wrap around us in a hug (as she did outside), her footsteps boomed like thunder as she threw daggers with her eyes. It didn't take long for me to realize that the small number of Black girls that she deemed problematic under her watch suffered her wrath more than anyone else. And the animus she reserved for me in particular was even deeper. She hated me. More often than not, her pale white skin turned hot red in my presence. It was no secret that my family played a powerful role in the community, and least of all to Sister Rose. Words and feelings made it clear my family's principles of self-preservation and determination were incompatible with Sister Rose. My convictions about her sentiments towards me were confirmed on the many occasions she saw to it that I was either punished or made a mockery of for one thing or another. I remember one year, a few weeks into third grade, picture day rolled around. My class was all lined up outside of the library, the girls all dressed in our yellow and brown plaid skirts with blue socks pulled to our knees, yellow collared button-down blouses and brown cardigans. The boys wore brown pants, yellow button-down shirts under brown cardigans with the school's logo embroidered on the left lapel. An assistant helping the photographer came out of the library to pass out little black combs one by one for us to tidy our hair. Just as the assistant placed a comb in my hand, Sister Rose emerged from the library, snatched the comb out of my hand, and said, "Now, Tamika, you know you don't need one of those."

Her words tore through me, inviting the entire crowd to inspect and critique my appearance. I might have respected her more if she had the decency to pull me to the side to tell me her thoughts, on the far-off chance she'd spoken up out of concern rather than chastisement, but of course she didn't. I held back the hot tears that day, but the aggressions had only just begun. Another teacher, Ms. Roberts, would drive me into a shell in math class, ignoring my raised hand first subtly and then with vigor as she called on anyone else she could find. Until I got fed up with her antics, shouted the answer out of turn, and gave her an excuse to target me again. My shell had gotten thicker as time passed, but with time the environment would prompt many of the intellectually driven insecurities that Black children have a tendency to acquire when forced to prove themselves in environments that are not culturally competent. I knew my math; I saw the correct answers on my desk when the class went through the problems together at the end of each session. But I was being told correct wasn't good enough for me, there's still something to prove that I had no control over one way or another. My voice could be loud, but it would not be heard.

But there was one class where I was allowed to shine my light fully. For one reason or another, religion class was an open door when I showed my command of the Bible stories that always seemed to escape my peers' minds. Sister Rose couldn't deny my mastery of God's word, and when she said something that was incorrect I let her know.

"That's not what my pastor taught me," I blurted out one day. You could expect—I did expect—to be smacked down and told to know my place again, as had become so commonplace day-to-day at school.

But Sister Rose never tried to silence me in religion class. Although she still did not treat me well, she was tolerant of and respected my ideas there.

In full transparency, I was by far not a perfect student. I had my own issues. I was extremely talkative and, at times, a little mean. But there was a lesson granted to me by what I experienced with her. It was an example of the power of a liberated mind. The truth was with me, what's right was with me, and even in the face of opposition my voice would carry.

There was a noticeable difference between the Latino families and Black families at the school. The Latino families found commonality with the on-site staff. The nurse, office assistant, lunch ladies, et al., they all shared a bond. Similar to the four or five Black teachers who had a bond with my family. There were just not enough of us to establish a sense of community. Not once in my life did I feel like the school was a place where people understood me or cared about me. I knew this to be the case because my behaviors were escalated. When I had an infraction—and to be clear, I got into trouble sometimes—it was made into a far bigger problem than any of my classmates who got into trouble for similar reasons had. Nothing, literally nothing, that I was doing was exclusive to me. All the kids talked, and all of them got into fights, but the punishment for little Tamika was different. When I wasn't battling the injustice of infractions in the principal's office, I was fighting a different type of war in another area of the school. Mr. Stevens's classroom.

Mr. Stevens, my fifth-grade teacher, was dusty. A heavyset man, he had furry brows that framed runny red eyes, and dry, flaky lips. He didn't wear glasses, but often squinted as if he couldn't see well. Even though he was overweight, he walked fast and always seemed to emerge from around corners. Our running joke was that he turned into a werewolf who roamed the halls at night when the building was clear. Since his skin was the same color as mine initially led me to assume that we were on the same agenda as Black people in a religious environment. I learned rather quickly that nothing was further from the truth. On most days he was late starting class and taught more often from his desk rather than standing up at the board. He spoke with a loud and booming voice. He often kept classical music playing on an old record player at the back of the classroom, stating the music was for thinking. Although I can't say I learned anything monumental in his class, Mr. Stevens became the basis for a memory I have never forgotten. Most kids thought he was easygoing and parents believed him to be a genius for the combination of music and lights off while working. They all believed he had some magic spell for keeping kids in line. Midway through the year, I saw another side of who he was. One day when all of my classmates exited, he asked me to stay behind to review a test score. Following his directive, I remained at my desk watching the students file out one by one. The lights were off and that day was particularly dark, so I could only see the silhouette of him sitting at his desk at the front of the room.

"Ms. Mallory, you may come up now," he sneered.

I stood up and walked over to the chair that he kept beside his desk for students who needed to conference with him and sat down. His breaths were heavy. He began reviewing my paper, then paused and looked at me with stone eyes. He didn't speak. Assuming he wanted more of an explanation about my work, I sat up and attempted to move the process along.

"Mr. Stevens, are you going to give me my grade?"

"In a moment, Tamika," he replied. "Why don't you come here and sit on my lap while we talk?"

Falling back into the chair, I had no way to escape the shock. I was in disbelief. Did this muthafucker just ask me to sit on his nasty-ass lap? I thought to myself. Disgusted, I replied.

"No. I won't."

He reached out to touch my arm.

"It's ok, Tamika. You can trust me," he said.

I snatched my arm away and ran all the way to the lunchroom. That day I didn't even have lunch, as I was in a lot of shock. It didn't matter; I just needed to get away. And thank God I did. The story could have ended much differently. For the remainder of the year, I didn't see Mr. Stevens the way other kids and parents saw him. He was a confirmed wolf in sheep's clothing.

Although I kept my distance from him, I never spoke of what happened to me. His vile attempt was another attack on an innocent little girl who was in the process of finding her voice. He had taken that from me and who knows how many other girls or boys. Far worse, there was not a single person in the school whom I could confide in or who I thought would believe me. Therefore, I remained silent, or should I say I was silenced? Telling my mother would have been a declaration of war. Although there were times I wasn't sure that my family wanted the inconvenience of fighting in the streets and at home. The prospect of drama everywhere was overwhelming. She had always been adamant about people not touching her kids. She taught us the phrase "stranger danger" and she meant it with her soul when she said, "If any person even tries to lay their hands on you, let me know and I will handle them myself. That goes for family members too." Growing up, I watched my mom shield my dad from information that could have angered him. Although I rarely saw him angry, it was clear that upsetting or disrespecting him was not a good idea. As for my dad, his role as a corrections officer was warning enough. To keep the peace and buy the rest of my time at Annunciation, I said nothing.

There is not a doubt in my mind that for me, Catholic school was an entry point and the cause of deeply rooted childhood trauma in my life. It is an exhaustive mistake to place children in any environment that fails to acknowledge their existence. No one at the school took the time to understand who I was as a student or the ways most conducive to my learning. Yet I prospered, but not without sacrifice of positive self-perception. And while my mother may have believed the diversity in experiences from the rallies to my community to Catholic school created a balance in me, I beg to differ. The lack of acknowledgment pierced my soul. But I understand that she was trying to keep me safe.

There was no space amidst those walls for the outspoken Black girl, raised to see and understand America's ills. Unless a Catholic school has a specific racial lens that does not shy away from the real issues affecting Black people, allows for a curriculum that talks openly and honestly about the inequality in America, studies race in America, and is committed to truth as a part of the curriculum, in my humble opinion, I caution Black people against immersing children into intolerant learning environments. If this choice is one of safety, always keep in mind that they need to be continuously reinforced and centered in self-knowledge.

Whether Catholic schools or private institutions, educational constructs need to be more cognizant of their faculties' racial bias and implement proper measures to ensure they don't become complicit in inciting depressions and confusion of students as a by-product of microaggressions.

I urge the children of our nation deserve better.

In my formative years, the groundwork of integrity was laid in the bosom of community. One that my parents masterfully assembled to ensure that I never forgot who I was and what I would be forced to overcome if I wanted to succeed. I watched as my family and village strived to live righteous lives. I saw Black people living righteous lives. The fibers of responsibility and accountability were ingrained into my psyche. In the next phases of life I chose to test the waters. It seemed that there had to be a way to spice things up.

———

"Fight the powers that be." Those words rang in my ears like sirens. When I was a little girl, Chuck D's voice and the words of Public Enemy were ingrained in my emotional cache, and I was crystal clear that the world saw me differently because I was Black.

My parents had now been working in the movement for almost a decade, but not much about the state of emergency for Black and brown people in America had changed. "Fight the Power" and its message were a track added to the playlist of my life, and its rhythm became an unforgettable melody in my soul.

By the time I was fourteen, Mom's push had materialized into a relocation to Co-op City. Nestled in the northeast section of the Bronx and bound by Interstate 95 and the Hutchinson River, Co-op City was a sea of never-ending gray buildings that looked like skyscrapers. The air was colder, and the sun shone less. The grounds were well kept, but there was another undercurrent of life beneath the surface. Co-op City was where the middle-class Black families resided. The residents were working nine-to-five jobs—nurses, cops, teachers, construction workers, lawyers, and everything in between, primarily without subsidies. The grounds were well-kept, with lawns of lush green grass lined by wrought-iron fences and flowers planted in the spring and summer months. Moving away from the projects was supposed to be an answer to the call for a change of scenery from the Manhattanville Projects. What my mother didn't realize was that the neighborhoods shared more similarities than differences. Much like in Manhattanville, there were benches where folks congregated when the weather was nice, but there were even fewer activities for young people. Residents paid assessments with the belief that they would get access to amenities and recreation, but none of that ever trickled down to me or my friends. Only the seniors in the community had access to amenities. There was no place to channel our energy. Instead, kids learned how to entertain themselves out of sight, behind the buildings where it was safer to sell and abuse drugs and have sex prematurely.

Instead of the noticeable strung-out crackheads in Manhattanville, there were high-functioning drug addicts who maintained their jobs by day and got high at night. The buildings were referred to as sections and became the basis for how we categorized ourselves. If someone from Section 1 had a beef with someone from Section 4, it was justification for violence. For me, the sections never mattered, but it was all too easy to be deemed guilty by association. Wherever you lived, that was your set. End of story.

Regardless of what transpired outside, Mom and Dad did everything in their power to create a haven of peace inside. The smell of Comet, Clorox, and Ajax and the sound of good soul music blaring through the apartment in rhythm with brushing bristling against the baseboards were our signals to wake up on Saturdays. Mom was a wall-washing, floor-mopping, baseboard-cleaning kind of woman. And once the apartment was cleaned, she meticulously returned the supplies back to their usual storage as we prepared to leave for rallies hosted by National Action Network (NAN). Mom would leave a few pieces of fried sausage, or liver, bacon, or Spam on the side of the stove for us to grab as we ran out the door. Food was love for us. The fact that she took the time to toast the bread with butter before melting the cheese made her sandwiches the best I'd ever had. Mom always laughed while she cooked, the sound and evidence it was being made with love. She laughed hard, rearing back with a sound midway like she would stop breathing between each one.

When we'd get back after NAN, Mom would be laughing then too, talking on the phone with her sisters about everything and nothing. Even then in the middle of a conversation, she somehow always seemed to know when I was preparing to do something I had no business doing. Whether thinking about boys or planning pranks, I was no stranger to mischief. So Mom knew to stay on me like white on rice. If I didn't know any better, I'd think she had a camera set up in my room watching to see what I'd find myself into next. The older I got, the more creative I became in constructing plans to push boundaries. But there was something about my ways I knew both my mother and father appreciated. If there was one thing they taught us, it was that our minds were the most powerful tools we had. As long as we lived with love, respect, and adoration of our Blackness I knew Mom and Dad would be there to back us up.

My parents personified the revolution they lived. As a collective, our pride and Blackness superseded every environment we lived in. And everywhere they went, they planted seeds of Black pride. I was their harvest. Racial pride, economic empowerment, and the embrace of Pan-Africanism was second nature to us. Instead of sitting in the house, staring out the window hoping for change, we personified it. Instead of waiting for America to wave the white flag of peace, power, and prosperity, they created their own. We were well-versed and educated on the issues.

The proof was in the scores of VHS tapes featuring speeches of people ranging from Minister Elijah Muhammad and Minister Louis Farrakhan to Reverend Jesse Jackson, Dr. John Henrik Clarke, Fannie Lou Hamer, Reverend Al Sharpton, Dr. Martin Luther King, and Malcolm X. Dad kept these voices in heavy rotation on the TV. When he wasn't listening to speeches, then he was listening to the voice of Ed Bradley over the ticking clock of *60 Minutes*, or Mom was locked in with Oprah on the TV. In retrospect, I realize how much of what I became was a result of this subconscious classroom. Oprah didn't look like many of the other hosts on daytime TV, nor did she fit the stereotypes of Black women so often put forward by the media around me. It caught my attention, and her content—societal issues, and women's rights—was different from other things I saw on TV.

It matched the tone and tenor of my home. Everything my parents did was an act of revolt. They recognized that there could be no victory in being Black in America without a fight. Fighting looked like education, so books inhabited every nook and cranny of our home where my mom sat on one end of the couch and dad on the other right in front of the stacks of writers and thinkers on the living room coffee table. *The Souls of Black Folk* by W. E. B. Du Bois, *Invisible Man* by Ralph Ellison, *The Color Purple* by Alice Walker, *The Mis-Education of the Negro* by Carter Godwin Woodson, *Freedom Is a Constant Struggle* by Angela Y. Davis, *Beloved* by Toni Morrison, *The Souls of Black Folk* by Du Bois, there were too many to name.

Fighting looked like loving. My parents were trendsetters in life and in love. In a time when the residue of the Man in the House Rule, where institutionalized governmental America and the so-called powers that be excluded women with men in their homes from receiving public assistance, left the women to fend for themselves as heads of households, my parents remained married. Even today after fifty years, their vows are still intact. They recognized that Black love was revolutionary. Fighting looked like an awakening. My mom's words kept our family grounded in the necessity to speak truth to power, and my dad's actions drove our ability to do so. On Saturdays, when the cooking and cleaning were done, he was adamant that we attend rallies as a family. From the moment we got off the elevator and walked through the metal doors of our building to the moment we hit the breezeway that led to the street, you could feel the energy and hear the shouts of people looking to experience the movement.

"Go 'head on, Mr. and Mrs. Mallory. Power to the people! Y'all going to a rally today?"

"Yeah, girl!" Mom responded, winking her eye and nodding her head in agreement.

Dad's responses were more gentle, but that never bothered me. There was an unspoken sense of pride that consumed me every day inside our world. I low-key felt like we were the shit. In the presence of my parents, I stood a little taller and held my head a little higher. Together, we walked like a militia en route to join the rest of the soldiers.

When we arrived at a rally, I could hear the synchronized voices chanting from the sidewalk. It was the beat of Black excellence. Thunderous war cries spilling into the streets. Our souls being baptized by the spirits of our predecessors. Reverberating, steady, ancestral.

Once we'd found our ways inside to join the gathering crowd under one roof, the voices could be heard with greater clarity. As we moved closer towards the auditorium, the masses became more distinguishable, and the voices became distinct words.

"The revolution will not be televised."

"No Justice, No Peace."

As my mother opened the door, the energy hit me and consumed me as the single voice transitioned back from one to many.

———

Truth be told, the revolution was televised. It's all on tape. Much of my life as a little girl filled with fire for equality and justice is documented. Back then, the approach was far more militant. And it had further-reaching

goals than one day, or one event. There was also a tremendous amount
of time spent on teaching Black people the art of self-development and
even self-control.

The movement of today takes on a new shape. With the rise of the
digital age, the intensity with which we view injustice, consume news, and
even advocate is different. I am the end product of two different iterations
of the movement. But the mission of equality remains the same. The fight
remains the same. The issues remain the same. There is yet work to be done.

"Power to the people."

A people with no limitations set upon them by anyone outside the
movement. There is no age limit on activism. There is no way an activist
is supposed to look or sound. There is no set point in time or rite of
passage that makes one feel the spirit of power running through their
veins; it just shows up. And when it does, you can either embrace it or
run as fast as you can in the other direction.

After our spirits were lifted and we took our seats, another voice emerged
at the front: "Brothers and sisters, you must be aware of the power of
your mind. You will not become what you are. You will become what
you think you are."

"Say that, Dr. Ben," another voice said in the audience.

"If we lack knowledge and self-awareness, we will never be able to walk
the righteous path towards self-actualization. This, brothers and sisters, is
not a mistake we can afford to make. Not today. Not tomorrow. Not ever."

Dr. Yosef Alfredo Antonio Ben-Jochannan, affectionately known as
"Dr. Ben," didn't need to shout. His words were measured, deliberate.
Most of the times I heard him speak were after rallies, when he would
seal the spirit of empowerment with his quiet, unwavering conviction.

Dr. Ben was said to have been of Caribbean and Ethiopian descent.
He was a force as a writer, historian, and scholar. Dr. Ben's speeches about
the African diaspora and reparations were a reflection of his decades of
work and commitment to the movement. No price tag could be placed
on a mind as potent as his. The opportunity to be in his presence was
invaluable. On the heels of his words, the people rose to their feet yet
again showering Dr. Ben in a sea of praise. Back then, when I was a
young woman, it felt as if Dr. Ben aged quickly. But in retrospect, he
had always been there. He was at the height of rendering his knowledge,
and I didn't know it. I didn't think it was important. What I wouldn't

give to have that guiding light in my life today. The way that Dr. Ben imparted information, his body language, his cadence, the way he chose which syllables to emphasize, superseded anything I had ever seen. As I got older, he would speak to me in a way that let me know he saw leadership qualities in me.

Shortly before his passing, Dr. Ben lost his ability to communicate. I had the honor of hugging him and sitting with him in his last days. He had not just taught me about myself as a woman; he was teaching me about my Black soul. And I am thankful I got to share my appreciation while it was still possible to do so face-to-face.

———

The work of the revolution had no end, but the bodies of the revolution needed respite and relief. When rallies or marches and protests were scheduled, we were always in attendance. And on other days we went right back to being a family like any other. Some days we'd visit my uncles' houses, where I had impromptu playdates with my cousins. On other occasions, we wandered to Paramus Mall first, picking out new clothes or shoes or going to Pathmark to stock up for a week of cooking ahead. Our lives and hearts were full. Midnight on Saturday ushered in the sunlight of Sunday morning; we went from "Fight the Power" with raised fists to "Praise the Lord!" Sunday mornings looked like content hearts and minds waking up to the smell of grits, eggs, and sausage. *Open Line* spoke to us through the radio, featuring conversations with all of the bigwigs in the movement, elected officials, and those who were doing racial justice work. The hosts on WQHT Hot 97 were intellectuals, one in particular being James Mtume, widely known for his song "Juicy Fruit." *Open Line* streamed through the house and Mom scurried from the kitchen to my room, making sure I was getting dressed, while Dad sat on the couch, reading. He was not a churchgoer; the rallies on Saturdays were his spiritual vitamin. But he would show up on special occasions, like when I had a solo part in the youth choir. Once Mom was dressed, she would call me into the bathroom to do my hair. As I stood at the mirror in front of her, I saw the reflection of myself standing in front of the reflection of what I could become. She was strong and admirable. The most powerful human I had ever seen.

As an adolescent, I began to see the passion from the rallies and church on the weekends spill over into the weekdays in the form of youth meetings hosted at our place. From statistics about racially motivated crimes against Black people and the ills of an inequitable governmental system to current events and strategizing how to mobilize support to uplift our communities, our age had no bearing on our capacity to deliberate.

The first knock on the door was always around 6:00 p.m., and from that moment forward the evening was filled with greetings, hugs, and roaring laughter from the adults. On the days we hosted youth meetings at our place, Mom rushed home to make her famous hors d'oeuvres and platters. A tray of tuna fish surrounded with Ritz crackers was the crowd favorite along with fried wings. Everyone went crazy over it. It was so good that nobody cared that it made your breath smell from all the onions. I still love it to this day, and now I make my mother's tuna recipe often.

At our meetings there were no secret agendas. No fronts, nothing to hide. This space empowered us to talk solely about Black issues without apology.

"We must understand that fighting the system is just as much about knowledge of self as it is about knowledge of what is unjust."

"A man (woman) who lacks understanding of economics lacks understanding about the world around him."

Prophet, AKA Willie Spiggers, would lead us in reading affirmational quotes.

It was much more than a youth meeting. We were tribe building. The more the powers that be attempted to destroy our communities, the more strongly we united behind the scenes.

As leaders we were also tasked with planning activities to keep our peers engaged and out of the streets. As long as we could articulate the need to the adults, anything was fair game: fashion and talent shows, house parties. Regardless of the fact that I planned, there were many times my parents would not allow me to attend. The end point was more important than the process. It felt good to do good. I'd been experienced watching this kind of community building take place from observing my parents and their counterparts, but this was one of my first experiences taking that role on myself. Building that confidence in myself and learning to instill it in the people around me was so important, far more important than I could realize back then.

People don't believe me when I say it now, but when I was growing up the idea of me standing in front of a crowd and taking on the work that became my life didn't make much sense to me at all. I was born into it, and learned of it, but was this the path I was meant to walk? The mechanics came naturally, but the leaders I studied felt larger-than-life. They seemed perfect. But at my home, beneath the surface, the reality of loneliness was becoming more evident as the days passed. Leaving Manhattanville meant saying goodbye to all my same-aged friends I'd accumulated over the years. And I found there was no space for a girl like me in Co-op. I was the "Black power girl." As much as people seemed to respect my family's position, girls weren't welcoming of me by myself. I wasn't into the things I saw earn people's acceptance in this new environment. I wasn't into repping a set or fighting. I had no desire to be initiated into a group or a gang.

"That bitch must think she's special or something."

"We should jump her."

I would try talking to everybody, but at times that got me in trouble too.

To the girls around me, rejecting this status quo meant I thought I was better than everyone else. But nothing could have been further from the truth. I didn't support violence or behavior that I had seen perpetuating violence all my life. It wasn't worth it to put down my principles in order to fit in or feel accepted. The commentary about me was relentless, and I had to dig deep into myself to remember what I'd believed in, even if it would have been easier to give in to the crowd.

The loneliness compounded, morphing into something even worse as I saw the people I needed support from seem to thrive in the same environment while I was struggling. I recognized a difference between the relationship my mom had with my sister, at this point near thirty, and the one she had with me. There was a lightness and joy to their time together, Sharon always boiling over with laughter and Mom joining her in time. Mom had been so young when she gave birth to Sharon, which meant they practically grew up together. It was Sharon who had been with Mom through some of the early challenges and changes in her life. Through the years their bond resembled more of a lifelong friendship than a parent-child relationship. On many afternoons when I came home from school and my homework was finished with Dad, I found myself looking for someone to talk to, hoping for a friend who was close in age and could relate to what I was experiencing and who could see life through similar lenses. Watching my mother and sister be so close made me yearn for companionship. In my mind, there was no one there to share my secrets. Despite my mom's efforts to keep us all busy, there was an emptiness inside that superseded it all.

CHAPTER 4

AROUND THE WAY GIRL

As a child immersed in the movement, I was well-versed in many of the issues affecting our communities. More so than my same-aged peers who were not. From attending rallies and church every weekend to exposure to art and culture and the culmination of a village, my parents did everything possible to raise my vibration and to make me a conscious Black girl. In spite of it all, there was still something missing. There was more of life I yearned to experience. My adolescent mind lacked stimulation. Looking back, after we moved to Co-op City, my decision not to return to Mt. St. Michael, my Catholic high school after the first year, due to my attitude and festering personality issues, established a new pattern of poor decision-making. Although my grades were good, I was not evolving and further indoctrination was not the answer. By then, my parents were tired of my constant complaining and mood swings. Eventually, they said fuck it, you can just go to the public school.

I was in search of thrills. The kind of stimulation that skirts the edge of danger and feels like excitement. Ones that feed the egos of teenagers, making us feel invincible. Our everyday life was so routine and mundane. Today I understand that our structured lives were what was best. The tight reins my parents kept on me didn't allow for the freedom to explore the world in alignment with what I felt was hip and cool. We weren't visiting overseas countries every summer like some of my classmates who had the opportunity to visit their families in their native lands, such as the Dominican Republic, Haiti, various countries in Asia, etc. And while the trips to Alabama and North Carolina to see our family in the summer, on holidays, and for other family occasions were filled with unexplainable joy, I needed more. Truth be told, I wanted to be outside where shit was popping. My definition of fun was shaped by movies and music videos that glamorized jewelry, cars, clothes, and mansions. Nino Brown, a crime boss from the film *New Jack City*, was the personification of the lifestyle I laughingly thought I was cut out for. As kids, we envied the glitz and glamour of street life. The acquisition of labels and shiny things was all we were after. My parents were wise enough to know what came with those lifestyles and they did everything in their power to show me a better way—a righteous way. In retrospect, I fully understand why for my parents the establishment of a righteous life was necessary. Even so, I am not completely sold on rearing practices that shelter children too much. As the saying goes, it is a hard needle to thread. When you come from humble beginnings, you learn to recognize the value of a quiet life, one that allows for clarity and consistency. Truth be told, being Black in America is adventurous enough. The act of surviving from day to day is a gift. My parents were knowledgeable about the ills of the world, and they remained focused on raising my levels of consciousness in hopes of preventing me from experiencing many of the pitfalls they encountered, but because I yearned to be in the company of people my own age, their warnings weren't enough. A wandering mind riddled with curiosity is a danger zone, and I wanted all the smoke.

All I know is that I yearned for more. More time spent with regular kids, not movement kids who were involved in the same work that my family was involved in. Even the young people in the movement had more freedom than me. More time outside, just kicking it, doing hood shit. More time listening to music instead of movement speeches. The first time I left our apartment without parental supervision was my way of going after more.

The summer when the late Notorious B.I.G. dropped his single "Juicy," it was in heavy rotation in households and on the radio. Every-body had it blasting on their Walkmans or in their CD players in their rooms. Getting my hands on new music was sometimes a challenge. The process of doing so meant convincing someone to take me to 125th Street in Harlem, where people sold music at various stands. Saturdays, when it was warm outside, were the best time to go. And if I had to choose a favorite month in New York, it would have to be June. To me, June in Harlem is the most wonderful time of the year, earmarking the beginning of summer. Dare I call it paradise? After months of brutally cold temperatures, folks are all of a sudden happy.

I can recall one particular Saturday in June, after my fourteenth birth-day, towards the end of the month families were leaving their apartments en masse for a day outside at the same time we were departing for the rally at NAN. And by the time we returned, even more families and other people were outside, enjoying the day. To my surprise, neither Mom nor Dad stopped to talk to anyone on our way back inside like they did on some occasions in Manhattanville because they had not yet met many people. Mom mentioned something about needing to get her cooking done. They spoke to a few folks in passing, but that was it. When we got back inside, I was pissed. Why couldn't we be outside like the other families? Why couldn't I hang out like the kids from other sections? Lying on my bed, even though I was on the twenty-fourth floor, I imagined the sound of the chatter of the people outside. It was torturous. Screams of enjoyment and bursts of belly-aching laughter that were reminders of how much fun I wasn't having. Just as she said she would, Mom began cooking in the kitchen, and my dad was on his side of the couch nodding with Minister Farrakhan playing in the background.

"Dang, I really need eggs for my macaroni and cheese. It won't come out right without eggs." As soon as I heard my mom's voice, a lightbulb went off. I ran to the kitchen and stood by the wall where the base of the phone was mounted.

"I could run to the store and get the eggs for you," I offered.

Standing at the cutting board, slicing potatoes, she turned to look at me. "Hold on a minute, Ola. Let me see what this girl is saying. Tamika, what did you say?"

"I said . . . I could go to the store and get the eggs for you." She put the knife down and walked towards me.

"Hmm. I guess you could," she said, placing her hand on her hip. She told my aunt, "Ola Mae, this girl said she can go to the store to get the eggs."

I could hear my aunt Ola Mae's voice on the other end of the phone.

"Why can't she? That girl is way smarter than y'all think. She could probably run your whole house if you let her," she snickered.

"I'll have to think about that, Tamika. I don't want you going out there and getting into nothing with nobody."

Aunt Ola Mae was still interjecting on the other end of the phone as they went into a full conversation about all the things happening in the world. Meanwhile, my heart was pounding in anticipation of an escape. The longer I waited, the less patience I had to spare.

"Dad. Tell Mom to let me go to the store and get the eggs," I said.

My dad was on the couch knocked out asleep with his mouth open wide. He didn't even budge, so I ran back to my mom.

"Vomp. How much longer y'all think you can keep that girl tied up in that house?" My aunt was loud enough for me to hear her on the other end of the phone. She was one of many advocates for my parents to loosen the reins on their restrictions on my independence, but not too much. My aunt Barbara, one of my mother's sisters-in-law, was another advocate for me.

"Tamika, let me see what your father has to say about this."

She walked towards my dad, who was on the couch.

"Stan. You think it's ok for Tamika to go to the store to get some eggs for me to finish making this macaroni and cheese?"

There was a long pause.

"Stan. You hear me?" Groggy, Dad lifted his head.

"Huh?"

Attempting to avoid being cornered into the conversation, he made an executive decision. "Come right back," he said.

"You think it's safe for Tamika to go to the store alone?" Mom looked at me as if to say, "Don't fuck this up."

She told my aunt to hold on, and said, "Let me go get my purse."

She put the phone down, and when she returned she gave me the money for the eggs and her trust.

"I'll be back," I said, running towards the front door before she changed her mind.

Closing the door behind me, I stood with my back against it for a moment in silence—disbelief. The act of stepping across that threshold in Co-Op City for the first time on my own transformed me. In the past I had only been able to go a few feet away from my parents while they were also outside because when they attempted to give me freedom back in Manhattanville, I ran away. This was the first time they remained inside while I went out. Inside our place meant confinement and hefty expectations of excellence. Standing on the other side of the door alone meant I called my own shots, and as they say, power is one hell of a drug.

My only goal was to soak it all in. The deep breath I took and the massive grin I wore while walking towards the elevator were proof I felt free. Even the elevator ride to the first floor felt different. I danced my butt off on the way down. Thank God the elevator didn't make a stop, or I could have embarrassed the hell out of myself. By the time I got to the ground floor and walked out, I saw the outside in a way that I had never seen it before. Instead of the sun hiding, that day it pushed its way through the buildings and I could feel the warmth of the heat on my shoulders. Standing in awe, I watched families congregating. I would eventually learn about the young people in Co-op. From good kids just outside for fresh air to dudes grouped together, rolling dice, and hustling while attempting to talk to girls passing by. That day, it was quiet. I walked slow as hell, making sure I didn't miss a moment of that feeling—freedom. I wanted to see everything for myself, especially the boys who were older and more well-kept. This was my first time walking the grounds alone. To get to the store, I had to walk past the basketball court. Even if I wanted to look away, I couldn't. I hadn't seen that many cute boys in one place since the first time I saw Jodeci standing in the middle of the desert wearing black leather, singing their banger, "Cry for You." The first time I saw that video, I waited until everyone in the apartment went to sleep before frantically hoping it would play again on a rerun of *Video Soul*, the go-to show for Black music. They played all the videos and they were singing their hearts out. There wasn't a girl in the world who took the time to consider why anyone would be caught wearing leather while standing in the middle of the desert. No one cared, especially me. All I knew was that they gave me all the feels to the point that I wanted to get my hands on my own version of K-Ci. And if I couldn't find him, a DeVanté would do. That day, the basketball court looked like a good place to find one. Before I knew it, I was standing with my fingers through the fence, in a trance. The longer I watched, the freer I felt. Closing my eyes and allowing the wind to graze my hair and the sun to kiss my face, I made a vow to myself right then and there that I would find a way to discover this same feeling again.

That day, I circled the block, went to the store, grabbed the eggs, and made my way back home. Smart enough to recognize my first outing as an opportunity to build trust, since I ruined it with my past antics. I simply tested the waters. Even though I had not been gone much past my deadline, Mom was on my ass by the time I got back inside.

"Tamika, that was a long time. I was starting to get worried."

"It's cool. I walked slowly. Took my time, ya know? I didn't know much about the area. I got lost between the buildings, but I found my way."

She rolled her eyes while I made it my business to craft a lie worthy of the unaccounted time.

Mom wanted to tell me off, I'm sure, but there was no reason to because my lie logically checked out.

"I did get you a honey bun, though." Reaching into the bag, I retrieved the honey bun as my peace offering.

"Be clear. Ain't nothing out there for you to soak up. You got it?"

"I got it," I replied.

Under her breath, I heard her repeat sarcastically, "Lost between the buildings." "Thank you," she said, staring at me.

Once I saw her eyes, I knew she was watching me differently. I also knew I was off the hook for the evening. It was the unofficial charting of new territory. In my mind, managing to escape once meant I had what it took to do it again.

Dad was still asleep on the couch, so luckily for me, I didn't have to answer him at that moment. My mom gave me a pass and directed her attention back towards finishing the meal she was preparing with eggs in hand.

"Go take a bath," she said.

I sucked my teeth loud enough for her to hear me. She didn't reply, so I knew I was in the clear. After my bath, I stayed up, staring at the ceiling, thinking, and strategizing new ways to earn my parents' permission and trust. The small taste of freedom I accessed that day made me thirsty for more.

Over the next several weekends, my new routine consisted of scoping out who was outside when we returned from the rallies and finding a way to get back outside once Dad was on the couch resting and Mom began her cooking. Most of the time, my out was when she needed something from the store, which made it easy. At some point along the way, both my mom and dad knew that my going outside was less about doing them a favor and more about me hanging with friends in Co-op. The more I made my way outside, the more people I met who were in my age group. In spite of it all, the evolution of my social life was of no concern to my parents. There was never a time I was not required to specify where I was going. In addition, they always gave me a time they believed to be reasonable to return, but I was getting to the point where I no longer listened. I was far more interested in my own agenda, and eventually I met a girl who seemed to think and feel much of the same.

This Saturday in particular, I was minding my own business while pacing the aisles of the grocery store with a list of ingredients for Mom's pie until I heard an unfamiliar voice.

"Hey, did I see your parents on the news?"

A voice interrupted my gaze. A girl I had seen around Co-op but never formally met was standing in my personal space before I had a chance to gather myself, so I just nodded.

Now fully aware of the moment, I braced myself for whatever she had to say. I was used to people and their opinions about us, but she surprised me.

"Yo, that's mad cool. Shit, I'd just be happy if my dad showed up to scoop me when he was supposed to," she said.

Now aware that she didn't pose a threat, I responded in kind.

"I hear that."

"So you like having your father around?"

"Can't lie. I do. A lot."

"You lucky, but I bet you they don't let you do shit. I'm Raven by the way."

Raven was short and brown with a beauty mark above her left lip. Her jet-black microbraids were pulled into two ponytails on either side like Moesha. Her baggy jeans, white cropped tank, and fresh new J's were proof she had style. Raven was kind of fly. I on the other hand had no fashionable clothes. But that's something I'd have to get to later.

"We need that shit, to be honest. Kids around here getting into a lot."

"Like what?" I asked.

"Fighting behind buildings. Drinking 40s, smoking weed or, even worse, Newports."

"Damn," I replied.

It wasn't that I didn't know about what kids were doing; I just personally had not consumed alcohol or smoked. The parameters my parents set were too tight for me to do anything other than attend the rallies and school and go back home. Raven, now even more immersed in the conversation while clapping her hands, kept the party going.

"You know what else I be seeing?"

I raised an eyebrow in anticipation of her answer.

"Girls, getting dudes to spend that money on 'em. Trust me," she said before pushing my shoulder gently. "I see it all."

Now she had my attention. She ran with it.

"I've been seeing these fine-ass dudes out here hanging every day since summer started. Obviously, you see 'em too. Look at you, standing there smiling and shit."

I looked away as fast as I could.

"Look, you ain't gotta be shy. I'd probably be looking at you mad strange if you hadn't noticed all of this."

Easing my head back in the direction of the court, I allowed myself to smile. "I can't lie. It's mad dudes out here right now."

We looked at each other and cracked up laughing. Raven was cool.

"Where are you headed after this?"

"Nowhere in particular. I gotta get groceries back to my mom. She's trying to make a sweet potato pie."

"What for?"

"No reason. She just cooks a lot."

"Yo. Your moms is making a pie for no reason?" She raised an eyebrow and said, "Must be nice. My moms stopped cooking as much when my dad left. I guess she said fuck that."

I paused for a moment before asking, "Where did he go?"

"Hell if I know. All I know is that the day he left, he told me he was sorry and that he was never coming back."

You could see the pain in her eyes as she stared off into the distance while giving me what little details she had. Although I couldn't relate, all I could think about was the one time when my mom and dad were not seeing eye to eye. Luckily for me, they worked through their differences and I never had to watch him walk away. Raven wasn't so lucky.

"Fuck that," she said. Raven cursed a lot.

The sound of her voice startled me back to our conversation. I looked at her like she was half-crazy.

"You should come to Boston Road to the beauty supply store."

"For what?" I asked.

"I gotta get some bobby pins for my doobie and some black gel."

"You think we can make it? Seems kind of far."

"If we get the fuck out of here now, we can walk at our own pace. We could probably even grab a gyro and be right back to get the brown sugar for your moms," she said, raising her eyebrows and placing her hands on her hips.

In my mind, I questioned whether or not venturing that far away from Co-op was the right thing to do. The fact that we would have to take a bus to get to the beauty supply store should have been enough to convince me that an impromptu field trip with Raven was a bad idea. Maybe in my heart of hearts I needed to prove to myself and to Raven that I could. That day, I was forced to make a decision about what I was going to do. In retrospect, I now realize that the decision was more about what I was seeking. It was all so telling about my intrinsic motivations at this point in my life. As I saw it, there were two options. The first was to go to the store, grab the items for Mom to finish cooking, and come back home. This decision reflected loyalty to the perception that my parents maintained of me. The second option was to venture out on my own. A decision that was ultimately a demonstration of loyalty to myself. I stood on Bartow Avenue, under I-95, thinking long and hard about who and what I chose to be at that moment. Returning home early had the potential to break the newly established boundaries that had gotten me out of the house in the first place. If I went home early that day, would Mom expect me back early from that point forward? If I got on the bus alone, would I be safe? Ultimately, I decided to fall in line with my parents' requests of me, but not for long.

"Give me your number. Maybe we can go next week," I said.

I saw the disappointment on her face, but I didn't care because at least she knew I had a mind of my own. Raven left the store and I got the items I was supposed to get and went home for the win. When I got back home, I almost wished I made a different choice. Whatever I could have gotten into with Raven would have been far more exciting than sitting in the house with grown folks. Right then and there, I made up my mind that the next Saturday I was choosing myself. That day, however, I decided the preservation of my newfound freedom was not worth the risk.

As soon as I woke up, I called Raven. We began speaking regularly. That day, I barely gave her a chance to say anything before I blurted out my offer.

"Let's go," I said, shrugging my shoulders.

"Go where?"

"To the beauty supply store," I replied.

She didn't hesitate either. "Meet me downstairs."

The route she suggested when we were standing in the store was at least an hour, which meant coming back it would be the same, putting me way past curfew, but I couldn't worry about it because we were already in motion. There are no words to describe how good it felt to talk to someone who was my own age. Someone who shared my same interests. Raven was seeing the world the same way I saw it, but faster. She had seen and done more than I had, and therefore, she was interesting. Raven was cool and different from the girls in school, who kept drama brewing. She showed me how easy it was to escape and made me even more excited about the world outside of the walls behind which I was confined. From that day forward, my ambition was not just to get outside of our place but to test boundaries by any means necessary.

As I was walking back to Co-op, the reality of how long I'd been gone set in. I hardly said goodbye to Raven. Thoughts of Mom beating my ass took over and I still needed items from the store.

My mind raced while trying to get to the store to get the food from the list at the last minute. Even though I was late as hell, I was counting on not arriving home empty-handed. When I got to the front door of the store, it was locked and the workers were inside sweeping. Frantically, I knocked on the door, hoping for a miracle. Praying that someone would allow me to come inside.

"Please. I just need to get four things. I promise I'll be quick. . . . Please. My mom needs this stuff so she can cook," I pled.

As the owner came closer to the front door showing his hands, I knew it was over. Instead of running, I walked. Hanging my head in shame, not only was I afraid, but I was also ashamed I had nothing to show for having been gone so long. As I exited the elevator, my nerves got the best of me. My bottom lip quivered. Placing the key in the front door was the worst part. There was no way to know what or, even worse, who was on the other side. Pursing my lips together, standing on my toes, gripping the handle slowly, and easing the door open was harder than heart surgery. I had to do it quietly, as Mom was standing in the living room waiting for me. This time, there was no need for me to twist the handle; Mom hurried to the door just as I reached out my hand. To make matters worse, Dad, who was usually chillin', was on his feet. She let me walk through the door into the living room just long enough for Dad to get a single sentence out.

"Tamika, where have you been?" he asked.

Before I had time to muster up a lie, I heard the crack of the leather belt and felt the heat of it grazing against my legs. That night, Mom beat my ass. There was nothing to be said. I fucked up and the punishment was warranted. Especially after learning that my dad went to the store to get the items I was supposed to be bringing home and after he looked for me. I took my punishment like a champ. The few tears I did shed were more as a result of the anticipation of the moment than actual pain. Afterward, all I could do was shower and get in bed. While I was lying there, a part of me no longer cared what my parents felt. Inside there was a sense of celebration for what I managed to accomplish on my own. I no longer cared what anyone else thought; I wasn't going back to the old Tamika. She had been caged long enough.

Like clockwork, Raven would be waiting for me in front of the basketball courts, where we would spend the first twenty minutes watching the boys and catching up. Raven's lifestyle was different. Therefore, we had different sets of stories. Most of hers were about people who lived in the neighborhood.

"What up, girl," she would say as she greeted me. It was a term of endearment, although I never said it back.

For three Saturdays in a row, we ventured into the city by train together, each time staying out a little longer than before. My only goal was to be back before the sun went down.

By the end of July, I had established a pattern of coming and going as I saw fit and breaking the rules much more than I'm proud of. When I left the house, it had nothing to do with running an errand for Mom and everything to do with what was on my agenda. My actions were somewhat respectful while under their roof, but my thoughts were anything but. All I cared about was kicking the shit with Raven and a few other kids whose parents couldn't have cared less about what time they came in the house because they were too busy caught up in their own lives.

One day, I saw her leaving the building and getting into a car with a man I'd never seen before. She was also dressed in a way I'd never seen before. Black jeans, a white button-up shirt, and a pair of brown penny loafers, which were hardly her style. She looked like she was headed to a fancy dinner. She must have taken her braids out, because her hair was slicked into a bun. I later learned that it was her father who had picked her up. Either way, seeing her leave was confirmation that she wouldn't be able to hang. What I didn't know was that plans had also been made for me.

With Raven gone, I went back upstairs to map out a new plan. It was then that my parents informed me of their decision to have me stay at my cousin Tish's house and that we would be departing shortly for them to drop me off. Their decision was rooted in their belief that I would be better supervised there during the daytime hours. If I stayed at home alone, it meant I was granted at least eight idle hours per day. Based on my track record, they were no longer willing to risk it.

The only flaw in their plan was that Tish was not who the family perceived her to be. She lied all the time about her whereabouts and snuck out of the house often.

Tish, three years my senior, was what we called slim thick. She had the whole five-five with brown eyes thing going on. She thought she was the shit and so did everyone else. The guys thought she was cool because she knew all the lyrics to Nas's *Illmatic* album, and the girls wanted to be her. She always wore light pink lip gloss that made her eyes appear lighter and it drove the boys crazy. When we went out together, we knew we were cute. Jeans, doorknockers, cutoff tanks, and statement tees were all a part of the look. My father and her father were brothers, so we were cut from the same cloth. In most instances, I knew what she was thinking or her next move, except the times she let me take the fall in front of the family to preserve herself.

Tish had been running the streets far longer than I had, but unlike me, she always seemed to get away with her dirt. For the life of me, I could never understand how she managed to keep her reputation in the family intact. No one saw her as disrespectful or untrustworthy. It was me who was labeled as the one who didn't listen, the bigmouth of the family. A title I didn't care to own. In spite of it all, there were more similarities than differences between Tish and me, which meant we were always in danger of having a good time together, even if it was at my expense. The week I spent at her house ended in turmoil. We went out; we got caught;

I got in trouble. End of story. Like clockwork, Mom and Dad picked me up from Tish's house with disappointment in their eyes and the perception was that I was the cause of conflict. Although I was not completely innocent, Tish was the ringleader and I was following her lead, but no one cared to hear my side of the story.

There were too many times I felt like the scapegoat for other family members' wrongdoings. In my mind, nobody ever seemed to focus on anyone in the family other than me when it came to mischief. It was baffling to me. Anything that happened somehow always seemed to be my fault. Today I recognize this is what being a special person represents. While it is true that we are all special, my life was designed to be public, which comes with a different type of scrutiny and responsibility.

It is imperative that we recognize the power of our influence as adults in the lives of children and we must be cognizant of how we communicate our assertions of blame. In my adolescence, there was a stigma assigned to me. Whether I behaved and followed all the rules set by my parents or I abided by my own, I was the child who talked too much and didn't listen. What I recognize today as purpose in training was passion suffocated back then. Through the continuous threads of disappointment, the bar for me during my adolescence was low and I was determined to meet it. The raging waters of hormones, mixed with a desire for independence, were brewing inside me. The dark clouds of my quest to discover myself on my own terms were ever present. As with every storm, conditions get worse before they get better. Unbeknownst to me, a tornado named Lucci was brewing in the distance.

The first time I met Lucci was at my dad's softball game. Dad often took me with him and I looked forward to going. The games were held in a park on 145th Street in Harlem that was separated into two sides. The field and bleachers were located on one side and an open space with swings, monkey bars, sprinklers, slides, and merry-go-rounds was on the other side. On most Sundays, the Icee man parked his cart on the opposite side of the field. I always wanted to look really cute when attending the games. When I went out with my father, my mother made sure I was adorable. Now old enough to walk from one side of the park to the other on my own, I looked forward to getting an Icee. It wasn't often that I met people I didn't know at the park, but one Sunday in particular, this fine-ass boy spoke to me.

"Hey," a deep, throaty voice said from behind.

Turning around, I was pleasantly surprised. He had a basketball player build. Taller than me, lanky, with long hands, hazel eyes, and a curly low top. He was beautiful.

"Hey," I said back.

"What's your name?" he asked.

"Tamika. What's yours?"

"I'm Lucci."

"Where are you from?"

"I just moved from Harlem to the Bronx."

"Where do you live?"

"A few blocks away," he responded.

My attention was drawn away from him by the little boy hanging around his leg. "Oh. That's your little brother?" I asked. He nodded.

"What are you doing in the park by yourself?"

"My father is playing softball over there," I said, motioning my head in the direction of the men on the field.

As the afternoon went on, Lucci and I discovered a commonality. He lived in Harlem and he loved sports. It interested me that he was so into what was happening with the game my dad was playing. Before the day came to an end and the softball match ended, we exchanged numbers, agreeing to keep in touch. And we did.

Over the next few weeks, anytime I was in Harlem, I made it my business to hang out with Lucci. On more occasions than I can count, I found time to sneak on the phone, whispering plans to get to Harlem to visit Lucci. After a few random visits, we had an airtight itinerary in place. After I left my house, I stopped to call him on the pay phone. When I got off the number 2 train, Lucci met me at 125th and Lenox. Sometimes he would pay for my cab to cut down the travel time. By cab, it was only a thirty-minute ride to Harlem. By train, the distance takes over an hour. Based on the curfew Mom and Dad gave me, I had approximately four hours to be outside.

On most of our visits, we just hung out and shot the shit. Laughing together about random things and being young. Lucci told me about his hoop dreams and I dreamed with him. Although I had several visits with Lucci, the last one was what I won't ever forget. That day it was harder to get out of the house than usual. For whatever reason, Mom gave me a shorter window to be out. I had already made up my mind that I was going to break curfew if I needed to while going to see Lucci. When I arrived in Harlem, he met me at 125th and Lenox per usual. That day, we walked to his grandmother's house, which was several blocks away. His grandparents were older, so it felt as if we were in the house alone. Even so, nothing was out of the ordinary from every other time we met up, at least in my mind. We watched TV, played video games, ate snacks, and laughed just like we always had. As the time closed in, I knew without question that there was no way for me to make it home on time. Getting anxious as the sun went down, I expressed my concern to Lucci.

"It's time for me to go," I said.

"Come on. Just stay a little longer," he pled.

We kissed and fondled on most days, but this day was different. He kept the lights out for much longer than usual.

Every time I tried to get up and leave, he held me down, begging me to stay. After a twenty-minute series of cat and mouse, I made my way to the door. He was pouting the entire time. And by the time we were on the staircase that led to the ground floor, he was holding my face, trying to kiss me and touch me in places he had not before. I didn't want him to, and I pushed him away. My lack of interest did not stop him. Instead, he became more aggressive.

Now standing behind me, he had turned into someone I didn't know. "Stop, Lucci. Please."

My words were loud and clear, but in his mind they must have been a joke, as he forced himself in me, sticking his penis inside my anus. My plea for him to stop fell upon deaf ears, and at the age of fourteen I was assaulted by someone whom I called a friend. Much later I learned that anal penetration was a popular act among teenagers to prevent pregnancy.

By the time he stopped, I felt like a lesser version of myself. He didn't speak, nor did I. He hailed a cab; I got in and he closed the door. That was it. No explanation. No apology. No acknowledgment of violation. All I could think about on the ride home was that I didn't have to pick up anything from the store for Mom to cook dinner. By the time I got home, my parents were waiting for me. Unlike most days, I was thankful for their chastisement. The boundaries and perimeters that felt like a prison before felt like more of a safety net that day. For the last few days of summer, I was on punishment and, surprisingly enough, I welcomed it.

From that day forward, I avoided Lucci and only saw him once or twice after the assault. The less I called him, the less he called me. Lucci never apologized. When I started to pull away from him or be less available, he didn't fight for me or make me feel wanted. He didn't care, and because of that, I felt devalued. The way that he moved on made me feel as if I didn't matter.

Lucci was proof of how women can sometimes still be in contact with someone who has assaulted them. Instead of holding Lucci accountable for his actions, I blamed myself. I knew I was not supposed to be there with him. Had I not been there, maybe it would not have happened. I had already been identified by my family as too grown and that label stayed with me.

I can't say that I took the time to heal from being assaulted. In truth, I don't know what healing from that looks like. Like much of my trauma during my adolescent years, I put it in the back of my mind.

It is a daunting truth to admit that Lucci shaped me. It is because of him I learned a hard lesson about being in places and spaces where I should not be. Even more demoralizing, I was forced to acknowledge that people will violate you, even if at some point in time you called them friend. After I was violated, my mind processed the trauma as a lack of participation on my part, therefore confirming that my body was what was most important to men. As I look back over the youngest and most vulnerable years of my adolescence, this sentiment pushed me into having sex prematurely. In my fourteen-year-old eyes sex was a necessary component to extend relationships with men and every decision I made in this season was influenced as such.

CHAPTER 5

A TEENAGE LOVE

The Bible tells us that love is both patient and kind. In my life, my dad was the personification of both. He demonstrated patience and kindness through the gift of his time. On more occasions than I can remember, he gave his time and showed me I was worthy of love. As I recount times spent just the two of us, my fondest memories are centered in the sound of beating drums in the streets of Harlem. The African-American Day Parade, a highlight in the month of September, was a time when the diaspora came alive. The variance of rhythm, tempo, and intensity of the drums still today remind me that I am the descendant of a people capable of triumph. At the African-American Day Parade, coordinating costumes reminiscent of Carnival in the Caribbean flooded the streets of Harlem: dashikis, kente cloth, and every representation of Black culture ever present. Reverberating harmonies of unapologetic Blackness consumed the air. Attendees like Dad and me were dressed in our best street clothes. Hightop Reeboks, fifty-four elevens, as we called them, and everything in between. The goal was to be fly.

We'd walk the entire parade route that ran from West 110th Street and Seventh Avenue all the way to its end point near the Armory at West 136th Street and Fifth Avenue. We sampled food and supported local vendors. Miles and miles of Blackness is what I remembered while walking next to my dad. The entire week leading up to the event was a whirlwind of activity, even after my mom passed off parade-day responsibilities to my father. Every year on the morning of the parade, she would buzz through the kitchen, meticulously gathering an assortment of our favorite fruits, sandwiches, juice boxes, and chips to ensure I was fully prepared for a day in the city. Her second objective was to make sure I was fresh to death. Short sets she ironed the night before were perfectly creased and my hair was coiffed in a fresh doobie or a half-up/half-down style. Dad was fly too in his African garments bought directly from African vendors.

Year after year, Dad secured the perfect spot at 125th and Seventh Avenue, walking the distance with me and carrying our food at the same time. When I was a little girl, my father's presence brought me a sense of serenity, along with a warm feeling of hope and joy that kept me shielded from the world's troubles. He did everything in his power to protect me, but as the years passed, the seasons of life began to change. By the time I reached puberty, I was no longer the little girl perched atop her dad's shoulders at the African-American Day Parade, eyes sparkling with joy. The love he so generously gave was no longer enough to quell the curiosity that adolescence awakened. Instead of unconditional love, I found myself yearning for fleeting acceptance.

Though my parents worked tirelessly to shield me from the hard lessons of the streets, those very lessons became some of my most profound teachers. Everything they tried to protect me from turned into the very things I craved and desired.

Within a month at Harry S Truman High School, curiosity had completely taken over. I had convinced myself that nothing my teachers offered held any value for me. Nobody took the time to help me channel my interests or energy the way I wanted, and while I am in no way blaming them, this is my truth as I lived it. It was in many ways a continuation of the story I've lived all my life—that people never actually saw me. Instead, I have always felt like a foreign object and that there was something about me that did not resonate in the rooms and with the people who held closed the gates to my advancement. I thought that by acting out I could prove that I was just like everyone else. Raging hormones, unfettered curiosity about the world around me, and aching impulsiveness drove my decisions. The friends I gathered as an adolescent were not good for me, and in retrospect, I was not good for them.

Truman was so vast, and the lack of supervision so evident, that you could skip school while still being on campus. On other days, I wandered the streets, grabbed food, and hung out on a bench in Co-op, people-watching and chatting with others who, like me, had decided to ditch school. Once we caught wind of truancy officers swarming around our preferred spots, we pivoted to day parties at one another's apartments.

In retrospect, that was only for the worse. I was hanging out with boys all the time, and I realized that I was placing myself in danger by not being where I was supposed to be. There were so many things that could have happened to me, but I can't lie; I felt cool. One day, when I should have been in school, I found what I was looking for, or should I say he found me.

"Tamika, wait up."

"How you know my name?"

"I asked those ugly-ass girls you hang out with," he said, motioning his head towards the girls I was running with at the time—none of whom ever seemed to like me, but that's another story.

"You know you shouldn't be calling people ugly, right?"

He looked at me like I was crazy, having hit a nerve and activated a future Tamika—the advocate—not even I was fully aware of yet.

"As Black people, we have enough to battle. We damn sure don't need to call each other names."

We were three minutes into the conversation and I was already standing on my soapbox, preaching what I'd learned from my parents and the movement.

"Yeah. Ok, preacher. I got you," he said.

We both burst into laughter.

"I'm surprised she told you."

"I'm not," he replied. "She didn't have much of a choice. I threatened to tell her big brother she was sexin' dudes in Section Two."

"Oh. Damn. You would actually do that to her?"

Although I didn't mention it, my antenna immediately went up. The fact that he was willing to make up a story about Raven told me a lot about his character. It was a flaw I was willing to overlook because he was the first guy to give me attention.

I had never taken the time to look at Reggie. I only knew who he was because Raven's older brother was supposedly dating his older sister. It was none of my business, but I always saw his sister out with another dude on the days I skipped school. Reggie was fine. A brown version of Bishop from the movie *Juice*. I took note of the way he licked his lips as I got closer, and the way he used his hands when he was talking and wanted to make a point.

"Come walk with me to my building."

That was all he needed to say. Flattered by his invitation, I didn't ask any questions. I was naive. I thought "come over to my place" was an invitation to chill. Like a playdate, but instead of two girls, it was just Reggie and me. When we got to his apartment the first visit, his mom was in the kitchen and his brother was in the back room. That day, we played video games on his Sega Genesis, drank cherry Kool-Aid with way too much sugar, and shot the shit while *Family Matters* played on the TV in the background.

Over time, our impromptu meetups in an apartment where people flittered around as we wasted time turned into visits where we were alone. The games on his mother's couch turned into moments of experimentation, and eventually we were no longer doing kid activities. The first time we had sex was in a room he shared with his brother. I didn't know what I was doing, but it was clearly not Reggie's first time. He told me what to do and that was it. I lay down a little girl and got up a woman.

When I returned to my parents' place, I showered and plotted things out so they would find me in my room doing homework. My sister Sharon had started a life of her own by then. She was married and on her way. As I reflect back, I can't imagine the roller coaster of emotions my parents must have experienced watching their little girl grow and force her way out into a world ready to drink her up; wondering if I was safe and if I was where I'd said I would be. Well, I wasn't. Hooking up with Reggie became a frequent activity. I never took the time to ask why he wasn't in school because I already knew the answer, told through the constant flow of people coming up to him as we sat in the park, and the small packages exchanged hand to hand for money. Soon Raven joined in with one of Reggie's friends and we all became the kids making out behind the buildings outside. It was all madness. When the weather got too cold Raven and I decided to kick it at another girl's house on our free afternoons. And on one particular day, in my mind, I decided that if Reggie wanted to find me, he knew how. There must have been about six of us hanging out that day.

"Yo. I got a bootleg version of this new movie that came out." Raven was always getting her hands on shit first.

"What movie?" I asked.

"Girl. *Scream.* You better recognize. I heard people been mad scared watching it."

I didn't say anything at first, because I wasn't a fan of movies with folks getting killed for no reason. Judging from the enthusiasm of everyone else in the room, I was the odd man out.

Eventually, I stood right in front of the TV and said, "So y'all like watching folks dying?"

"Tamika, girl. Move your ass," Raven joked.

I moved from the couch to sit by the window and saw that Raven hadn't been lying when she said you could see all of New York from the girl's apartment. Most importantly, I could actually see my place from there too. I sat there and watched as both my mom and dad got home from work and eventually my dad went back out to run an errand before returning for the night. The only person missing was me. What I had not prepared to see from above was Reggie, making out with another girl just like when we first met. She was a short and fair girl with a fresh perm, half up, half down. It was obvious they were more than just friends, as he caressed her face.

That night, I didn't go home at all. I fell asleep on the couch at Raven's house, and when I woke the next morning I woke up pissed. If I had seen Reggie that day, I probably would have punched him in the face.

When I finally arrived home, I braced myself for Mom and Dad's disappointment. By this point, she had stopped hitting me and he was beyond punishment because I was too far gone. Instead, Mom stood in silence, staring straight into my soul. The concern on her face showed up as two wrinkles between her eyes. There was also an emptiness I hadn't seen before. It was a look of loss, maybe even despair. She didn't speak of it, nor did I. Shaking her head, she let out a big sigh and walked away from me towards the kitchen. Walking to my room, I could hear her on the phone telling my aunt that they were considering sending me away to a boarding school.

"Ola Mae, I swear, I don't know what's gotten into that girl. I don't even know who she is anymore. All we can do is pray for her now."

I can't say she had written me off, but as a mother today myself, I can confirm there are times you have to let go of the rope to keep from severing your fingers, the moment you realize that your words no longer carry the power to change your child's behavior. Mom knew it was not possible to want a better life for me than what I wanted for myself.

Coming home at respectable hours, getting an education, neither of those things was my priority anymore.

———

A few days after seeing Reggie, I left school early, casually walking past the same metal detectors I had passed earlier that morning. Retracing my steps, just as I had when sneaking out for lunch on my own schedule, I followed my usual route, passing by the basketball courts. The basketball courts were empty—it was too cold to play on a December morning. As I reached my building, I spotted Reggie standing just inside the doorway. Any hope of avoiding him vanished in an instant. He grabbed the back of my arm.

"Tamika. Wait up. I've been looking for you for days. Where have you been?"

I stopped. "I guess I could ask you the same question."

He looked as if he had no idea why I would be upset.

"I saw you."

"You saw me, what?"

"I saw you out here last week with that other girl."

He stepped back, releasing his grip from my arm, taking a long pause before rubbing his hands together. I braced myself to receive his apology.

"Man, you are bugged out. You already know what it is between us."

In disbelief, I said, "Are you fucking serious, Reggie? So we're not together. I should have never fucked you."

On this day, I was unusually calm. On a regular day, I would have been far more irate and screaming, but on this day, I did not have it in me to do so.

"I never said it was just you and me. We good though," he said.

"When you see me, don't say shit to me," I said.

My pride wouldn't allow me to plead with him. Instead, I walked towards the elevator, hoping, wishing, that maybe he would try to stop me, but he didn't. He let me go without so much as an apology.

From this moment, I learned a valuable lesson about life: Always ask; don't assume.

"You a muthafucker for this, Reggie," I said before the elevator doors closed. After a few months, my first official relationship in my head was over. Tears streamed down my face. Hurt, disgust, deceit, were all a part of the sick feeling in my stomach. When I got to the front door of our apartment, I leaned my forehead on it and watched the tears fall from my eyes to the floor.

The next morning, I woke up and called Raven to see if she was down to hit the streets, and of course she was. After I seized the opportunity to lighten my load, explaining myself and confessing to her about Reggie, she gave me the same bad advice that all girlfriends give one another.

"The way to get over one man is to move on to the next."

It sounded good at the time, but there would be hell to pay for it later.

The first time I saw Reggie after the night at the elevator was about a week later. Raven and I walked across the basketball courts, and there was no doubt he saw me—his eyes locked directly with mine.

"Just keep walking, girl. He ain't worth it," Raven compelled as she grabbed my arm to her chest.

Unbeknownst to Reggie, or even Raven, he was not the only guy who caught my attention. And I had convinced myself the way to strike back was to take *control of my destiny*.

Earlier that same day as Raven and I were walking down 125th Street, we spotted a gold Lexus easing past. The guys in the car noticed us from behind and came to a rolling stop. The guy on the passenger side didn't say much, but the driver was spitting his shit.

"Say, Ma, where y'all heading?"

Before I could answer, Raven inserted herself. "We're heading wherever y'all are heading."

The driver was chocolate with a dark fade and waves that could still be seen under his red do-rag. His thin lips set against sizable teeth were the perfect backdrop for his gift of gab. He kind of reminded me of Big Daddy Kane back in the days of *Yo! MTV Raps* when Fab Five Freddy was the host. He had on a white A-sweatshirt and a fat-ass rope chain around his neck. He was loud and boisterous.

"How you heading where we heading and you don't know where we going, Ma?" Raven shrugged her shoulders. "Come around here," he said. "What's your name?" She looked at me, before walking around to his side of the car. "Yo. You need to pull over before you be askin' my friend to walk in the middle of the busy-ass street," I said before rolling my eyes. Raven didn't care. All she saw was the Lexus. He asked her name again.

"You asking me a bunch of questions. Tell me your name."

"Marlon," I heard him respond.

The passenger, a hue fairer than the driver, wore a blue button-down shirt with the sleeves rolled up and a pair of white linen shorts. He wore three medium-sized gold rope chains with huge charms hanging from each one of them. One charm was a cross, the other was a diamond-trimmed dog tag, and the third a replica of the continent of Africa, which caught my attention. Peering inside the car, I could see his arms and legs were toned. Not toned like he ran track, toned like he spent a few years on the football field or he had been to jail. His slanted eyes and soft lips captured my eye.

"Oh. So I see you're a little firecracker." He spoke gently, but his voice was brisk and masculine.

"What do you mean by that?"

"What's your name, Ma?" he asked.

"Tamika. What's yours?"

"Cane."

"How old are you, Tamika?"

I had to think quickly on my feet. I know he was looking at me, thinking I was young. "Eighteen. I'm eighteen," I insisted.

He knew I was lying, but he clearly did not care. It was the first time I ever lied about my age. Prior to that day, I never had to be any age other than sixteen. If I told him I was sixteen, he might have cut the conversation off, but that's not what I wanted. I wanted to keep it going, and I did. I knew he was older.

Leaning into the car, I said, "So. Are we going with y'all or not?"

"That's my bitch right there," Raven hailed from the other side of the car. Ghetto as hell as always.

"I guess y'all are heading where we're heading," said Marlon.

It was Cane who had the final say, which led me to believe he was the boss. Raven hopped in the back seat and so did I. We ended up at Junior's, a restaurant in Brooklyn famous for its cheesecake and late-night hours. Many years later, Puff Daddy Combs would put it on the national map in an episode of one of the first reality TV shows, *Making the Band*.

When we arrived, Raven and I had an impromptu girls' meeting in the bathroom and agreed to step our shit up. I told her she needed to stop being so loud. We recognized that we had not been on a date or in the presence of grown-ass men. For them to believe that we were old enough to be there, with them, we needed to handle ourselves differently. When we sat down at the table, we were women. Raven sat across from Marlon and me across from Cane.

We spent the rest of the afternoon getting to know one another and having a good time. It was Cane who asserted they had to leave and requested the check. After Cane paid, he sent Marlon to retrieve the car and pull around the front to pick the three of us up. It was at that moment I knew I picked the right guy, or at least I thought I did. I still remember the view as we rode back across the Brooklyn Bridge. It was so beautiful at night. Staring at the bridge was a reminder that there was a whole world I had yet to explore. They took us all the way up to Co-op. When I got out, I thanked them for a good time. As I began walking towards Section 3, I felt a hand on my arm. "Wait. Hold on. You're not going to give me your number or anything?"

I smiled and dropped my head.

"Like I said. Thank you for today. If it's meant for you to have my number, I'll see you again."

"You a smart-ass bitch," Raven said as she walked around to the other side of the car, reached into his car to retrieve a pen, and wrote my number on his hand before locking her arm in mine. We walked off towards the buildings. After everything that went down with Reggie, I figured this time I'd be the one playing hard to get. Another reason I didn't want Cane to have my number was because I knew my parents would not allow calls; I was already in too much trouble.

Over the course of several weeks, I was more tired than usual. Some days I felt like myself and others I was just out of it, so I slept. It had been three months after the end of the relationship with Reggie. Thankful that I had managed to erase him from my system, when I was awake, I daydreamed of seeing Cane again, if I ever went back outside. Some of the foods I ate on a regular basis now made me nauseous. All the obvious clues that my hormones were shifting became apparent. I brushed them aside as puberty, but it was much more than that. Too young to know what a baby growing inside my body felt like, I missed many of the signs that I was pregnant. The two months prior, my period arrived like clockwork. The Saturday afternoon I threw up a slice of pizza, I knew something was off. Immediately, I grabbed my purse and hopped on the elevator to head over to Raven's apartment. I was beating on her door, like the police.

"Girl, open the door. It's me." When the door opened, it wasn't Raven; it was her grandmother. She stood with her hand on the door looking at me like I was half-crazy. Even though it was ten in the morning, most folks were sleeping in.

"Lil girl, why you got your lil fast ass out here banging on my door this time of the morning?"

"I'm sorry. . . . I . . . I just need to talk to Raven."

"Talk to Raven about what?" she chastised. The look on her face was stern, like she meant business. Before she could go harder, Raven appeared.

"Ma. Leave Tamika alone. Let her in," she said, gently wedging her body in front of her grandmother's. Both Raven's mother and father were in and out of her life; therefore, she spent the majority of her time with her grandparents.

"Girl. Come in. Grandmoms is trippin'."

I threw myself onto Raven's bed as she closed the door. "What the fuck is wrong with you?"

"I think I'm pregnant."

"Pregnant," she yelled.

I put my finger across my mouth. "Shhhhhh. What the fuck, Raven. I don't want anyone to know."

"Hell no," she said as she started pacing. "You can't be pregnant. No fucking way."

"You know I wouldn't even be saying this shit if I didn't think it was real."

She fell down on the bed beside me.

"Damn. That's fucked up, Tamika. Pregnant by who? I know not Reggie's ass."

"He's the only person I ever slept with, except this one guy in Harlem."

"Damn. Are you sure?"

"Hell yeah, I'm sure."

"Would you tell your parents if you were?"

"How the hell could I? They are already sick of my shit. This would hurt them on a different level." The tears began flowing while I was sitting on the bed with Raven and continued when I got back home and cried myself to sleep.

For almost a month, I walked the straight and narrow. Each morning I woke up, went to school, and did my best to not leave early. If I stopped with the bullshit and became who my parents wanted me to be, maybe the pregnancy would disappear; at least that was how I rationalized it. The more I willed it away, the more the pregnancy became real. There was no other choice than for me to go to the doctor. Oddly enough, they never asked me any questions as to why I was completing my paperwork alone. All I remember is telling the doctor I thought I was pregnant and him telling me to pee in a cup that I wrote my name on and placed into a silver metal mailbox in the bathroom. It seemed easy enough. The next day and the day after, there was no news. The false sense of hope I had came to a screeching halt on the third day when I was standing in the kitchen and the phone rang. My mom was nearby cooking and my dad was in the back room, out of earshot, with Barbara Walters on *20/20* playing in the background.

"Is this Tamika Mallory?"

I was too afraid to confirm or deny my identity.

"Tamika, this is Dr. Watson from the Midway Clinic."

My mom, who was stirring pasta in a pot, stopped and turned around before putting the spoon down and walking to the other room to pick up the other phone as the doctor continued.

"The results from your pregnancy test came back. They show a positive reading."

Silence. You could have heard a pin drop in the kitchen. There was a ringing noise in my ears and I felt as if I was going to pass out.

"Hello. Hello, Doctor. This is Tamika's mother," she spoke into the phone. "Are you sure you have the right Tamika?" she asked.

More tears began streaming down my face as the doctor doubled down on his findings.

"When, I mean, when was she even there? Are you sure you have the right Tamika?" she asked again.

"Tamika, do I have permission to speak about your health with your mom?" the doctor asked.

Mom interjected, "Tamika is a child."

"Tamika, I need you to know that you have many options."

"Tamika, hang up the phone," Mom demanded.

I did as I was told.

When we hung up the phone, the apartment was somber. It was as if someone had died. Maybe there was a part of her that mourned the loss of the little girl she once knew. Her tears were proof that she suffered insurmountable loss. She stumbled towards the kitchen table, sat, and wailed. All I could do was stand there and take it. I wasn't deserving of an escape to my room and I knew it. It had never been my intention to hurt her this way, but the recklessness that was my new normal left little room for anything other than major disappointment.

"Go away from me, Tamika. I can't talk to you right now anymore about this. You are still my daughter and I love you, but I can't stand the sight of you at this moment. You have caused this family too much heartache and grief. I will have to figure out how to tell your father."

"I'm sorry, Mom," I whispered. I was lost and confused. There was no way for me to know what would become of me and where to go from that point forward.

"Just go," she warned. I left the kitchen and retreated to my room. From there, I could overhear her pleading with my father for over thirty minutes. Eventually, I heard my sister Sharon walk into the apartment.

Instead of a full intervention-style family meeting, it was just the four of us: my mother, father, sister, and me. The dread etched across my mother's face made her almost unrecognizable. When I walked into the living room, my father slammed his fist into the table and walked out. That moment, right then and there, I felt sorry for all of the trouble I caused my parents. For the first time in a long time, I felt remorse. The three of us remained in an emotional exchange for about twenty minutes before my sister went into strategy mode.

We sat on the couch in the living room as a family and discussed the options for my future. The overall consensus was that I was too young to become a parent and that our family did not have the financial resources to sustain another life, but ultimately the decision was mine to make. It was clear that my mother was not in favor of me having a child. An abortion was what I saw as my only viable option. Even then, I did not have the capacity to process what having an abortion would feel like. All I knew was that after having one I would no longer be pregnant, and that's all I wanted. There was no need for me to sleep on the decision or to think about it any longer. My decision to have an abortion was not one that required processing. I just wanted the nightmare to end. We agreed as a family that it was my body and my choice and the decision was final.

My mother made me schedule the procedure myself. A week later, on a Wednesday, against her will, she and my sister Sharon, as well as my other sister, Dana, who happened to be in town from North Carolina, were making preparations to take me to the clinic. My father drove us. They all stayed with me for the duration of the process, which I recall as torturous since I was now four and a half months pregnant, almost too far along to have had an abortion. The cold table, the snapping of rubber gloves around the wrists of white hands, the needles, the tugging of my uterus, and the blurry vision of doctors talking over my limp body were all I could remember as I came to the recovery room. Alone, uncertain, and petrified, I attempted to sit up but felt too weak to do so. With a single tear streaming down my face, I promised myself that when I got up from the hospital table I would never return under any circumstances. Although my family was present, I went into the room alone.

CHAPTER 6

A HARD KNOCK LIFE

By the time I turned sixteen, there was nothing sweet about it.

After escaping the cliché of becoming another teen mother statistic, I was invincible, or at least I thought I was. While lying on the recovery table after my first abortion I made a pact with myself to never get pregnant as a teenager again, but the thrill-seeking side of me was still alive. Two weeks after the procedure, I was free to do whatever the fuck I wanted, again. What I wanted led me back outside with Raven. The first time I saw her since confessing my concern I might be pregnant wasn't strange at all. In fact, we never had another conversation about a baby at all, but she must have known. Between my absence and change in behavior, it didn't take a rocket scientist to figure out where I'd been. Either way, it was behind me and I was committed to move forward and on to a whole season of my worst inclinations. Hood shit and ratchetry with my best friend. It was summertime.

The day I returned to my old antics, Reggie was outside. The sight of him made my mouth dry and my skin crawl. There he was living life like mine hadn't just been turned upside down. He had no idea about the trauma I experienced from our negligence. I wondered if it had all been an accident or if getting me pregnant was his intent all along. Either way, he was the one who knew what he was doing, and I really didn't. With clenched fists and hot air seething inside me, escaping through my nose, I pictured myself storming onto that court and landing a punch so hard he'd collapse in front of the other guys shooting hoops. I wanted them to laugh at him while he lay there, humiliated. I wanted them to laugh at him while he was down. I wanted him to feel something. Anything. He deserved to be embarrassed the same way I had been when the doctor told everybody in my house that I was pregnant over the phone. He deserved to feel an ounce of the pain I felt lying there on that table as they took the baby from my body. He deserved some form of punishment for what he had done to me. I gagged at the sight of him, mustering up all I could to keep myself from throwing up.

Raven must have noticed my evil gaze in Reggie's direction.

"Remember what I told you, Tamika," she said. "The only way to make your ex jealous is with your next."

"Yeah. I remember."

We slapped hands and walked in a new direction to leave Co-op. A direction that didn't force me to have to see Reggie. Raven's words were my new marching orders, and a week later I had a new dude.

Deion had more money than Reggie and more clout. He made a name for himself in the streets. His reach went way farther than Co-op City. After he'd been living there with his family for several years, they bought a house and moved to Bed-Stuy. Deion managed to build a small street empire along the way, so he moved differently than most guys his age. He wasn't standing in the park selling weed like Reggie. Instead, he had a few Reggies working for him. The night of Raven's brother's twenty-first birthday was my first time laying eyes on Deion. Everybody in the house was packed into the kitchen, smoking weed and drinking in celebration of the day, Raven's grandparents were out of town, which meant the kids had free rein. The only reason I came over was that I was bored in the house and wanted to get out. The front door to their apartment was unlocked, so I let myself in. When I walked into the kitchen, the monstrous cloud of smoke covered their faces. Raven called out to me, and I walked towards her until the smoke cleared and I saw her face.

"Tamika!" she exclaimed, as she turned to notify no one in particular, "That's my best friend, y'all!"

"Raven, you be too muthafucking loud, yo," her brother blurted out while desperately clinging to his high.

"What's up, Sis? What is all of this?"

"It's my brother's birthday and you know we always turn up for birthdays around here."

"I see," I replied.

I tapped Raven's brother on the shoulder and wished him a happy birthday before noticing a guy sitting next to him.

"Thanks, Tamika," he replied, but I could barely hear him because I was too busy admiring his friend.

"Deion, you want to hit this?" Raven's brother asked, passing him the blunt. Deion was skyscraper tall with almond eyes, pink lips, and a flat top fade. Deion stood out because he wasn't as loud as the other guys. He didn't need to be because he looked better. When I saw him smile the first time, I wanted to see it again. I was mesmerized by the way he towered over me, and my only goal became getting him to notice me before the day was through. Positioning myself by the door, I knew he had to pass me on the way out.

"You leaving?" I asked.

He was quick on his feet with his response. "Why? You want me to stay?"

"Tamika, get your ass out of the way so this man can go please." Raven's brother was cockblocking, but I was determined to overcome that.

"Maybe if you give me your number, we can talk about it over the phone."

Raven walked over just in time with a grimace and a pen in hand, passing it to Deion. He wrote his number on the inside of my hand and the rest was history. Every day thereafter, we talked on the phone. For over two weeks, we planned the next time we would see each other. He lived with his family in Bed-Stuy, so it wasn't as easy to see him because of the distance. The first time I caught the train to his house, I went alone. Truth be told, I didn't want Raven in my business. Even though it would not have been hard for her to find out, I wasn't the one who planned to tell her immediately. The train ride wasn't as bad as I thought, and once I got off the train his house wasn't far away. That day I met his whole family. His mother, sister, baby brother, and grandmother were all under one roof. Deion was the man of the house and they respected him as such. His mother served him the same way my mom served my dad, and everyone catered to him.

"Can we get you anything else, baby?" his grandmother asked. Grandma Pearlie could not have been any taller than five feet. On most days she wore a fuzzy housecoat and matching slippers that sounded like someone was scratching on cardboard as she shuffled through the house on the wooden floors. She had Deion's heart and eventually mine.

She was too stubborn to use the walker she'd been prescribed and always sat in the window in her bedroom facing the street. Her face in the window was how I could always know Deion was at home, because when he left he always made sure she was set up in the TV room, front and center to catch her favorite soap opera, *The Young and the Restless*, or her backup, *All My Children*. The running joke said *All My Children* was Grandma Pearlie's forbidden pleasure, a vice that meant she was cheating on her "husband" Victor Newman.

To be honest, Grandma Pearlie was far more interesting than Deion and always dropping knowledge about lessons she learned in life. More than just Deion's grandma to me, she became someone I trusted.

Eventually I disclosed my relationship with Deion to Raven, and she became my alibi when I needed to spend the night at his house. There were many weekends that I left on a Friday as if I were going to school and returned on Sunday afternoon as if I were preparing for the week ahead. All the while, I'd been in Bed-Stuy kicking it.

The first time I suspected I was pregnant from Deion, a small yet obvious weight loss, coupled with the onset of constant nauseousness led me to the drugstore to get a pregnancy test. When it came back positive, I didn't panic. Instead, I told Deion about it on a Friday afternoon. "So what do you wanna do about it, Ma?" he asked.

"I'm not old enough to be anybody's mother."

I'd been on the pill, but I had not been consistent with taking them. He sat for a minute in silence.

"Alright. Lemme know what we need to do. I got you."

By Monday morning, I was back at home, mid-miscarriage. I couldn't run the risk of disappointing my parents again. I did the best I could to clean up after the majority of the pain subsided, my mind singularly focused for a time. The next few days I pretended to be getting ready for school, but I never left the house. And by that weekend, I was back up and catching the train to Deion's house.

I still felt alone, but it was different this time. Unlike with Reggie, it was obvious that Deion cared. That weekend I shared in detail what happened when I lost the baby. The gruesome act of clearing my blood from the bathroom so no one at home would know. He brought me food and lay down with me. He told me to put my feet up and rest. But no matter how hard he tried, a distance remained.

It had been understandable that we had spent our time in his house, because it was where we had the freedom to be ourselves and lay up the way we wanted to, but it was still work. The constant lying to my parents and juggling alibis to keep everyone at arm's length proved to be overwhelming. My visits slowed down, and the less I visited, the less Deion asked when I would be coming over next. The final chapter with Deion was written after I turned the page to a story of love named Jason.

Jason was like a male version of me. We lived in the same building in Co-op and he too felt like the black sheep of his family. His sense of humor, his good heart, and the way he managed to see the beauty of the world through pain made him one of a kind in my world. Although he was in no way corny, he was not a hustler like most of the guys who hung around the way. He was working at a law firm when we met. We discovered a commonality in our laughter, and together we could talk for hours on end about everything or nothing at all. Every time I saw him, it was like the first time all over again. Our bond grew during moments in the hallway of our building, when one or both of us had been put out due to a lack of understanding by our parents. Jason was close with his mother, but lived under his grandparents' roof. His mother's battle with addiction made consistency challenging, and Jason's grandparents had a vision for his life that didn't align with running the streets or going and coming as he saw fit. Just like with my parents, Jason's grandfather told him he was locking the door at a certain time and if Jason didn't make it home by that curfew, then he was left without a place to go. On the nights when we were both locked out, we managed to find a couch in somebody's apartment.

In retrospect, we were protecting each other, he to me as much as me to him; I never let him couch surf alone if I could be by his side. By the time I was seventeen years of age, I was spending more time outside than under my own roof. Jason and I fell in love hard and fought harder.

After terminating my first pregnancy and having a miscarriage, I learned I was carrying Jason's baby. I was seventeen, and pregnant for a third time. This time I discussed the details with Jason right from the start, and he gave me the money for the abortion with no negotiation or delay. I went to Planned Parenthood that Monday and by the end of the week it was done. My parents never got wind of any of it.

This time, while I was at Planned Parenthood, the nurse stressed that I needed to take my pills on time and get control of my health. Subconsciously, because Mom was never big on taking medicine, I had not established a consistent routine. She eventually found the pills in my room on one of her random spot checks, but we never discussed it in detail. She used to do this thing where if she found something she didn't like in my room she'd avoid the topic but make sure to leave what she found out in the open to make it clear she knew what was up. Had I known better, I would have done better, but I didn't. I acted and thought as a child, even though I was fully engaged in adult behaviors. Whether I was wrong or right in anyone's eyes is not the most important factor here. I acknowledge that my decision making was poor. To be clear, what was most important back then and still today is what I did with my body was my choice. I had the option to make a decision about what happened to me. A choice that no woman should have to fight for. I deserved the power to make decisions about my health and my future, just as women and girls should be able to do today.

The decision to fully disclose my multiple pregnancies here is not a comfortable one, yet this is my truth. As I write the pages of this book, women in this country are being forced to navigate a world after the overturning of *Roe v. Wade*. This is yet another example of women not being protected in America. So in an effort to project the narrative and discussion surrounding the pro-life versus pro-choice debate, I put aside my fear of judgment to simply proclaim: My Body. My Choice. There is no way for me to say how my life would have been different had I chosen to move forward with the previous pregnancies, but what I can be sure of is that I could not have given the love, care, and nurturing that every unborn child deserves at that time. There is no man, law, or legislature equipped to make this decision on a woman's behalf.

No one.

CHAPTER 7

WHEN THEY REMINISCE OVER YOU

My lack of regard for living under my parents' roof was at an all-time high. Even so, while I made personally questionable decisions there was never a time I engaged in illegal activity at will. I rarely smoked, because I did not like the feeling of being high. I also drank very little because anything that impaired my thoughts made me feel out of control. Nonetheless, I was in places and around people that could have gotten me killed, even though I didn't know it at the time. And because there were times when Jason didn't feel "exciting enough" for me, or was too hot and cold to keep my attention, I allowed myself to open the book of Cane.

One Saturday I met up with Raven. It had been a while since we kicked it because my hanging out with Jason had started to take up all my free time. Raven and I were on 125th Street when a familiar gold Lexus pulled up behind us, just like it did the first time we met Cane and Marlon. Only this time, Cane was driving the car by himself. When he pulled up beside us, we didn't exchange pleasantries. He simply said, "Get in."

"Shiiiit. You don't have to tell me twice." Raven was already tugging on the handle to get in the back seat. My approach was slightly different.

"And why should I?" I said, leaning on the window of the passenger's side.

"Come on, Tamika. Trust me. I got you."

When I got in the car, I had no idea where he was taking us, until I recognized the Brooklyn Bridge through the windshield.

In my world this was an adventure. Brooklyn had a reputation for being rough and far off my map, with its own cliques and gangs and customs to learn. It was a place one just did not go to without a real reason or an escort to watch your back. I thought it was cool that Cane had taken us under his wing to see his world. We made a few pit stops before heading back across the river to Harlem. The idea that I didn't really know who he was or what he was really doing set off an alarm in the back of my mind, but I was living my life and teenage affections go a long way.

By the time we turned back that day and he pulled up on 155th Street, I had regained my bearings. This time, I didn't need any help recognizing where I was—Holcombe Rucker. People were pouring in from every direction, and the crowd had to number at least a thousand. Folks were lined up outside waiting to get in, crowded on the metal bleachers, and some were even poking their faces through the holes in the metal fence, just to get a view of the most talked about athletic talent in the country.

Standing outside the park, you could look up and see people in nearby apartment buildings on Eighth Avenue peering from behind curtains. Even if they couldn't see every move being made on the court, they could hear the roars of the crowd and feel the infectious energy. On those courts, only the best of the best went hard in the paint. It was a rite of passage for everybody who would become anybody in the basketball world. From the likes of Dr. J and Kareem Abdul-Jabbar to Kobe Bryant, LeBron James, and Carmelo Anthony, anyone who is anyone has at one point been through the Rucker. And then there were the fallen soldiers. Legends who balled on the courts but never made it out of the city. Stories of being gunned down in the streets over senseless arguments or due to jealousy.

It was a public place, but with the crowds and demand for prime position in order to see what was going on, it helped to know someone in order to be someone.

"*Yoooo.* Damn, Cane. You're the man. Like on some real shit." Raven damn near lost her mind. Even though I was more excited than she was, I played it cool.

"So you gettin' us in?" I asked.

Cane raised an eyebrow and laughed to himself as if my question were silly. Slightly embarrassed and unsure of what to do, I asked again.

"So are you?"

"Nah. I'm not getting you in. I'm taking a whole team in." I was still unsure of what he meant, but apparently Raven was not.

"That's what the fuck I'm talking about. You hear that, Tamika? We goin' in with the team!"

Cane pulled up to the front and motioned his hand for another dude

I'd never seen to come out and take the car. He came around to let me out of the passenger seat. Raven was so excited that she let herself out and was already standing at the front entrance by the time I exited the car. Cane didn't walk beside me, but I could see him keeping close watch of my whereabouts and making sure I was good. Eventually a group of about seven guys emerged in matching black jerseys with silver writing and surrounded Cane. They were slapping hands and greeting one another before they were up. Raven and I squeezed into a small opening on the bleachers that gave us a view of everything that was going on. Neither one of us knew much about the game, but it didn't matter. Running up and down the court, yelling out in frustration, pumping up their chests—we were watching greatness up close, and the scene made me wish we'd had time to prepare before we got there.

"Girl. I wish I had known we were coming here. I would have put my outfit together better," Raven said as she nudged me. The scene was beautiful and the men putting on the show were beautiful to watch. "It's all good. I got a feeling we'll be back," I said as I watched Cane watching me from across the court.

That night after the game, Cane took us to a hole-in-the-wall, Charles Pan-Fried Chicken, to eat. Everybody and their momma seemed to be there as Cane and his people took over the whole restaurant. We ate and laughed like we did before. The only difference was that Marlon wasn't with us. Cane was patient with us and treated us like the young women we wanted to be seen as. He let us order whatever we wanted, moving like a boss, and we wanted for nothing. In his presence, I managed to forget about Deion. When he dropped us back off at Co-op, I knew that I was through being cooped up in Deion's bedroom. I was becoming a woman and deserved to be treated like one. No longer interested, I didn't call Deion and he didn't call me. The only time I saw him was when I went back to sit with Grandma Pearlie on occasion. My allegiance to her never wavered. I even ran a few errands for her when she needed my help. There was never weird energy between Deion and me. There was no ill will. We both just realized that there was nothing left and we left it at that. In my mind, it was some grown-woman shit.

I embarked on a dual life from that point, dating Jason and Cane at the same time in a constant disappearing act.

The first apartment I began spending time with Cane at was out in

Jamaica, Queens. He would always say, "I want to take you somewhere," and I trusted wherever he desired to take me. We went to the movies and took long rides in the car while holding hands and sitting in silence or listening to music on the stereo. We never formally assigned a title to our relationship, but the energy exchange was pure.

In the mornings, on most days Cane woke up before me. He was an early riser. By the time I walked into the kitchen, I knew to expect the daily newspaper floating all around. He read it relentlessly from front to back each morning. From the bedroom, I could hear him shouting about the things that angered him. It was the only time he raised his voice, at least in my presence.

"It's fucked up how they treating these niggas on Rikers Island, man!"

Anytime anything was printed in the paper about Rikers Island, Cane was visibly upset. I had never met anyone besides my family and a few others who took the time to be knowledgeable about current events or who cared about injustices around them.

Our new normal consisted of me going out frequently to buy new clothes for both of us. Every three days I would buy new sneakers. Dressing him was one of the things I most looked forward to doing. Perusing the aisles of the mall, knowing that I could buy anything I wanted, made me feel powerful. That wasn't the norm for girls coming from where I came from. I never really understood why this man always needed new clothes, but I was so naive I just assumed he needed more fly shit.

On occasion, while reading his newspaper in the mornings, Cane asked me what I thought of the news of the day. During that time, I was not following the way I used to, but my background in the movement and growing up in my parents' home left me more than capable of holding my own in any discussion with him. Not only did I comprehend what was discussed, but I also had the power to articulate value adding commentary to the discussion. When Cane brought things to my attention such as political scandals or candidates running for office, I was headstrong enough to spar with him verbally.

"I swear, you're a firecracker, Tamika."

That was his go-to way of letting me know he was feeling me. He liked that even though I was young, seventeen at the time (even though he didn't know it; he thought I was now nineteen), I could hold my own, analyze, and give my perspective.

Cane didn't get excited about much, but dining—especially his cuisine of choice, Jamaican food—always seemed to get him stirred up. We were vibing, and learning how to give each other what was needed to make us feel cared for. Then came one evening at dinner where things went sideways.

"You have to taste this," he said, gathering a forkful of rice doused in savory butter sauce and feeding it to me. The plump shrimp mixed with garlic and onions, green peppers, tomatoes, and lemon was an explosion of happiness in my mouth. "Damn. That's so good!" I exclaimed as I closed my eyes and leaned back in my chair. He took pleasure in seeing me happy and I took pleasure in being in his presence. That evening, when the waitress brought the check, he realized he left his wallet in the car.

"Yo. I'mma run to the bathroom real quick before we get out of here. Take the keys and grab my wallet from the car for me."

I nodded my head and stood up from the table. As I did he grabbed my hand. His hand on top of mine was stiff. It wasn't a caress. While holding my hand, he pulled me a little closer to him.

"Make sure you get the wallet from my car." He squeezed a little tighter before emphasizing, "Not the valet. You."

"Damn—you're hurting my hand. I got it," I said as I pulled away towards the front entrance.

There were times when Cane had this way of telling me to do things that let me know he wasn't requesting. Most were simple asks that I had no problem fulfilling, so I never pushed back. That night, the valet at the restaurant reserved a spot for Cane's car right out front. It must have taken me three or four minutes of searching before remembering that his wallet was inside a pocket of his leather jacket. I watched him place it there while pumping gas before we arrived at the restaurant. When I popped the trunk to retrieve the wallet, I was in utter shock by what I saw. Laundry bags, zip ties, rubber bands, trash bags. It took a moment for my brain to make the connection between what I saw and who I believed Cane to be. Looking around, I lowered my head into the trunk, taking a closer look at what appeared to be a shitload of evidence of either a crime that had already been committed or one in progress. When I lifted the stack of laundry bags, I saw a gun. The first time I ever saw one that close up. Now paranoid that someone else might walk by and see what I saw, I slammed the trunk closed and walked back into the restaurant.

"Damn, Ma. You look like you've seen a ghost."

I thought to myself, Shit. I have, but I remained quiet.

"So where's the wallet?"

"I . . . I . . . I didn't see it. I looked everywhere."

He snatched the keys from the table and walked back to the car to retrieve it himself. As I sat there, my mind began to wander. Did I really know Cane the way I thought I did or had I only been introduced to his representative? After six months of dating, I came to the realization that I didn't know shit. I'd never questioned where Cane got his money before that night. It was of no concern to me. His business was his business. But still, there was no way for me to unsee evidence of his illegal dealings.

My suspicions were further fueled when I learned he'd been keeping another apartment in Central Harlem. The first time I visited him there, he sent Marlon to pick me up. The apartment situated off Bradhurst Avenue had a couple of guys standing outside, like guards keeping watch. As I entered the living room, the floor was open, with money stacked up in the middle of it. I walked past it as if this didn't faze me, but taken with what I'd seen in Cane's trunk all roads were leading to a life of crime I'd not known before. Cane was a high-stakes robber. My suspicions led me to believe that he was high up, one of the masterminds behind the organization. It explained why everyone always catered to him, the way he constantly swapped out his cell phones, never lifted a finger, and took off on random trips to Boston here and there with short notice.

One might assume that with an informal confirmation that the guy I was dealing with and spending all my time around robbed banks I'd run for the hills, but I didn't. The influence and power made him more attractive to seventeen-year-old me.

The more time we spent together, the more time he wanted us to spend together. Cane wanting me around as much as possible was another factor that drew me closer to him.

Bad Boy Records was the soundtrack of this era and I was surely enjoying riding through Grant's Tomb, hitting up Harlem lounges, and getting dressed up to look fly to hang out with my man. Thinking back, I had to be looking like I was twelve years old, and nobody asked a word.

As the weeks progressed, Cane's random trips out of state for business turned into structured, weekly meetings. We were spending less and less time together, but he had created a culture in our relationship where I could still live my life as I wanted to. I was an "it" girl and a part of the "it" crowd. I was popping.

But then, the cadence of our routine started to slowly change. The money he used to give me was drying up. I spent more time back in Co-op at my parents' house. Eventually, Cane just stopped calling. There was a part of me that always knew that he didn't belong to me, and that I had no real power over what we would become or when our relationship might end. All I knew was I'd gotten wrapped up in the fairy tale of it—that Cane would take me with him somewhere one day and leave the pain of New York behind.

The final nail in that idea came after running into Marlon months after Cane and my relationship had run cold.

"Tamika?"

"Marlon? Is that you?" We embraced.

"Yo. Ma. What's up? It's been a minute," he said as he held my hand, giving me a once-over.

"Yeah. It has. What's good? How have you been?"

"I've been good, Ma. Just out here getting to this money."

"I hear that," I responded. I knew he was waiting for me to ask about Cane, but I waited for him to initiate the conversation instead. Like clockwork, he started singing like a bird.

"I know you heard about your mans. He got caught up on some bullshit yo."

"Yeah. I heard, but I still don't know what really happened?"

I actually didn't know. There was no one who could have alerted me about what was happening in his life. Due to our age and proximity difference, we didn't share mutual friends. Furthermore, his circle was not the type to disclose details of his personal life.

He rubbed his nose with his thumb before taking a step back and responding, "It's always a bitch that gets you popped, I swear."

"I'm not sure what you mean."

"Real spit," he said as he nudged me gently on the shoulder. "Cane has a wife, kids, the whole nine, while he was fuckin' with you. To keep it a buck one hundred with you, I don't even know how he got away with as much as he did."

I remained quiet.

"The whole time y'all was together, I was thinking to myself that you deserved better. Like you really needed a real one to hold you down." He licked his lips while staring at me like I was a piece of meat.

"I coulda been that for you, Ma."

Was he being serious right now? And did he really think now was the time to try to pick me up?

That was all news to me. I always thought that Cane's and my connection was real, and that he wanted me alone. But did I really? His movements were so clear. I figured he had other girls, but a family? Nah.

As Marlon kept talking nonsense, I realized he and Cane were manipulators and that Marlon had now moved on to driving a wedge between me and Raven too. "That bitch was jealous of you," he said.

"Who: Raven?" I replied.

"You probably never saw how she wanted Cane for herself."

The startled look on my face was a dead giveaway. I had never known Raven to be anything other than a friend.

"Damn, Ma. Peep game. She was always on your heels. She wanted to be you. And if there's one thing I can't stand, it's jealous bitches."

From that moment forward, everything else Marlon said went in one ear and out the other. Why would he feel the need to alert me about my own friend? Something was off, but I still couldn't put my finger on it. I gave up and left, retreating to go figure out what I could about this man I'd been dating and falling for all these months. Cane, which was not his real name, was thirty-two years old, and just as Marlon disclosed, he was married, with six children from different women. I thought he was twenty-eight with two children. I guess we both lied.

Not only was Cane a high-level robber as I suspected after finding the evidence in his trunk, but he was the ringleader. The kingpin. The operation he curated spanned over a few states and millions of dollars had been seized over the years. Many of the dudes who worked for him were locked up on Rikers Island, which explained why he was so passionate about what happened there. Who would have thought that one day he would be imprisoned with them?

Cane lived a grand life and so did I when I was with him. The end of our relationship was also an opportunity for me to reevaluate my path in life and seek out a fresh start. There was nothing glamorous about being locked up, leaving your family and friends behind, and lying every day to keep one step ahead of a disaster. I began to consider the prospect of going back to school and realigning with the path of academic, social, and emotional abundance my parents had so desperately wanted for me.

I'd spent years of my life running away from my home and the destiny written in my DNA. Dropping out of school, teenage pregnancy, neither of these attributes was a by-product of the life my parents envisioned for me. And no one was to blame but me. I continued to put myself in compromising situations. Not heeding warnings, not paying attention to the red flags, not staying alert to the traps being set around me. I was spending more time in Co-op City again, getting my bearings but still skipping school too much and not walking the path I needed to be. And who else would pop up but Marquis, another kid around the way who was always buzzing in my ears at the worst times.

"Yo. Tamika. What up?"

I turned around; it took me a moment to realize who was calling my name. "Marquis?"

"Who else could it be? You should remember my face after ghosting me."

"Nah. It wasn't like that."

"Well, what was it like then? I called you a few times, but you never hit me back."

"I just got kinda caught up."

"Caught up?"

"Yeah. Caught up. You know life is crazy sometimes," I said.

For me, "caught up" meant I was on the run like Bey and Jay with a guy named Jason and simultaneously floating in a whirlwind romance with a guy named Cane. That's what "caught up" meant, but I didn't tell him that. To him I was still Tamika the smart girl who knew what was up but still had her shit together. On several Saturday mornings, I showed up to attend rallies, regardless of whether or not I stayed out the night before. I started to come around a little bit. I was a youth organizer, often taking a spot to speak during Saturday morning broadcasts on local radio, and I worked religiously as we were preparing our platforms, identifying issues and current events to be discussed. I attended other youth group events and connected with other young leaders during fairs, and Harlem Week, which was a big festival in Harlem during the summertime. People in my innermost circle knew about my dual life, but it was still a mystery to almost everyone else. Mom went as far as to enlist the help of professional therapy, but back then I wasn't receptive to the experience and it made no difference. Life in the streets kept calling my name and I answered every single time.

"Damn, shorty, it's like that?"

Marquis was Morris Chestnut in *Boyz n the Hood* fine. He was chocolate with washboard abs. They caught my eye when I first spotted Marquis during one of those games at the Rucker with Cane. Raven spotted him first, but he'd flirted with me on the sidelines between games and I'd given him my number. It slipped my mind because so much time had passed since I'd last seen him. With Cane in jail and no other prospects to consider, Marquis was looking more inviting than ever.

I stepped to him. "Maybe you could call me later and we could figure something out from there."

"Later?" he questioned. "I was thinking we could kick it now. You obviously ain't doing shit."

"You don't know what I'm doing."

He was startled by my response. He didn't have a comeback.

"Why don't you just talk regular?" he asked. As if me being straightforward and confident in my speech were somehow "not regular."

After a long pause, I released the tension in the air. ". . . I guess we could hang."

Relieved, he said, "Cool. My moms just went grocery shopping, so we got mad snacks at the crib."

While I was walking with Marquis to Section 4, where he lived, we passed by the basketball courts. Like clockwork, I glanced at Reggie playing, but he didn't notice me. If he had, I might have been inclined to shoot a bird in his direction.

When we got into Marquis's apartment, it was humble, but dark and imposing. Unlike Mom and Dad's place, there was no window to let in the sunlight. The air was thick. The only furniture in the living room was a blue love seat with a striped floral print and a black TV stand with a small TV and antennas on top. It might have been the oldest TV I had ever seen. It didn't matter. A group of guys were sitting on the love seat playing video games.

"What's up, y'all," Marquis said as we walked into the living room. I nodded my head, but I didn't know any of them. To me, they were just kids hanging out. What did scare me was the pit bull roaming around.

Ever since the day one bit my sister Sharon, I kept my distance from dogs like that. In fact, that they had a dog at all in Co-op City, where pets weren't allowed, should have been a red alert right from the start.

Marquis greeted each of them by reaching his arm over the couch and slapping high fives.

Standing in the living room, I noticed a green outdoor bistro set positioned in the kitchen as a dining area.

"Let's watch TV in here," he said, tapping me on my shoulder, directing me towards his bedroom. "My TV is better than the raggedy-ass one out here."

Since it was just the two of us, I saw nothing wrong with watching in his room. People kicked it at each other's houses all the time. We both sat on the bed as he grabbed the remote for his personal TV. It was much larger and newer than the one in his living room.

"Where'd you get that TV from?" I asked.

"I won it. My coach at the Gaucho Gym told me if I won the free throw contest he'd get it for me, and well, you see it."

"So you nice on the court, huh?"

"That's what they tell me. My coach says if I keep it up, I'm on track to get a scholarship to college."

"College?" I asked.

It had been a minute since I heard anyone mention a future dream that involved education.

"Yeah. College. How else am I going to get the fuck up out of Co-op? I'm not trying to sell drugs like the rest of these dudes and get popped. I'll never make it then."

Leaning back on his headboard, I replied, "College was always something that my parents wanted for me, but I can't see it."

"What do you see?"

His words stunned me. There was no way I could answer because I didn't know. I remained silent until I thought of some goofy shit to say as a distraction from the question.

"Right now, I see you next to me and that's about it."

As we laughed together, he leaned in to kiss me. I turned away.

"Nah. I'm not ready for all that just yet. I'm just trying to get to know you right now. Wasn't it Janet Jackson who said, 'Let's wait awhile'?" I said, laughing.

Marquis leaned back to his side of the bed. He wasn't amused by my commentary, but I meant every word I said. Marquis was cute, but I hadn't known him long enough to go all the way. And I'd been through enough with my past choices and the consequences I faced because of them.

"Bet," he said. "I'mma go in the kitchen and get us some snacks then."

"Ok. Cool."

From the room, I heard a knock at the door.

Hand slaps. Whispers. There had to have been at least two other guys besides Marquis in the living room.

"Yeah. She in there, my boy."

Uncertain of what they were whispering about, but certain the energy shifted, I stood up to go towards his closed room door to hear better.

"Damn. I can't wait. Who's going first?"

With the door slightly ajar, I noticed a total of four bodies moving. They were slapping hands and jumping up and down like they won five dollars from a scratch-off ticket from the corner store.

"Tamika. You good?"

"I'm fine," I replied. It was a lie. In my mind and my heart, I knew something was off. I was not fine. I was in danger.

"This is my homeboy Derek. He just wanna talk to you for a minute."

When Derek came in, his energy was off. Immediately, he made me feel awkward. I had never been in a situation where a group of dudes were plotting on me.

"Why are all those dudes out there?"

"Oh. Those are just my homeboys. I told them you were here, so they just wanted to fall through."

"Fall through for what?"

"Come on with the bullshit. Why are you acting dumb? You up in here acting like you don't know what time it is."

"What the fuck are you talking about, Marquis?"

"You wildin'," he replied. "Just come here and be still." He started unbuttoning my shirt.

"Marquis, stop. This is not what I came here for."

"Then why the fuck did you come?" he said with rage in his eyes. "Look, we not gonna be in here all day. I go first, and then my homeboys are up next."

Now I was fearful not only because of his intentions but also because I could hear the pit bull scratching outside the door. Even if I wanted to run out of the room, I couldn't.

The tears welled up in my eyes. There was nowhere for me to go. The strength in his hands as he unbuttoned my shirt told me that either I could lie down or he'd force me down if I pushed back.

"Please, Marquis. Don't do this," I said as the tears streamed down my face. I wasn't giving up without a fight, but I knew that if I caused a scene, it was possible that the other dudes would come into the room, only making it worse.

Marquis and I struggled in the bed as I squirmed in constant motion attempting to move his hands away from me.

"Marquis, please. I'm begging you don't do this."

"Shut the fuck up," he yelled.

His asks were now demands as I continued to break free from his grasp.

"Oh shit," I heard a voice from outside the room yell out. Before I knew it, a woman who I'd never seen busted into the room. Startled, Marquis jumped up.

"Mom. What are you doing here?"

"Marquis. Get your dumb ass up and go in the kitchen with your lil friends," she scorned before walking over to me in the bed. She stood directly over me, looking at me for moments before speaking.

"Lil girl. If you don't get your ass up out of my house, I'm gonna start looking for your momma."

"Yes, ma'am," I said as the tears that had been welling up came crashing down my face.

"Button up your shirt first. If you need a second, you can sit here. I won't let anyone come in here. As soon as you can, get your shit and go."

She left the room. I didn't wait. With my hands shaking, I jumped up and buttoned up my shirt as fast as I could before grabbing my jacket from the floor and heading towards the bedroom door. She kept her word and was standing just outside the bedroom door when I opened it moments later. My chest rubbed her shoulder as I slid beside her out of the door. Most of the guys were in the kitchen, but I counted six on the way out. There were more than I suspected. Before I closed the front door, I looked back at her one last time. The look in her eyes was one I could never forget.

It was an unspoken agreement between us. Whether I knew exactly what the guys were preparing to do or not, I did recognize that they meant me no good, her son included. She got home just in time to save me.

I ran like hell back to my parents' house. When I got inside, I walked past my dad, who was in his normal space on the couch after work. It was my hope that he couldn't detect how upset I was and start asking questions I wasn't ready to answer. My parents had already witnessed way too much drama from me. I went into the bathroom and shut the door, before turning on the shower. Once inside, I sank to the floor, and bawled. My eyes were bloodshot red the next time I saw myself after I finished trying to wash away what I'd experienced. I was too upset to eat dinner that night and tossed and turned when I finally got to bed. My mind was racing. Thoughts of what could have happened to me replayed in my head.

Was there no one I could trust not to harm me? Anyone aside from my parents? Was this how the world really was? Maybe this was why my parents had tried to keep me away from the world for all those years.

Shit went from bad to worse when I finally ran into Reggie again, foolishly expecting he might lend a friendly ear or share in my frustrations with navigating the world as a young Black person in the 1990s.

"Yo," Reggie called out to me from behind.

Startled, I jumped before responding.

"Oh shit, Reggie. You scared the shit outta me." He walked closer.

"I heard you been letting mad dudes in Co-op hit. When I see them niggas, I'mma tell 'em I had you first."

Was he fucking serious? He didn't take the time to see if there was really truth in what was said or to find out if I was ok? As bad as he was for me, even Cane would have never lent his ear to gutter gossip like Reggie was repeating. Furthermore, he didn't even have all of the facts.

"First of all, back up. Second of all, what the hell are you talking about?"

"Raven said you slept with four dudes a couple of weeks back."

"Raven?

"You must have the wrong person. Raven ain't say no shit like that."

He lifted his finger towards my head.

"No, you thought Raven was your homegirl. That's what's wrong with y'all females, man. You always mistake enemies for friends."

"Whatever, Reggie. Truth be told, none of it's your business."

"You're right. It ain't and I don't give a fuck, but when shit hits the fan, don't say nobody ever told you the real."

I threw my hands up and walked off as if his words didn't matter, but they did. I was wounded at the prospect of betrayal in his accusations. The only people who could correct the record on what had actually happened in Marquis's room were his mom and the guy who'd planned to take advantage of me. I'd been hoping to figure this all out with Raven, the person I thought I could confide in without judgment to see things through. But now even that relationship had slipped into mistrust. I saw her again weeks later on a walk to the store on request from my mom to buy flour. Raven was wearing the same hairstyle she did when I met her. I called out as I waited for the signal to change so that I could cross.

"Raven. Girl, wait up."

She kept walking. Could I have been mistaken? I attempted to catch up. The crosswalk side had a ticking sound, *tick-tick-tick*, until it was ok to cross over again. Waiting for the sound to end made me anxious. It felt like an eternity. My nerves were shot by the time I could cross and finally come face-to-face with Raven.

"Girl, what the hell? I know it's you. What's up? Why aren't you talking to me?"

She was distant and cold. I knew almost immediately that there was some truth to what Reggie, Marlon, and so many others had started to warn me about her.

"So it's like that now? Are you out here telling my business and spreading lies about me? What the fuck? I thought you were my girl."

She took a step back and chose violence with her first words.

"To be honest, I never liked you anyway. You a selfish bitch." I was stunned.

"What? Oh, I see now. This is about Cane, huh? You really wanted to fuck with Cane?"

"Bitch, I don't want your dusty leftovers," she said.

It was clear that she was not telling the truth. In my mind, I could not shake the fact that she had been playing in my face the whole time.

"If you want him, you can have him. He's in prison now," I said.

Fuming at her words, I made the decision to walk off until she went for the jugular. "Bitch, I already had him," she said before hitting me in my face two times.

That was when I lost it. All I could see was blood. There we were, brawling in Co-op like some hoodrats. We had done a ton of hoodrat shit together, but never in a million years would I have suspected that would be what became of us. She was bigger than me, but that was of no concern in the moment. After I threw her to the ground, she got back up and charged me like a bull. I did my best to pull as many patches of her hair to keep her off of me. Once I got back on my feet, I pushed her down to the ground. She scraped her face and this stupid fight was over.

I no longer cared about Cane. That wasn't it. But it was my belief back then that while guys came and went, Raven's and my secrets were forever. We were supposed to protect each other's names.

After we were separated by some onlookers at the corner store, I got what I needed and returned home. When I got back to our place, I was fuming. Mom could see that I was ruffled, and the second the name "Raven" escaped my lips Mom's reply hit me right in the gut.

"I always told you that girl was no good."

Although I didn't tell her all the details about what happened, she knew enough to draw her own conclusions.

At that point, it was clear to me that I did not have any friends. From that moment on, I was no longer sure if I wanted them. I never saw this moment coming.

After being deceived by so many people I considered friends, I resolved to be a loner and to protect myself. It was a hard pill to swallow that the common denominator in everything getting in my way was me. In my heart, I knew it was time to make some different choices. And I did. One of the first being Jason.

After I bumped into him one day as I was walking home, stewing in my loneliness again, Jason and I picked up as though we'd never left off at all. From that day forward, we started being together every day, hanging out at each other's houses. Most things came easy between us, but what did not was related to wounds left behind from when I'd been the problem in our first act together. He wanted answers for where I had gone all those times he could not locate me during our first try at getting together. There was no way in hell I was telling him about Cane, so I never really answered his questions. He was understandably frustrated, and if I'm being honest now, my damaged soul was still holding out hope that Cane might return one day and save me from all this and erase my missteps. But he never did.

But in the course of my healing, Jason became my lover and my protector, for real this time. I no longer wanted anything to do with street life. I only wanted to live. The foreseeable life in front of me was with Jason by my side.

When I learned that I was pregnant with Jason's child this time, I was forced to think long and hard about my options. My heart wouldn't allow me to have another abortion, and things were different because I loved Jason and truly wanted to be with him. Imagining myself as a mother was hard, but every time I thought about what could be for us, it brought a smile to my face. I stood firm in my decision to leave my parents' place permanently to begin anew with Jason. To say the life Jason and I were building together was rooted in humble beginnings is an understatement. Telling my father was one of the hardest parts about the transition for me.

By the time I was five months or so, I waited for my dad in the living room of my parents' apartment. Dad came home from work like clockwork. Once he was seated in the kitchen at the table, he opened a box of food and began to eat. Standing across from him, I forced myself to spit it out.

"Dad, I went to the doctor. I'm five months pregnant and I'm just telling you that I have every intention of keeping my baby."

"Oh yeah?" he said.

He took the food away and threw it out and I left the house. He never said another word about it, nor did he have to tell me that Mom was worried; it was crystal clear.

Our parents on both sides were pissed off, which further sealed our decision to get a place to stay so we could be together. Neither Jason's side nor mine supported our decisions, and in no way, shape, or form would they have permitted us to lay up together in their homes.

We bounced from substandard apartment to substandard apartment until we found a railroad spot in the basement of a house in a Jamaican community of the Bronx. It was equipped with a makeshift kitchen and a shared bathroom. Each room was separated by a door. Government assistance for food and medical care was our only source of survival. The random jobs I had at the supermarket and, eventually, a telemarketing company paid pennies. Jason was still employed at the law firm, but it was still temp work, with fluctuating hours and wages.

The basement apartment was owned by the Jacksons, a Jamaican-Chinese family who rented it out from time to time to make extra money. Even though we were their tenants, they treated us as a part of their family. The mother, Jody, reinforced many things I'd learned from my mom, and the Jacksons' support throughout my pregnancy was immeasurable for me. Before and during my pregnancy, the majority of Jason's and my time together was spent fighting. We were equally to blame as our fights turned from just emotional to physical. Fists thrown in rage, slaps, tussles, and biting were all fair game. We were toxic together, but we loved as hard as we fought, which made leaving far more difficult than staying to fight. We survived that time, but when I brought Tarique home from the hospital a renewed focus told me the state we were living in was unacceptable. After some work on the boiler in the room next to ours, the apartment had taken on a smell I worried could be harmful to our baby. My parents' house, only three miles away, felt like the perfect escape again. Since I'd had to leave the call center job late in my pregnancy, I developed a new habit of bundling Tarique up each day to head over to their place. We'd spend the day there while my mom and dad were at work, leaving just before the sun went down to return to the basement at the Jacksons'.

These breaks lent temporary relief from my issues with Jason, but our demise continued on as it had been. The final straw was a night Jason came home around three in the morning pissy drunk, an immediate indicator that things were off. Jason had never been the type of person to get drunk and disappear. He always believed that folks who lost control of themselves to intoxicants were embarrassing. Moreover, he never left my side even in the worst times. Something was wrong.

Earlier that same evening, I'd attended a rally hosted by a local organization. Instead of walking back to the Jacksons' after being at my parents' all day, I'd stayed and accompanied my parents to the rally with Tarique in tow. It felt different being there as an adult than it had as a child. So much about how I saw the world had changed. I had changed. That night, more than an active participant, I was an observer. My mom came over to me and whispered in my ear. It was one of those moments that only a mother has the talent to execute. She was smiling and nodding while greeting guests but having an entire conversation with me through her teeth. No movement of the lips.

"There's a lawyer here from a firm that represents folks in the move-ment. He's one of the leaders and he's looking for someone to answer phones. It might be a good fit for you, Tamika," she said as she waved to guests coming in the door. Mom knew I was ready for a change.

"Law firm!" I exclaimed as she motioned for me to keep my voice down. "Now, Ma, you know I have never worked anywhere like that before."

"It doesn't mean you can't," she said, smiling, patting me on the shoulder, and taking Tarique out of my hands before walking off to greet other attendees with my dad.

In the movement, opportunities were abundant, but people with the head and heart for it were few. Activists were always looking for fresh talent to expand their reach, enhance their organizations, and strengthen their businesses. From contractors to therapists to tailors, there is never a lack of business or opportunity when we combine our time, talents, and treasures for the greater good of all. Group economics is the name of the game.

Thirty minutes or so later, I was approached by Attorney Michael A. Hardy after his meetings with families in need.

"Hey, Attorney Hardy, I heard that you are looking for some clerical workers."

He laughed. "Clerical workers. You must have heard that from your mother. I am indeed looking for someone to handle office responsibil-ities."

Attorney Hardy, dressed in a button-down shirt, with a brown pull-over and a pair of loafers, looked like he could have been related to Uncle Phil on *The Fresh Prince of Bel-Air*. He was tall and he spoke with a soft, but firm voice. He was well known for his advocacy through the legal system and was hailed as a hero in the movement. I knew it would be an honor to work for a man like this. And that night, it was apparent that the job was mine for the taking. It wasn't a question in my mind, because I recognized that if I wanted a different life for Tarique, one that was the polar opposite of what I had created for myself in the years past, I would have to do something different.

When I got back to the Jacksons', I was bursting with excitement to tell Jason about my new position and how I felt in my spirit that life was opening up a new path for us as Tarique's parents. But my excitement turned into frustration as I stayed up for at least four hours, waiting for Jason to come home. By 1:00 a.m., I'd had enough and fell asleep. By sunrise, I was livid. When I woke up, he was lying next to me in bed, knocked out cold. Who knew what he had been doing. I was disgusted. On top of that, the fumes from the boiler room were coming on strong again and it sent me over the edge.

"Wake up," I yelled as I pulled the covers off of him in a rage.

Getting up on my knees in the bed, I attempted to wake him once more.

"Wake up. How dare you come home that late, while Tarique and I sit here, waiting for you. I know you were probably out with some other bitches."

He was too knocked from whatever he had been doing to fight. Instead, he sat up and shoved me with the little energy he did have. It was enough force for me to tumble backward, knocking over a glass on the side table. Tarique's screams were not regular cries; they were pleas for help. I don't care what anyone says; babies can sense tension. And although they might not know or be able to articulate what is happening, they are alert to imminent danger. Jason and I were doing more harm than good by attempting to be together.

After the fight, we did what we had always done and swept it under the rug. It no longer mattered to me whether or not Jason shared in my excitement about the job. There was enough excitement inside me to cover the entire family.

A week later, on a Monday, I was up at six in the morning, preparing bottles and sets of clothes changes for Tarique to go to the babysitter, while agonizing over what to wear for my first day at work. The days of cropped tops, distressed jeans, and sneakers were long gone. No one had ever taught me what was appropriate to wear to a job like this one. It was my first big-girl job and I was nervous as hell. The attorney's office was nothing like the supermarket or the call centers where my career had been lived out thus far. None of those jobs came with the benefits or salary I was now eligible to receive.

My first day taking the train downtown to the office I was nervous and once I arrived, I was intimidated. Attorney Hardy was a partner in a firm, in a shared office space on Forty-Seventh Street in Manhattan.

Even though I felt intimidated about starting work in a Midtown office, answering the phones turned out to be easy. After all, I had spent so much time running my mouth as a volunteer at NAN—chatting on the phone and chopping it up out in the streets—that this part of the job felt like second nature. Still, within the first hour, I recognized that working at this level would require a new version of me. That day was a wake-up call that alerted me that there was far more to the movement than rallies and underground meetings. It did not take me long to understand that the movement was also a business and the leaders who thrived in it were not just people who stood at microphones or those who held megaphones to coerce people into action. The movement consisted of CEOs, managers, and professionals with tremendous business acumen. In addition to the finances necessary to fund campaigns and initiatives, I was also witnessing firsthand the legal side of the movement, which was an entire operation in and of itself. Real movers were depending on us to get the job done to let them do the crucial work they needed to do out in the world.

The first time I was invited to attend a formal staff meeting was like a transformation. It was a now or never moment when I stepped across the threshold from the foyer of the office and into the conference room. I was growing up. I could literally feel the sweat in the palms of my hands, but I closed my eyes, took a deep breath, exhaled with all my might, and put one foot in front of the other until I was standing shoulder to shoulder with other professionals. By the end of the meeting, the nerves had dissolved and I knew in my heart that I found a new home. This was my new norm and I was ready for it.

CHAPTER 8

ROSA PARKS

The normalization of cops who shot up windows and murdered us in our own communities was known to us, but not widely displayed. Those called to protect and serve were instead focused on destruction. Their ancestors and people like them—those willing to push criminal means to destructive ends for people of color—had been the same ones who stole our land, robbed our communities, and committed genocides devoted to uprooting any sense of community or opposition to the status quo. But even with that said, if we were to save ourselves, it would also mean relinquishing our patterns of self-destructive behavior. It would mean establishing new patterns that rerouted our paths away from the people, places, and things that caused harm to ourselves and our communities. And while it is certain that, as individuals, we wake up from the deep sleep of oppression at different times and in different places, not one of us can afford to remain asleep when injustice comes to our front doors.

The moment Tarique was born, I was born again. Every moment before he took his first breath, I was existing, but I wasn't alive. With every passing day after his birth, I was evolving. Evolution is a peculiar concept. It is often in motion before we realize it. This affects relationships because, in many instances, changes coming are hidden from the naked eye. This was now a truth both Jason and I were coming to terms with. The tapestry that once bound us together was unraveling at the seams. His interests and my interests placed us worlds apart. The volatile relationship we had before Tarique was born went from bad to worse and it was clear our aspirations for more could not coexist with a home life of constant turmoil. My time, energy, and all of my concerns were now directed towards Tarique. Instead of hanging out and having fun, my attention was absorbed in safety and stability, two things Jason was struggling to provide.

It must be plainly stated that Jason wanted desperately to provide for his family. At the time, we experienced life through the lenses of young people without a pot to piss in.

But at now nineteen years old, I knew what we once had was fading away. The version of Tamika he fell for was not around anymore. I'd been forced to grow up, and he wasn't on the same track just yet. With mounting pressures to be a provider and a source of comfort for Tarique and me and the lack of tools to do so, he did what most do: numb the pain. Numbing for Jason included staying out too late and smoking weed and expressing anger to the point that he was no longer rational. One night as I put Tarique down to sleep, Jason was on a rampage.

"Shut the fuck up. I will play this music as loud as I fucking please."

"Jason, come on now. Use your head. Think," I said, pointing to the top of his head with the sharp edge of my nail.

"Every time, you take shit way too far. You act like you are my momma or something. Telling a grown-ass man to turn down the music."

"That's dumb as hell. Why would you blast music when I just got the baby to sleep?"

Then he pushed me, hard. The blow to my chest felt like an elephant standing on top of me. Struggling to catch my breath, I grabbed the wall, attempting to stand again, but he pushed me back down and said, "You changed. I don't even know who the fuck you are anymore."

I didn't have the strength, so I used the energy I had left to yell from where I was.

"You're damn right I changed. It's not about us anymore, Jason. It's about Tarique." Sitting with my back against the wall, I used the last breath I had to speak my final piece.

"If we don't grow the fuck up, what will happen to him?" Those were the last words I spoke before crying myself to sleep on the floor.

It didn't matter to me if it sank in for him that night. I was no longer concerned about forcing him to understand. My only hope was that he would change. That was the last fight before I unofficially moved back in with my parents. Maybe I thought the distance would make Jason miss me. The way I saw it, more time apart had the potential to make our hearts grow fonder. In my mind, I was two steps ahead of the process. If, for any reason, things didn't manifest in the way I believed they could for Jason and me, I was fully prepared to walk away to focus solely on

Tarique. What I didn't realize at the time was that it would be less of a choice and more of a decision made based on principle and a lack of respect for our relationship.

The day I knew Jason and I had come to an end, Tarique and I spent the night at my mom and dad's instead of going home. We slept in a little later than usual, but Mom was making breakfast by Tarique's first feeding. Walking into the kitchen and seeing Mom standing in front of the stove with her hand on her hip brought back so many memories.

This particular morning she wasn't on the phone with Aunt Ola per usual. She was humming and casually swaying.

"Look at Grandma in here making breakfast," I said as I entered with Tarique wrapped in a blanket in my arms. She jolted towards me, stealing him away.

"Let me see this boy," she insisted before enveloping him in love. "Look at MaMa's baby. Just look at him. He is so sweet. Oh yes, he is. He is so beautiful."

She went on and on, caught up in the rapture of a grandparent's love.

My dad entered the kitchen with a smile like the one he used to have when he came home from work and I greeted him at the door.

"Look at how strong he is," my mom said. Dad took him right away. He didn't say much. He just stood shoulder to shoulder with my mom, misty-eyed. They were so consumed with Tarique, you would have forgotten I was even in the kitchen with them. All I could feel was blessed in knowing that Tarique was surrounded by love. My first instinct was to call Jason to have him be a part of the moment. The first time I dialed his number, he didn't answer. Slightly agitated, I dialed the number again.

"Mom. Can you keep Tarique for me? I need to run out for a minute."

"I ain't no babysitter!" Mom said, a knowing lilt to her voice as she turned to Tarique with joy. "Are you staying with Grandma? I know that's right."

As my mother went through the laundry list of reasons why she was not a babysitter, Dad took Tarique in his arms to defuse the situation. In those moments, he didn't have to say much. It was his way of letting me know that he had my back.

I went back into the room and threw on a sweat suit and overcoat before leaving. In my heart, I wanted to believe that Jason wasn't picking up the phone because he stayed out too late and was still asleep, but a woman's intuition is a muthafucker. On the way, I called my sister Sharon to let her know about my suspicions. We always know when we know. What I knew was that Jason had been different lately. Not the kind of difference that men feel when they become jealous of the new baby who has taken their spot. Different in the way that he loved me. Although I changed, it was apparent that his responses towards me changed too. He was more busy than usual, whereas before he had always made time. The moments when we laughed together about stupid shit dissipated into thin air. The closer I got to the house, the faster I walked as my mind raced with possibilities of where he was and who he was with.

Instead of going in through the front door and alerting everyone in the house, I decided to stand at the small window in the basement where our studio was located. The thin, sheer curtain that covered the window gave me a glimpse into the room. Standing there, I could distinctly hear moaning and grunting, clear indications of someone having sex. Further proof was in the silhouette of multiple bodies in the room. Rather than exploding immediately, I kept listening while tears streamed down my face. When I could no longer control my fury, I slammed my fist against the window like a madwoman.

"Oh shit. Get up, nigga," a male voice other than Jason's warned from inside.

Both my rage and curiosity grew. Was he hiding his sexuality this whole time too? By the time I made it inside, I was furious. The TV running in the background was on porn.

"After everything we've been through, this is how you play me, Jason? You're having sex with men?"

I didn't care if he answered my question or not. All I knew was that I was packing my shit that moment, that day. It was a nonnegotiable and unforgivable offense for him to be fucking other people in the space where our son slept. There was no way for me to have been prepared for what I witnessed when I opened the closet door.

"Bitch, what the fuck are you doing in here?" There was a woman whom I'd never seen hiding in the closet. Had I not been done, which I already was, I was beyond done now.

"Y'all got a fucking threesome going on in here? That's what y'all in here doing? 'Cause I guess nobody got no real job to go to. Nobody in here got no productive shit to be doing? None of y'all motherfuckers worried 'bout raising no kids. Just me, huh?" I said, slamming my hand into my chest. "Just me. I got it. Well, y'all can have this shithole."

I made it back outside with as many of my belongings as I could take with me in a duffel bag and a small suitcase, and my sister Sharon pulled up just as Jason reached me to plead his case. Sharon, now nearby enough to see my face, saw the girl leave the apartment—proof that Jason was not alone and my concerns had been valid. In my heart, I'd known that we were growing apart, but I couldn't help but wonder how we had grown so far apart in such a short amount of time and after witnessing together the biggest blessing our love created.

Today I speak with experience when I say that young people should take their time before having children. Doing so can be the difference between the success and failure of a relationship. A baby is often a wedge between the people you used to be and who you will become moving forward as parents. Many of the connective fibers that draw you to a person can be lost when another human being becomes the priority. That day, I lost Jason as a staple in my life, and through his actions it was apparent he felt the same about me. My only goal for us from that day forward was to find a way to give Tarique what he needed from the capacity of co-parents. As far as I was concerned, there would be no reconciliation of the romantic love we once shared. When a woman leaves a man for another man, it's possible she returns in hopes of reconciliation. When a woman leaves a man for *herself*, the chance of her returning is almost zero.

After the breakup with Jason, there was no point in looking back; I was no longer headed in that direction. My future and focus were on building a sustainable career to make the money Tarique and I needed for us to live on our own. Returning to live with my parents full-time was my only option until I got on my feet. There was peace of mind in knowing that Tarique was surrounded by their love. In the mornings, he was with a sitter, but as the demands of the job increased, he spent more and more time with my parents and Jason's family, who eventually became very reliable partners in his life as well.

At work, I was advancing rapidly. The woman who was running the front office when I began working there transitioned into a new role, and in the interim I assumed her duties. They found me to be a quick study, and in under two months I was offered a raise and promotion to the role of office coordinator. When you are aligned with the path the universe has designated for you, everything just seems to flow. When it's your turn, things just happen. And most importantly, I was committed to the cause. The more skills I acquired, the more my confidence grew. The more my confidence grew, the more interested I became in learning about the cases we managed. The more I worked, the more I wanted to work. Receiving a consistent paycheck confirmed my potential to create a better life for Tarique and myself and I was determined to do so come hell or high water.

It was important to me that my peers and Attorney Hardy saw my grind. For me, that looked like taking the initiative on various projects, the exercise of intuitiveness when working with our clients, and anticipation of the needs of the office staff to ensure that everyone was empowered to execute their respective roles with excellence. Longer hours on the job meant coming home later in the evenings. There were some days I didn't get to Tarique's babysitter until almost nine at night after having worked a full day. My parents were in total opposition to him being with the sitter for that many hours a day. In an effort to support me, they began assuming the responsibility for picking him up after their workdays ended. My mother's disdain for my lack of work/life balance was a mounting frustration in our home. One evening when I returned, Mom was waiting for me at the door, reminiscent of the days when she'd wait up for me to dress me down for staying out too late in the neighborhood partying and getting into trouble. This time, the conversation was different. We were no longer discussing the act of irresponsibility. The conversation now evolved into the management of responsibilities.

"You can't possibly think that this boy will get what he needs from you in a couple of hours a day. That's not what a child needs from their mother," she scolded.

I didn't have the strength to argue. I was already exhausted, and now the things I'd done to keep my baby safe and secure and put us onto a secure track in life were being questioned as well.

"I see you working hard, baby. Your dad and I are proud of you. We just want you to find a way to spend more time with Tarique. He needs you. God knows he needs you," Mom followed, with tears in her eyes.

I hugged her as she passed Tarique off to me to begin his bath routine. Too tired to take one myself, all I could do was take off my clothes from work, pull my hair up into a bun, and sleep for as long as Tarique would allow me to do so before he woke up in the middle of the night hungry.

I would take a shower around three or four in the morning. Lying beside him, knowing with certainty that he had peace and quiet to rest and grow and that he was nurtured, was my way of parenting. Knowing that I was out in the world making an honest living and becoming someone he could be proud of was my way of parenting. Although my physical presence didn't match my parents' expectations for me as a mother, I knew in my heart that I was doing what was best for Tarique.

The tension surrounding my inconsistent schedule, far from the predictable metronome of work-dinner-family-sleep my parents had lived through my childhood, was a growing point of contention. I knew I needed to move out on my own again. And at this juncture in my life, I knew I did not want a man to live with me either. Every morning on the train to work I listened as the metal wheels against the metal tracks became the soundtrack while I dreamed about what was next for us. On a train in New York, anything feels possible, and now my focus was getting my son and me together in peace for good.

New York often gets a bad rap, but this daily subway-directed meditation on the future to come focused me. Before long the rhythms of the commute bloomed into something even bigger as the same faces popped up on the benches across from me each day. And on other days when the train was overcrowded, you might find yourself standing shoulder to shoulder with a complete stranger. One magical day, that stranger would become a sister-friend I so badly needed.

Nyheike was of mixed Chinese-Jamaican heritage. She didn't always share the same sentiments I did regarding the experience of living while Black or brown, but her broad-based cultural experiences made for meaningful exchanges and discussions. But it wasn't just heated debates about racial justice and economic fairness—we mostly just tried to have fun. We found touchpoints in food and fashion and, being young women in the heart of New York City, shared an experience hard to explain anywhere else.

One day our chats turned to our living situations, and I learned Nyheike was living on City Island, a fishing village just off the coast of the Bronx known for seafood and its summer social scene.

I knew it mostly from venturing out for day trips to eat and hang. Ocean spraying in the air while we relaxed in the sunshine far from Manhattanville.

Well, it turned out Nyheike wasn't just talking about City Island for kicks—she had a room opening up in her place and thought Tarique and I might make for an easy fit.

My eyes lit up like a Christmas tree. Nyheike's offer felt like a divine alignment. God saw me trying to do my part and he presented me with an opportunity to achieve a desire of my heart.

"I would love to see your place," I replied.

That weekend, I ventured to City Island on a Saturday with Tarique in tow. City Island felt like suburbia although it was still considered a part of the city. Most residents were homeowners instead of renters, and it had a family-friendly vibe no matter where you went. But the high season of summer also meant it didn't feel disconnected from the lifeblood of New York.

Nyheike was a woman of her word. Everything was just as she said it would be. The room was larger than the red and yellow oddly shaped apartment we shared with Jason in the Bronx. The white paint gave the room a fresh, airy feeling. It felt like home. There was a shared kitchen, but separate bathrooms. The room she offered me was huge. There was enough space for Tarique and me to live comfortably.

I spent the entire ride on the bus back to my parents' place on cloud nine.

Sharing the news with them was bittersweet. On the one hand, they were sad to see us go, and on the other hand, they were proud. This was solid proof that I was putting in the work to turn my life around and a testament that I had what it took to stand on my own two feet.

The first night sleeping in our new bed on City Island, I can remember staring up at the ceiling, reminiscing about all the shit I was leaving behind. All I could do was cry. I had been so wrong about everything I thought I wanted so many times, but somehow those painful experiences felt necessary for me to appreciate all that I was becoming. I could literally feel my body and my mind recentering, shedding layers of the old wants, needs, and desires of the thrill seeker in search of love.

The new start also meant new social circles. I was now hanging out with young professionals who, while they still knew how to have fun, also knew there were bigger goals in mind to be aware of at all times. My immediate circles were mostly made up of Black folks in search of opportunities for elevation and upward mobility. As I matriculated throughout the New York social circles, I formed a deeper connection with four women. Nikki, Jamie, Kienya, Shanell, and I began calling ourselves the Startin' 5. On the heels of the Bad Boy shiny suit era, everyone was in search of a good time at night after handling their business by day. People not only wanted to feel good, but they wanted to look good while doing it. The nightlife was just as much about fashion as it was about having a good time. A group of promoters who referred to themselves as the Final Four had the city on lock, curating some of the best parties and social experiences the city had ever seen. Nikki, a cousin of one of them, was our in. And over the years, I'd form my own connections to the people who granted us access to places where culture really moved.

On Fridays, we would leave work early to go to Forever 21 at Galleria mall in Westchester, New York, to get geared up for the weekend. Forever 21 then was what Fashion Nova has become now. The only difference was that it was in person instead of online. That's my favorite way to shop by the way. It pains me to have to purchase everything on the internet today. Our usual routine was to go out to eat at the best restaurants before hitting the clubs. We thought we were living our own version of *Sex in the City*.

As the momentum of my personal life picked up, so did the need for my presence at work. I remember one standout day, when Attorney Hardy came to me about taking on more responsibility for a sad case that was in need of more attention in the office. It involved the shooting of four unarmed, ambitious young basketball players. Three of them were Black and one was Latino, all at the peak of their budding careers. These young men had been racially profiled and shot on the New Jersey Turnpike while traveling to North Carolina Central University for a showcase of their talents in hopes of earning scholarships. The hopes, dreams, and ambitions of Rayshawn Brown, Jarmaine Grant, Keshon Moore, and Danny Reyes were cut short after two state troopers violated their constitutional rights by shooting them without provocation. The case now known to the world as that of the Jersey Four sparked widespread anger. It was a clear case of racial profiling, a grim truth in this country then and now. Eventually, a suit was filed, but no settlement is ever worthy of the harm caused to the violated. This was a Friday, which meant that all roads led to the rally on Saturday. As an active volunteer, I jumped right into galvanizing the people to support the Jersey Four. Even though I worked at the law office, I never abandoned my participation in the movement.

From distributing flyers and setting up microphones at rallies and even running errands for the families of those directly impacted by the case, I needed to do my part to ensure that come hell or high water justice was served. Everything that my parents had exposed me to in the movement became real. Instead of listening to stories of injustice as a bystander, I was part of those boots on the ground.

As a part of my evolution, and my process of settling into a new life, I returned to the foundation of reading my mother and father instilled in me. In April of 1999, Sista Souljah, a thought-inducing, conscious leader whom I admired, released a book titled *The Coldest Winter Ever*. I must have read it from cover to cover in a weekend the first time I got my hands on it. Her depiction of the drug war and its lasting effects on the Black family was almost too accurate to have been fiction, but it was. Over the years, it became a classic and the story of Winter, the protagonist, was another narrative that allowed us to see pieces of ourselves. Winter's story reminded me of the life I had left behind, for good, to fight on behalf of those who needed it.

Unfortunately, this line of work knows no end, as there is no shortage of egregious acts of violence on innocent people of color. I think back to Amadou Diallo on February 4, 1999. Only twenty-three years old and enrolled in college when plainclothes officers fired forty-one rounds, nineteen of them entering his body, in New York City. He was simply standing there. No imminent threat. No weapon. No erratic behavior. Standing. The officers claimed to have mistaken him for a serial rapist they'd been chasing. This is the case that comes to mind when I think, When did I really "lock in" on the life I've become known for? Amadou's story was paralyzing. Even so, the only course of action was to step forward and I did. I took a more active role in the organization's process by helping with various tasks. Within a week's time, we had a succinct plan in place to advocate for Amadou.

While I was in the office preparing to close out for the weekend, Attorney Hardy entered.

"Tamika, I've seen how invested you are in Amadou Diallo and that is great. We have to start thinking about what is realistic for you going forward."

I turned around with a confused look on my face and said, "You're getting rid of me?" He chuckled.

"Tamika, you've shown tremendous promise. I just want to make sure that you are in the right place for your professional growth. I'm not getting rid of you; I support you."

At that moment, I realized that Attorney Hardy had become more than my boss. He was now an uncle to Tarique and me. And I knew deep in my heart that he was right. His words were full of wisdom. I did wonder what was next for me. That day anxiousness set in. Fear set in. In no way did I have answers about where to go or what to do next. The consideration alone scared me.

CHAPTER 9

TO BE YOUNG, GIFTED, AND BLACK

In life, there are two guarantees, death and change. Tarique was growing and changing day by day and so was I. By the time I mastered caring for him at one stage of his development, he was reaching another. The same was true for my career. Just as he reached eight months old, he was preparing to walk and I was preparing for the prospect of career growth. One day Attorney Hardy came into the office to share that he was going to push me forward due to the potential he saw in me.

But then several months passed with no action after that heart-to-heart conversation. I was anxious to get more immersed in the community. The legal work was cool, but that wasn't my jam. I learned a lot about specific ways to write documents and do intricate administrative tasks. Dealing with cases and families was preparing me for my future of having to execute this task on a regular basis. Little did I know I was learning bedside manners. At the law firm, the cases were high-profile. However, the work was predictable and somewhat slow. I was looking for something more fast-paced that would allow my passion for activism to blossom.

In February of 2001, I received a call that changed the trajectory of my career forever. Attorney Marjorie Fields Harris, executive director at NAN, was on the line.

"Tamika, we are in need of an executive assistant for the executive office here. Would you be interested?"

I can remember closing my eyes giving God thanks. At that moment, I was being rescued to fulfill my passion.

I had already been in the presence of and volunteered under the leadership of Reverend Al Sharpton. The prospect of becoming a full-time employee in the executive office was one I did not take lightly. I was excited, but I also felt sad because I knew it meant leaving my backbone in Attorney Hardy. He protected me much more than I gave him credit for.

"It is an honor to be considered for such a position. I would be willing to come in," I replied.

I was hesitant to tell Attorney Hardy about this new opportunity. I knew I had to move with haste because in the movement news travels fast. I didn't want this information to reach his ears from anyone else.

Shaking in my boots, I approached him.

"Attorney Hardy, remember that conversation we had?" I thought I was softening the blow. "Well, an executive assistant position came available at NAN and I would like to learn more. You are right. I just don't feel like I'm giving all that I can give and doing all that I can do."

Lawyers can be very stoic. It's part of their daily job. Whether it's anger, happiness, or anything else, they don't always show emotion.

Attorney Hardy looked at me and said, simply, "Ok. When is your last day?"

I had not yet taken the meeting or gotten the new job, but I knew in my heart that it was time to move on.

I understood; nothing about the position at NAN was going to be easy. They say to be careful what you wish for—I had asked God for speed, and I got God's record-breaking answer, Usain Bolt meets Sha'Carri Richardson. This wasn't just a job; it was a lifestyle. Unlike my time with Attorney Hardy, where the day ended when the office closed, this role came with a twenty-four-hour responsibility.

My tasks included coordinating complex travel schedules and itineraries, managing the executive office phone calls, transcribing notes for meetings, and attending to the personal needs of the executives. The two most complicated tasks were keeping the written schedules in order with all of the changes and overseeing the mail. There were mounds of letters from those in need, whether incarcerated or facing trauma. Every piece of mail had to be personally sorted to determine the needs and ways in which we could serve families.

The more acquainted I got with my roles and responsibilities, the more I grew professionally. Although I was "just" an assistant, I was still a faithful activist as a member of NAN, complete with the new opportunities that came with it. I was learning more about what I wanted from life. In doing so, I had to think on the forgiveness I'd never really given myself. So of course one day, out of the blue, Jason reached out to me again. It was the first time I had spoken to him in several months. We instantly reconnected through the same laughter that had held us together when we were together. The difference was that in addition to the laughter, there was also great pain. My heart wanted to understand where he had been. When we went our separate ways, there was no phone number or point of contact.

I learned that during that time we'd lost contact he was homeless. Our conversations, reminiscent of old times but with an understanding that romance was no longer an option for us, brought joy and solidarity back to us again. Soon enough we were checking in on the phone all day between my handling of responsibilities at work. On some days we argued, and on others we were working to discover the connection that had at times been lost between us. Oddly enough, we never spoke at night. Self-imposed boundary or just a fact of his still-spiraling life after dark, it kept things in order in the way I needed.

After redeveloping a practice of consistent communication, I saw him in person again at Tarique's second birthday party. That day, he did not stay long. He came, dropped a gift, and he left. I thought that come Monday the calls would resume, but they never did. They stopped. Two weeks went by and there was no sign of Jason. Some days I called, until I imagined that this scenario was a repeat of his previous disappearance. When I called his phone, it just rang and rang and rang until it clicked over to his voicemail box, indicated by the opening bars of "Love" by Musiq Soulchild.

In April of 2021, we all learned that Jason was killed by his "friends" who were falsely convinced that Jason had stolen drugs from them. At trial it was learned that the last hours of his life were horrific. He was beaten and shot to death. They left him lying on an embankment for two weeks before his body was discovered. My presumption that Jason had returned to his old disappearing ways was wrong. Instead, he had taken his last breath. I often wonder what might have become of us, Jason, Tarique, and me, if he had the chance to continue his journey of reconnection I'd witnessed before that fateful day of his murder.

There are still times when I long for his partnership.

The real tragedy in Jason's story is that he never received the help that he needed. And there was no place for his parents to real get support.

Not only was Jason dealing with deep depression and separation anxiety, but there were so many layers that required attention for his healing left unaddressed. His life and demise are a reflection of the systemic ills of America.

There is a part of me that shies away from speaking about the struggles of Jason's life as I have here. I want to preserve his self-respect and legacy. And I know it hurts to see a loved one's low points be brought to light again. But part of Jason's legacy should also be to encourage us all to seek help when it is needed. Jason's discomfort with his childhood trauma, his unaddressed mental health issues, and his inability to secure and stabilize his life eventually would be the end of him. This is unfortunately all too common in the communities I work in.

After Jason was murdered, a part of me was lost. I was numb. Before his death, I was a follower, a worker bee there to make a difference, yes, but more so to perform a designated task, collect a check, and leave each day only to come back and repeat it all over again the next. After his death, I began stepping into my potential as a leader. Although I had always been an organizer, I was now convicted by my conscience to act like one. There was not a single person who could have persuaded me differently. Pain, loss, trials and tribulations, and ultimately triumph were the undercurrent of who and what I became. There is a fire ignited inside the bellows of a human soul when loss of this magnitude is experienced. It's not only melancholy; it's remembrance and the power of reflection. It's the reality that life goes on. Despite being young and processing, I knew that if I allowed death to place a hold on my heart, then I would succumb to it. There were times I would sit in disbelief that Jason's loss was our reality. Him being gone forever was difficult to conceptualize. With a son to raise, life was my only choice. There was no other alternative. It was in this knowing that I began to pick up the pieces and to see with sharper vision a future for myself and Tarique.

When I returned to work, retribution was on my mind. Not retribution through revenge, but retribution through activism. My mornings before leaving the house were spent reading the newspapers in an effort to proactively inform myself about current events. Before I found out about issues when arriving in the office. Back then, I was reactive. Arriving laced with more knowledge was a game changer for me. The same tugging that I felt when I worked for Attorney Hardy's office began to resurface. In my heart, I knew there was more for me to do. Jason's death confirmed that I needed to grow.

In his passing, I gained clarity that I was called to go out into the world and fight against all the things I identified as factors in his demise. Even so, I had not categorized the tugging I felt as a calling. What I did know was that in my role as an assistant, I did not have the flexibility to move forward as I needed. I'd seen the tools and weapons I needed to add to my arsenal as an activist—the day-to-day grit of leadership, the relationships forged with everyone, including businesspeople, politicians, funders, influencers, celebrities, pastors, scholars, and everyday folks. Getting to the next step was the next part.

I wanted to go to the state capitol in Albany, New York. It seemed to me that everyone who was fighting for something worth fighting for was doing it up there. My interest level in the job had diminished to the point that I began coming into work late, hanging out in the office, and scouting around for what opportunities might be up next. I was asked if I had an interest in working in the communications department as the assistant communications director under Rachel Noerdlinger. At this point, I'm sure I was about to be fired. The new role would be helping to manage our press conferences and coordinating communications for events, large-scale meetings, and rallies. I was finally getting close to the platform I needed to make a difference of my own. But as my responsibilities grew I did also suffer the sting of imposter syndrome. An opposing energy slipped into my life, one that would have me believe I was somehow unworthy of the tasks before me. An energy that forced me to question my capabilities and my worth. I began to hesitate before speaking. A chaotic mind led me to ask, Who do you think you are? A narrative of self-doubts—that I wasn't as educated on the issues as other people I saw leading in this field—became a tangled web to pick through as I found my way. I've had preachers tell me for years they battled with the idea that they were being called to the pulpit. Many who confirm they accepted callings they didn't want. Some knew that being called to preach meant a change of lifestyle. Others recognized the burden of the cloth and the new level of accessibility and judgment necessary to oversee a congregation of people.

I knew it was time to fight again. The fight for the position I'd grown into. To fight to be heard and seen the way I'd earned through hard work.

The more I raised my hand to volunteer to roll up my sleeves and get my hands dirty and to lead projects, the more my network expanded. At rallies, I began to introduce myself and become more assertive about how I could be of service to ailing families and advocates alike. This push for recognition of my work brought me to the issue that would really change my life like never before—the fight against gun violence.

I set a personal goal to become aligned with activists who were in the gun violence space. Leaders like Erica Ford, an international peace keeper and founder of LIFE Camp in Queens, New York, as well as A. T. Mitchell, New York City's official Gun Violence Prevention Czar and founder of Man Up! in Brooklyn, New York, challenged me to learn and grow in my work. After they challenged me, they collaborated with me. At the end of the day, we were all moving in accordance with our callings.

Once my purpose was ignited, I didn't have to search far for a training ground anymore. Public speaking was nonnegotiable as an activist, and while I'd done it in private settings and moderately sized meetings before, the thought of speaking, proclaiming, declaring, in a crowd larger than what gathered in our office meetings on a regular basis scared the shit out of me.

But despite the commotion taking place within me, the elders took interest in my ideas and trusted I would grow from there to the rest of the task. As far as they were concerned, if you were a good organizer, you were at least a decent speaker. Point-blank, and period. There was no formal coaching or baby steps towards preparation. The name of the game was baptism by fire. Before you knew it, you would be standing at a rally and pushed up to the microphone to speak.

NAN fostered an ideology of continuous learning. If you were immersed in action, reading and listening, you were always prepared. To me, it felt like a form of hazing. And although I don't quite remember the first time I stepped up to the podium, I do remember being a hot-ass mess in the moment leading up to it. Literally crying and shaking, with thoughts racing through my mind faster than I could assign the words to their meaning. But my creativity for how to garner the attention of target audiences and how to build stronger protests always carried me through. The superpower lifting everything else up. Even so, I did not always readily share my sentiments, because throughout my career I struggled with trusting my gut. Little by little I learned to trust myself more.

As I found stability on my own two feet at NAN, I realized a recurring source of disorder in my mind. I was without question at a deficit in formal education as far as members of the leadership group went. Instead of my being surrounded by those who were street-smart, my professional circle was now overflowing with degrees I probably hadn't even heard of back in Co-op City. In the presence of chief diversity officers, executives, equity council leaders, community stakeholders, and young leaders who graduated from respected educational institutions, the conversations always led to the question "Where did you go to school?" Forget that people placed judgment solely based on the type of school you attended. Whether you attended a Historically Black College or University (HBCU), Predominantly White Institution (PWI), or Ivy League school, those were the classifications you needed to fit.

To admit that you were not formally educated to the highest status possible was to invite turned-up noses. There I was, a high school dropout, without so much as a GED, climbing the ladder over people who'd spent years building professional résumés. Not having a college degree today leaves room for interpretation, but back then degrees were a necessity. Even I knew that it was only a matter of time before my educational status or lack thereof would come into question. Instead of allowing that to be my story, I made the decision to take control of my narrative and return to school.

This era of my life was laser focused on personal growth and development, which further fueled my professional growth. My territory increased after my sister Sharon offered me an opportunity to move in with her to share a multifamily house. In our new space, I had my own everything. There was no more sharing kitchens, hallways, etc., and Tarique had his own room.

After Jason passing, I took some time to learn more about who I was and what I wanted. And when I did try my hand at dating, it proved to be more of a learning experience than love. In true Tamika fashion, I found myself getting closer to mothers and grandmothers of the men I was dating than the men themselves. Stability was more attractive to me than anything, so I guess it was easier to tap out early than risk being hurt by another short-timer the way I had been so many times before.

But as they say, when you least expect it, love will find you. Kienya, one of the Startin' 5 members, was introduced to a guy named Darrin at an event and she instantly believed he was someone I should meet instead. She wasted no time giving him my number. He called me and we spoke briefly. Eventually, I accepted his invitation for lunch on a Saturday. Little did we know, our in-person meeting would be delayed for weeks.

It was the week of 9/11, the horrific terrorist attack, and nothing would ever be the same again. Only after another month of the world trying to piece itself back together were Darrin and I ready to try a reconnection. This time, I invited him to bring his daughter whom I'd been told so much about. It was comforting to know Darrin had a daughter who was close in age to Tarique. This meant he understood exactly what I was experiencing as a parent.

When we did finally meet, the first thing I noticed about him was his style. Although he looked young, something about him felt a little older. He was a gentleman in every way.

While we were at lunch he told me about his four-year-old daughter, Cheyenne, and I shared my life with Tarique in return. It was apparent that Darrin was a family guy and more mature than some of the men in my previous relationships. Darrin was calm. And because he had a pretty good job, we found commonality in doing fun things with our kids. And as we got deeper into the relationship, he disclosed to me that he had two big girls in addition to his youngest daughter. Crystal and Cheri were ten years younger than me, which explained why he hadn't been so forthcoming in the beginning. More importantly, he wasn't sure if they would accept me, which prolonged the delay. But no matter what and above all, he and Tarique hit it off so well it warmed my heart.

After a little more than a year of dating, Darrin and I made the decision to combine our homes. Things were unsteady with his daughters Crystal and Cheri at first, but after the sudden and tragic death of their beautiful mother the family unit pulled together as we all watched Darrin step into a bigger role for us all. It was beautiful. When I look back, I realize that we all had growing pains and a massive learning curve. Although times were tough, the girls knew I was trying and that they were loved, not just by me but by the entire Mallory family. On most Sundays we went to church and did all the things that families do together. We became a family of five living in a small apartment. Even though we had conflict, each family member found their space and purpose. Crystal was a phenomenal cook, and Cheri was a great hairstylist. Together, the girls helped us to keep the little kids together while Darrin and I worked to make ends meet.

Once the girls settled into their transition, my focus was back to work. But the issue of education never went away. In some ways watching the girls in pursuit of their education was a reminder that I still needed to pursue mine. At some point, I happened to see a commercial on the TV for a program at the College of New Rochelle that allowed enrollees to earn GED and college credits simultaneously. It was a perfect match for someone like me, younger and with a firm interest in continuing my studies into college.

With Tarique to care for and my full-time job still on deck, I didn't have time to waste. I met with an on-campus adviser, thumbed through a big-ass catalog she handed me, and plotted what needed to be done—I was here for myself, but I was also here for Tarique, Darrin, and his kids now too.

Some of the professors at CNR supported me by assigning work that aligned with what I was engaged with at my job. They took the time to recognize how taxing work was and how much stress was associated with simultaneously being in the movement and hitting my academic goals.

Although I wasn't one to complain about the fullness of my life, I was certainly tired as hell. As much as the people around me supported me and as grateful as I was for it, there are few words to describe the stress of going from schoolwork to movement work and back again day after day. Reverend Sharpton, whom I was working for at NAN, had also launched a campaign for president, which added another layer of stress at work. There was a part of me that denied myself the opportunity to express my feelings of being overwhelmed, recognizing the burdens felt by so many single Black mothers I encountered in my justice work. Instead, more often than not, I turned my frustrations inward. On some days I secretly cried in private while driving to class. And on other days I cried in public, during office hours while sitting across from one of my professors. The school had its fair share of adult students who were also maintaining full-time jobs and families. The staff recognized that we needed a sense of leniency to balance it all. And there were also those times when I recognized an extra sprinkle of favor bestowed upon me, as some professors recognized me from the newspapers and TV. Many were just as frustrated with society as I was. They too wanted change and supported me in working towards it on behalf of all of us.

One professor in particular who specialized in tough love almost always refused my requests for extensions: "The sooner you finish, the sooner you can graduate. I am not going to let you slack."

Even when I tried to interject, he would stop me in my tracks.

"You know when you slack, you fall off. You need to get out of here. That's what I'm going to help you do and I'm going to hold you accountable to do it."

He was right, even if my crowded mind and exhausted body didn't want to hear it right then. Working with these levels of stress hurt like hell, but as I saw it, there was a will, so God made a way.

Prior to every semester's end, I made my rounds at the registrar's office, with the same catalog in hand from day one. It was already jacked up by the end of the first semester. The corners were worn from frequent use and several pages were folded inside to represent classes I either was currently taking, needed to take, or was inquiring about.

Over time they probably got tired of seeing my face, but there was too much on the line to leave my education to chance. My work and my pursuit of education forced me to mature in ways I had not accounted for, calling me to a higher version of myself.

After four years and unabated toil, on January 31, 2006, I graduated with honors and a bachelor of arts degree. I felt unstoppable again, not because roadblocks did not get in the way, but because I'd learned to use them as stepping stones to keep going.

My graduation day did not go as planned. I wasn't where I was supposed to be or on time, having decided to help a friend in need who was dealing with health challenges. We studied and struggled together during our years in school; therefore, I saw our graduation day no differently. We had been there for each other and I wanted to be there for her on the day we were scheduled to write the final chapter of our educational pursuit. As good as all of this may sound, our plan for arrival was flawed. Due in part to the choices we made on that day, we did not arrive in time for the ceremony. Anyone who lives in New York knows the importance of taking public transportation on graduation days, especially when the ceremonies are held at Radio City Music Hall. We decided to drive. We arrived late, and when we finally parked, my friend did not have the ability to walk fast. My family was there waiting for my name to be called, and it was, but I didn't walk across the stage. In fact, I was nowhere to be found, nor was my friend. When we made it to the stage, we were left with only the option to walk behind the last student in line. My family was looking for me the entire time, but I did not appear onstage until the end.

Although I was somewhat sad to miss such a pivotal moment, I remained loyal. In doing so, I missed the opportunity to hear my family screaming on cue, but eventually I got over it because I had my degree in hand.

When the ceremony was over, I met with my family and spoke to my mom, attempting to explain the story.

My mom had heard so many excuses over the years, cried so many tears, placed so much faith in me, and been let down so many times that I was sure she was numb to it all. But this time I began to attempt to explain why I didn't walk across the stage earlier. My mom interrupted me, looking me square in the eyes, and said, "Did you get the paper?" I nodded and that was that.

After I had dropped out of school in the tenth grade, my educational career had come full circle and I was now degreed. It was on that day I found my confidence, and I never looked back.

CHAPTER 10

I KNOW I CAN

I find that every ten years or so, I just grow out of shit. Although things with Darrin were not terrible, the dynamics of our relationship shifted for me.

I'd escaped the emotional and physical abuse of my past, and I was now getting to where I'd wanted to be all along in life. I was traveling more; I was moving on in the world. But the continued pressure to be what everyone else needed further strained our relationship. Eventually, we discovered that we were no longer compatible. In hindsight, I believe I felt this to be the case more than he did. Something about me keeps seeing my moments of extreme personal growth only come alongside periods of focus and isolation where I can take a breath and figure things out. Darrin's and my family was progressing beautifully, but the intimate relationship just slowed down. We had become room-mates, no longer lovers. He was definitely frustrated. And between raising our blended family and the development of my career, and him working as well, there was little room left over to get our relationship back on track.

My career, on the other hand, was moving full steam ahead. If there is one thing I am not, it is an overnight success. While it's true my college degree had given me a sense of self-assurance I never had before, I was still learning how to show up differently in the world—with less apology for who I was and who I wanted to become. Standing taller and speaking more assertively was still a struggle for me. Instead of waiting to be called on in team meetings at NAN, I was raising my hand and volunteering to take the lead on projects and committees. I was making well-thought-out suggestions on strategy. I resolved to never again question whether or not I belonged in the room, reorienting that attention towards productivity and execution. A fire had been ignited within me. It was tough, but I was determined.

Progress was something I had mastered, but the categorization of success was not. After all, how could I measure accomplishment when my life's work was rooted in serving as a voice for those struggling to speak out on their own? Is it possible to deem oneself prosperous amidst insurmountable tragedy? My answer would be no.

I wrestled with a question I'd always been avoiding—can a single person ever make real progress against injustice? The answer is no, an individual cannot. An individual has the power to spark change, but it takes a village to ignite a full paradigm shift. But that also meant I needed to recalibrate my mind to recognize the value of the small wins as well as the large. There are no declarations of victory in justice work. Even the wins we do secure go right back into the battle, always at risk of being undone by the forces of inequity.

Over time, I learned to define my successes through a framework of purpose. I needed to reidentify the why and reason for my existence in my field. For me, unlocking purpose was like opening a box of butterflies. Once they take flight, they will never return to the confines of the box the way they had been before. A purpose, not simply a task or goal but a purpose, unleashed will always stay in motion.

Every day felt like I was fighting a war. After seven years of time already put into my work at NAN, I was clear about my assignment and my goals for advancement. My role as the associate director of public relations was to amplify the stories of families who experienced loss and tragedy, and to coordinate experiences that helped keep our organization's mission front and center. This took place through rallies, town hall meetings, and other forms of mobilizing people for the cause. Our mission was to provide hope for those who called out to us for help. I learned that smoke is almost always a sign of fire and I worked day and night to put the fire out. On November 26, 2006, I was standing directly in it.

The phone rang around 4:00 a.m. Getting out of bed and tiptoeing my way to the living room trying not to wake anyone else in the house, I knew something was gravely wrong.

"This is Tamika," I whispered with my mouth placed as close as possible to the speaker of the phone. By this time, the number on the other end had already called me three times. "Chick. You gotta get up. This is bad," she said.

Rachel Noerdlinger, the director of communications, was my boss but also my friend. There were times that our passion and aggression took over to the point that we would literally fight in business suits in the middle of the office. Rachel was a former athlete who had not lost her strength or power. On more than one occasion, we found ourselves nearly coming to blows in the office over anything. We were just that passionate. It was just our (imperfect) way of handling the stress of the work and the magnitude of the responsibility we held. We worked really hard and created memories together that will last a lifetime.

There was a quavering in her voice that I had not heard before. "What happened?"

"NYPD fired fifty rounds at three young brothers. They were unarmed. The brother who lost his life would have been preparing to get married this morning."

My heart sank into my feet. Her words sent shivers down my spine. *"Fuck!"*

I had no better words to describe what I felt in the moment. "Fuck is exactly right."

This was beyond real.

"Hurry up. Get your shit together to go into the office. The press will be at our headquarters by ten a.m.," Rachel said. We were always so intense.

When I hung up the phone, I sat there squeezing my forehead in my hand to distract myself from crying. What do I need to do? Who do I need to call? The thoughts came flooding through my mind. Immediately after I snapped back into reality, I took on my responsibility to contact other staff members as well as a few of our community partners. There was no time for me to get caught up in my feelings At times, we were like robots—called to action.

I took a quick shower, pulled my protective scarf off my hair, threw on my work clothes, and headed into the office. By the time I was preparing to leave, Black America was up and alerted to this crisis. Everybody in my house was up watching the news, and my parents had already called. This was going to be different.

By the time I arrived, the office news of the senseless murder of Sean Bell had spread like wildfire. Officers in plain clothes and undercover claimed to have been investigating a club where Sean Bell was out partying with friends Trent Benefield and Joseph "Joey" Guzman. As the guys left the club, they were confronted while in Sean's car by police who fired inhumanely and without cause, killing Sean and severely injuring Trent and Joseph.

Sean's story struck me differently, because he was close to my age. Our lives could not have been that different. He could have been any one of us. He could have been my friend, my brother, my cousin or coworker. The senseless manner in which his life was taken rocked me to my core. All I could think about was the punishment of those responsible for his death and the injuries of Trent and Joey.

Most of the executive team had rushed to be in the hospital with Joey, who was chained to the bed with seventeen bullets in his body. I interfaced with Rachel via text on what needed to be done: interviews to be set up, and cameras arranged for a planned press conference the size of which we were not really prepared for. But we always got it done.

At the same time, another line of communication was going down among my younger clique of activists as well as some of my street people. People thought they were ready for war.

For a moment in the office, there was silence. There was an emotional undercurrent. Like many of my peers, my body was in a crisis mode. Inside, I was ready, willing, and able to support Sean's fiancée, Nicole. Just twenty-two years old, she needed support in attempting to navigate a loss all too familiar to us but for her a first time. She hadn't asked to be pulled into activism, and now she was a single mother to two children overnight. Even in sorrow, Nicole's beauty and energy preceded her. She was so innocent and now forced to face the ills of the world. My heart broke for Nicole. To experience love only to have it stolen away from you is a pain I wish upon no one. An experience that ran raw again for me as I thought of Jason. As a mother, your living is at times driven by protecting your child from the evil of the world. When the very person who has given them life is stolen—murdered—there is nothing you can do. The sea of sorrow is all-consuming. And yet, you will be expected to carry on with life. To move forward in and through the pain.

It had been five years since Jason was killed, and as dark as it sounds, our shared experience with sudden and violent loss brought Nicole and me together.

A little less than a year later, on March 17, 2007, the city and many of our communities across the nation were further agitated and outraged when three of the five detectives were found not guilty of charges of manslaughter, assault, and reckless endangerment. It was a hard blow to all of us. In the courtroom, Joey was ostracized. The judge spoke to him harshly. With Joey being a big guy, they wanted to make him a scapegoat. My heart hurt for everyone, but to watch him being broken down in court was crushing. As we exited the courtroom, people screamed and cried in anger amidst the news. I went over to Joey to show my support and express my disdain for the lack of accountability that is far too often a reality in this country when crimes are committed against Black men.

Not one of us plans to be a victim of violence, particularly not by the very entity that has been designated to protect us. In our day-to-day lives, most will not experience deadly police violence firsthand. That's just a fact of math in a big country, but one deadly instance of unfairness perpetrated by law enforcement and based on race is too many, and we are far far far beyond one. Sean Bell's case will forever be etched in my heart.

It was an honor to serve Nicole, Joey, Trent, and Sean's family in a time of intense need.

Sean's case was a critical turning point for me, as it revealed my passion and capacity for helping people when they are in their most vulnerable state. With all the skills I had acquired, I was now all in on my personal activism journey. And although I did not necessarily know what that looked like, I could feel a deeper calling in my level of commitment. Reverend Sharpton and Rachel noticed my eagerness to spread my wings. The communications department opened my eyes to new possibilities and ways in which I could play a more active role in my personal activism. During my time in the field, I acquired a great deal of knowledge. Rachel was brilliant and our strategic planning sessions with Reverend Sharpton helped us to tell the stories of these American tragedies and make the vital connections to their historical context in relation to the injustice and inequality of the country. We were literally documenting the movement and the moment.

Approximately a year later, I was appointed to my first solo project at NAN as the director of the Decency Initiative. This initiative was in response to Don Imus calling the Rutgers Women's Basketball Team "nappy-headed hos." In challenging Imus, we received an overload of pushback. Many questioned why his references were offensive if in fact we as a community referred to ourselves in this way. My mission was to bring awareness to the exploitation of Black people in arts and entertainment. The Decency Initiative was created in order to reduce the degrading, racially insensitive and misogynous language and culture that has become pervasive today and to hold corporate America and the private sector equally accountable with racial sensitivity. We attempted to force the labels to see that similar derogatory terms were not acceptable for other races; therefore, the labels should not be profiting from the degradation of Black people. The focus was not on policing people; instead, it was established to spark widespread discussion and help the masses to think differently about what they desired to consume and how we as a community have the power to eradicate change of our perceived value. It was about pushing positivity. I believed in the power of the cause and it was a phenomenal learning experience; however, it was not easy to be personally attacked by the hip-hop community. These were my people, many of whose work and music I loved and admired. Regardless of the scrutiny, I knew in my heart, I was doing the right thing.

Over the next several years, my professional journey was comparable to that of a fitness regimen. I kept my head down and put in the work. The more I worked, the more I realized the results. Not only did I learn more about organizing campaigns, but because of my experience at the law firm with Attorney Hardy, I was conscious of legal limitations and liabilities. I had the ability to decipher moments when there was potential for justice to not be served based upon the narrow scope of the law. I saw leaks and holes in the justice system that others could not see. My dear friend Attorney Benjamin Crump (we'll talk more about him later), whom we affectionately call the Attorney General of Black America, often says he is the "attorney in the courtroom," I am the "attorney in the streets."

For me, this work wasn't about running fast towards a particular destination. It was about the gradual continuum of progress. Organizing is more than holding a megaphone at a rally. It's deeper than standing on a stage in front of crowds to spew words calling frustrated people to action. Organizing in its purest form is about change. Change that is needed so desperately our lives depend on it. I was beginning to feel the weight of this calling and it was heavy. There were more lives and more stories of injustice that further fueled my ambition. I was young and angry. I believed that my generation was going to fix America. What I did not know or understand was how hard it actually is to move and shift systems. I knew about campaigns, and helping families, but what I did not know was politics. This is why it is imperative that we learn history and understand its nuances. I say this while recognizing the power of naivete; I had to learn the importance of working ahead, the ebbs and flows of progress, and the time it will take to fuel and refuel the movement forward. But that's how it works, and I hope discouragements along the path to freedom never succeed in extinguishing our energy.

As my workload grew, I struggled harder to maintain work-life balance. My greatest challenge was not in the unpredictability of my days at work. It was in figuring out how to be a present parent and run my household. Thank God for Darrin. Although at this point, we were living separate lives, we remained a part of each other's villages. He remained extremely helpful with the responsibilities for Tarique. Even so, finding balance was challenging. Eventually, Crystal and Cheri moved upstate to live with a close family member. Living in New York City and being cramped into our space was not working out. My days now consisted of meetings with families, running campaigns, and working directly with members of the community. People were now coming to me asking my opinion and checking in with me regarding various projects. Instead of being a worker bee, I was becoming a leader.

There were so many times growing up that I wasn't sure where I belonged. I was all over the place. I was now addicted to the affirmation my work gave me. Had it not been for the continuous support of my parents and sister Sharon, the outcome would be much different for both of us. Tarique was surrounded by love. My father helped transport Tarique to and from the babysitter and made sure he was with him when I could not be present. And my mother made sure Tarique was fed and nurtured with the fullness of her heart. In the process, she gave me hell of course.

"Tamika, at some point you have to put your son first," she would often say.

To which I replied, "Mom, that's not cool. Of course I put Tarique first. I'm doing all of this for him."

"It's not enough," she said.

At times, I spent eighteen to twenty hours in the office. On occasions, I took naps on my couch. It's not like I was out partying or rubbing elbows with celebrities. Nevertheless, she was right. Her words stung because while I was out doing everything in my power to make a difference in the world, I was young and failing to discern the difference between physical presence and emotional presence in my son's life. In my heart, I believed that making more money to provide for Tarique and to give him the things I didn't have trumped everything else. My conscious and intentional time with him was compromised too many days to count. My mom wanted me to realize that although what I was doing was important, nothing was more important than the emotional well-being of my son, an attribute that could only be cultivated while fully present.

It was a wake-up call to change my ways. I recalibrated my investments of time and work-life balance right then and there, realizing that my work to protect young Black men from the world's neglect needed to begin at home. It was a moment of recentering, reconnecting to the people and institutions that had raised me and my community. Reconnecting also looked like attending church more often. Tarique was singing in the choir, I was more engaged with the activities in the church, and it was time well spent for both of us.

As God would have it, my next big appointment was as the Director of the William A. Jones Social Justice Initiative. It was an honor to serve in this capacity because I was handpicked by the Chairman of NAN, who also became my pastor, and confidant, Dr. W. Franklyn Richardson. In this role, I discovered a deeper purpose, bridging the gap between the Black church and social justice activism.

During the mid-1900s Civil Rights Movement, Black churches and their leaders played an intricate role in the execution of activism on behalf of their congregants and their loved ones. Segregation and Jim Crow laws limited Black people's rights to freely assemble, so churches stepped in to serve as safe spaces and meeting facilities. Under the roofs of our churches, rallies were held, headquarters for marches and meetings were established, and spiritual, emotional, and social well-being was promoted.

As the years passed and we began to see a decline in the role of the Black church in the Civil Rights Movement, a shift in leadership took hold. New generations of activists did not always hold the same sense of connection with the church. People began turning to other methods to exercise spirituality and activism. The four walls of the church were no longer the only place to practice faith. The wave of prosperity ministry that emerged in the eighties and nineties directed more attention towards the generation of wealth and diverted attention away from the civil and safety issues that had been a focus of service of our churches. Don't get me wrong, money matters, but so do policy, voting, advocacy, and protest.

Some church leaders had moved their attention towards development and the acquisition of property and wealth. While these were all good initiatives in my mind, they left little room for social justice work. Communities felt left behind. The activists felt like the church was too soft. Too in bed with elected officials. Our LGBTQIA+ communities did not feel welcomed in churches, as the discussion surrounding same-sex marriage was still taboo. There were and still are overall acceptance and shaming issues.

My role was to bridge those gaps between social progress and faith leadership.

Our strategy was to travel around the country hosting a programming series at select churches. I enlisted national speakers to attend and share. The church offered local people in consideration of the specific community needs.

Dr. Richardson believed in the entire pie of advocacy. He had previously served as the general secretary of the National Baptist Convention, and not only was he powerful, but he was also well respected. He was a big shot to me. To have been appointed by him was a distinguished honor. Not only did we work closely on the initiative, but he also made a concerted effort as my mentor. He was instrumental in teaching me how to communicate with church leadership, and the cadence and refinement necessary for me to evolve in my role as a leader. Under his tutelage, I learned the ins and outs of the pastor's role and the effective way to bring community and church together. He showed me the necessity to build alliances with church and community. Doing so helps to give your movement legs.

There was a sense of freedom that accompanied this new position. It was the first time I was "the boss," overseeing and developing. Working in this capacity was about accessing the power of ministry and organizing. It was exhilarating. And the work put a different spotlight on me. It's one thing to oversee a program or initiative that someone else has conceptualized, but to curate an initiative from the ground up drew the attention and respect of my peers. So I ran hard and fast. That same pattern of relentless ambition returned and I felt the urge to regroup and audit my life. I arrived at the realization that Darrin and I could not be together any longer. I was overcome with sorrow not only for myself but also for Tarique. Darrin was the only person whom Tarique has ever called Daddy. Jason was killed before Tarique started speaking.

The day I shared my thoughts with Tarique, I was brutally honest. "I don't think we're going to make it," I said.

Patiently, I awaited Tarique's response. It was not what I expected. "Mommy. I'm with you," he said.

I wanted to cry but didn't and listened to him continue.

"I'm going to miss my daddy, but I'm with you."

Our conversation reminded me of that night my mom came to my room to tell me that she and my dad might not make it. The difference was that they figured out a way through. Darrin and I did not.

I can't be certain if Tarique knew the magnitude of his words amidst a time of such great personal uncertainty. That day he affirmed that he would be with me through my challenges, and he has. Tarique has remained by my side through every valley and every mountaintop of my life. Our vow to always be there for each other is what sustained me on the days when even the rainbows of life were not enough.

The truth is that I needed to be on my own to see a clear path and direction for what I was to do in my life and career. The appointments to oversee the various committees and initiatives were a start, but there was still a tugging on my heartstrings that I should have been doing more. I've never been one able to walk through life knowing I wasn't giving my all to my life's work.

Knowing that I was compromising my time with Tarique took a toll on me. There was no question that I knew how to do the work. There was no question that I was where I was supposed to be, but I often wondered if I was living up to my full potential. My central causes of anti–gun violence legislation and the protection of Black people from unfair policing were getting attention locally and within my community, but I was not seeing the change that needed to happen at the macro level.

Society tells us to run fast and that if we don't take action immediately opportunities will expire. I was impatient with myself, but now with some distance I realize that if the path of my life can teach anyone anything, it's that what God has for us will not miss us. Living, through trial and error, is the only way to get where we are supposed to be.

CHAPTER 11

CAUGHT UP IN THE RAPTURE

The puzzle pieces of my professional life were aligning seamlessly. Not only was I strengthening my speaking skills, but there was also an overall growth in confidence. The William A. Jones Social Justice Initiative jump-started my close-knit relationships with so many Black preachers across the country who have become some of my most trusted friends and confidants. Many of whom do not play about me to this day. Whether the world recognizes it or not, there are many megachurches and leaders focused on social justice ministry, and in their presence I was right at home.

My network was expanding and the number of people now familiar with my work increased. Yet there was a part of me that considered companionship. What I knew for sure was that I had not mastered the art of love or war in relationships. Truth be told, I was not even sure I had the tools in my arsenal to do so. My previous relationships that I dare not refer to as failed served a purpose in their seasons. Those seasons had come to an end. The sum of the lessons learned was that if I were to attain any levels of success in relationships, I would be required to approach them differently from the start.

Imagine how much different dating would be if we asked our potential partners about the intricacies of their childhood traumas and inquired about the action they were actively taking to heal from them. If we engaged in honest and transparent conversations early on, it is likely we could prevent a great deal of heartache. Consider how things might be different if we took the time to identify triggers in our relationships and allowed that information to guide us in the establishment of parameters used to define whom and how we date. I'd venture to say these strategies implemented would prove to be transformative. And while these are all hindsight revelations, they force me to reflect upon the error of my ways over the years as I was attempting to discover love.

The first time I fell, it was with Tarique's father and I was fifteen. We lacked the tools to communicate properly; therefore, we screamed at each other to get our points across. When amplified words failed us, we used our fists. Even when I was pregnant, physical abuse was our resolve. We fought so much that we were known for it. We had normalized grappling in our relationship. Young, toxic, and void the levels of emotional intelligence needed to prevent us from intentionally causing harm to each other was the sum of us. For a long time, I blamed him for what took place in our relationship. It was my assumption that because he was physically bigger and stronger than me, I was under attack. What I failed to acknowledge were the countless instances when I was the aggressor. Neither he nor I had a clue about how to be in a relationship with another person. We loved each other, but the expression of that love at times spoke otherwise.

The next reciprocal relationship was with Darrin. Although we loved each other, the strife associated with the balancing act of a blended family proved too challenging at such an inexperienced age. In addition to that, I still had not mastered the art of conflict resolution. And even though the relationship was void of physical abuse, it was abundant emotionally. Darrin was a really good guy who is undoubtedly the husband of someone's dreams. He was humble and loved Tarique, but in retrospect, I was ill prepared to bring to the relationship the levels of balance and peace needed for it to thrive. I had not yet learned them. We did not master the ability to disagree respectfully. One might assume that after having had the example of my parents' multi-decade relationship, I would have these skills intact, but it was a work in progress. I was a work in progress. My actions were proof that sometimes the influence outside is stronger than the one inside your home. Instead of acquiring a spirit of defusing, I remained on standby to turn up. I always had to be right. As I got older, much of the fight in me was a result of my work in the movement. In this space, my job depended on my ability to channel frustration into action. I was a real street activist, and in that space my specialty was the transformation of pain into power.

The more I realized progress professionally, the more I kept my head down and did the work. My matriculation into adulthood also meant that anyone who dared to occupy space in my life would have to be a good fit, not for who I was but for what I was becoming. At work, I gave my all. By the time I made it back home, truth be told, I was exhausted. By day, I was evolving as an organizer in ways that even the world around me took note of, but more importantly, I was evolving as a woman.

And then an unexpected courtship with a board member evolved. Never had I ever been in a relationship with anyone remotely close to my professional stomping ground. Therefore, I had never dated anyone who was a high-level executive within the organization. In truth, I was a worker bee who worked to fulfill her tasks. Even so, there were days when I still didn't meet the mark. When I was a young professional, discovering love was the furthest thing from my mind, until Don came along. Don Coleman. The myth. The man. The legend. Don was the type of man who made you take notice when he entered a room. From the suits, shoes, and jewelry he wore to the high-end bookbag he carried, he always looked like money. Don was bold, and sure of himself. He was powerful and kind, and he spoke well. He moved with ease, even though he was nothing to play with. Don was from Detroit by way of Ohio. Home to legends like the Isley Brothers and DeBarge. Need I say more? The proof of his success and business acumen was in his work. As a former NFL player and founder and CEO of the number-one advertising agency in the country for African-Americans, he was a certified boss and a multimillionaire who said what he meant and meant what he said. Although I previously heard him speak at board meetings, I had not made it my business to be in conversation with him directly, except for a few times. Even those occurrences were uneventful. One day in particular, after the meeting was adjourned I was standing by the door, shaking each board member's hand as they exited. That day, Don was the last to leave. As I reached out for his hand, there was a look in his eyes I had not seen before. One that crossed the threshold of the business conducted in the room. Instantly, I looked away, as I'd made it a practice to look down or in another direction while working. When you are a woman in a professional setting, there is an unspoken set of guidelines that are adhered to in an effort to maintain the imaginary line in the sand that separates business from everything else. Standing on the other side of that line means not looking people in their eyes too long, limiting occurrences of touch, and even keeping laughter and small talk to a minimum. For me, professionalism is not optional.

A week later, we were in the same space again at a corporate event. My actions were robotic in nature. His gestures were different this time. Every time I caught him looking at me, I looked away quickly. He followed my eyes. Later that evening he called me and made it clear that he desired to get to know me outside of work. While flattering, there were too many factors that made it impossible as far as I was concerned. He took the time to walk me through the series of personal events taking place in his life.

If I'm being honest, it was exciting to think that someone like him was interested in someone like me. Don was known and respected by the world. His reputation preceded him. He had been featured in *Black Enterprise* magazine and the *New York Times*. The more I considered the potential of how dating someone like Don would manifest, the more I convinced myself that he was not for me. Prior to Don, I believed myself to have dated in my category of men and they were fine, but never had I dated someone of his stature or someone who was twenty-eight years my senior. In my mind, he was out of my league and not part of my work description.

That night when I got home, I sat on the bed, daydreaming about him, smiling to myself, and acknowledging the butterflies in my stomach. I also knew that based on the slate of events scheduled, I would see him again in a week's time. When I did, I was ready.

Everything about my look was coordinated, down to the most uncomfortable pair of heels I owned. Every woman knows that uncomfortable shoes are often the most popping pairs. My efforts to step up my look worked. When I arrived at the office for the meeting, he was already there.

"Wow, you look good," he said as I entered the boardroom.

There we stood in a very public place having a private conversation about nothing. For a moment, it felt like everyone else in the room disappeared, although my colleagues weren't paying much attention—yet. Rachel knew what time it was. In a previous conversation, I disclosed to her that I thought Don was attractive. By the time I realized that a few people in the room were alerted by how softly he spoke to me, I changed gears. For the remainder of the meeting, the chance moments of eye contact and soft smiles of acknowledgment sealed the deal. From that day forward, there was no question in my mind that he was interested in me and I in him. When the meeting was over, I greeted the board members at the door as usual. Don and I also managed to keep it professional as he shook my hand exiting. After that meeting, I thought about him every day. Sitting on my bed in the same spot, thinking about all the possibilities.

About two weeks later, while I was sitting at my desk, the phone rang.

"Tamika, it's Don. I'm leaving town, but I want you to meet me for lunch before I go."

Somewhat nervous, I agreed. "What day would you like to meet?"

"Today," he replied.

Taken aback, I pushed the phone away from my mouth, took a deep breath, and accepted his offer.

"Sure. Where should I meet you?"

I was floored by his response. His restaurant of choice was just off Fifth Avenue across the street from Bergdorf Goodman. Never in my life had I been to that area for anything outside of work. No man had ever asked me out on a date to that part of the city.

When I arrived, Don was already waiting for me. We sat for over an hour, dining, laughing, and exchanging. In transparent conversation, I expressed my concerns about getting involved with him.

"I'll be honest; I'm apprehensive about this," I said.

He allowed me to speak my piece without interruption. We also discussed what it would mean for me professionally to date a board member. How would I be seen if folks thought I was screwing a rich board member? Literally.

"Why are you interested in me?" I asked.

"For many reasons," he responded.

"What reasons?" I asked.

"You're beautiful. You're smart. I like your drive and determination. I want to get to know you better. I want to see more of you," he said.

I can neither confirm nor deny how hard I was smiling, but I'm almost certain I tried to play it cool as he continued.

"Remember that I told you there are a lot of changes happening in my life right now. One of them being that I'm moving to New York full-time."

As the conversation continued, he was straightforward about wanting to develop a deeper relationship with me. Although I heard his words, I'm not quite sure if I believed him. That same apprehension I had about someone like Don wanting to date me was still looming. And I was uncertain about what else he had going on in his life. After lunch that day, I didn't reach out or pursue any further communication for over a month. He texted once or twice, but it was sporadic. Don's lack of contact was proof of my suspicions, or so I thought. Later I learned that he was in the process of moving and figuring out his life.

Eventually, he called me one day out of the blue and told me he was in town. He invited me to lunch at the same restaurant we met at before. Together, we sat and talked for hours, getting to know each other and enjoying each other's company. From that day forward, we were inseparable.

One day while I was at work, he sent me a gift. Don is a giver. No matter what was going on in his life, I was cared for. From lunches and unpredictable special moments to late nights turned into early mornings on the phone amidst our conversations, we were forging a bond. Some nights we fell asleep together and others we talked until the sun came up. We were riding waves potent with the adrenaline of love. Our budding romance was a lot for both of us considering he was running a global company and I was full throttle with my work at NAN.

The universe heard the silent pleas of my heart and elevated me to move forward at work after receiving the nod of approval for appointment as the executive director at NAN. On a casual Sunday morning, while I was standing in the middle of Don's living room, Attorney Charlie King called me to share the news. Attorney King was serving as the interim executive director at the time.

"I'm going to recommend you to take my place as executive director," he said.

Although his words brought an immediate smile to my face, I didn't expect them to come true. In my mind, this one was on me, especially considering that he and the former Executive Director, Marjorie Fields Harris, were degreed, and had graduated from powerful institutions.

They were both lawyers and professionally sophisticated. These were not the categorizations I considered myself to be in, but I was and Charlie was not joking about his recommendation and the prospect of me becoming the executive director at NAN was no longer a dream. It became my reality.

My nerves were in overdrive while preparing myself mind, body, and soul to lead a group of people whom I had once worked for and studied under. Many of them, now peers, were much older than me. My saving grace was knowing that the current leadership of the organization trusted me, and believed in me and that they would be there to help me along. By this time Attorney Hardy was also in a full-time position at NAN as Executive Vice President. We would be reunited. They were not doubtful of my capabilities, even though I was. Although there was still a great deal for me to learn, I was aware of what I didn't know and I built a strong team to accommodate those needs. Although there were bumps and bruises, overall NAN grew exponentially while I was in my role. There were always highs and lows, but change and the charge to overcome injustice were ever present.

It didn't matter that we had heavy lifting to do in our respective careers; all that mattered was that we found time and space to be in each other's presence. My soul was drawn to Don and the guidance and support of the foundation he offered. Admittedly, I was worn out from living without a protector. I had been figuring things out on my own for so many years, I welcomed the support and companionship.

As time went on, things had changed drastically for me. Don and I made the decision to date exclusively. He sealed the deal as we silenced the whispers of those suspecting that we were together when he threw a thirtieth birthday party for me. Due to the growth of my career, I was now highly sought after to speak and make appearances at events. I was also writing for *Essence* magazine. From the outside looking in, one might have assumed I had attained success, but there was too much untapped ambition brewing inside me to proclaim that to be the case. The appointments to oversee the various committees and initiatives were a start, but there was still a sentiment in my heart that I should have been doing more.

There comes a time when you find yourself at a fork in the road. Unfortunately, my relationship with Tarique was still in need of work. I made a concerted effort to be more attentive to his needs and social and emotional well-being. I'm not sure he would agree with this. One day Tarique should write a book and tell his own story.

In 2011, the nation's attention and mine were redirected to the gun violence crisis. Eight days after the New Year, I was up at the crack of dawn like clockwork, watching the news, but decided to go in to the office late. At times the sound of the TV can turn into white noise, fading into the background, until something of interest strikes you. This was the case that day, until around 11:00 a.m. The tone of the voice of the reporter changed and there was a somber energy that made me stop and take notice.

"We are saddened to report U.S. Democratic congresswoman Gabrielle Giffords from Arizona has been shot point-blank in the head during a constituent meeting at a local grocery store." The reporter struggled to get through the statement. As I was waiting to hear if Giffords was alive or not, all I could do was pray. It wasn't every day you heard about a woman getting shot in the head on the news, let alone a government official. Gabrielle Giffords was someone whom I had met and considered a sincere person.

"I have another update. There are casualties."

My heart sank into my feet, as I awaited the reporter to confirm Giffords's passing.

"There are more casualties from this horrific tragedy."

Supplemental details about the case emerged over time and I followed it closely. Six people lost their lives and thirteen, including Congresswoman Giffords, were injured. The image released to the public of President Obama standing at her bedside was jarring. It was proof that we needed to do more. I needed to do more. Congresswoman Gabrielle Giffords fought and lived to tell the story and became an advocate for gun control. Work for me that day was a blur. The weight of believing that a single issue is up to you to solve is grueling. Somehow in my mind, I believed that gun control was my responsibility. The more incidents that took place, the more I felt compelled to do something about them.

From that day forward, my certainty of my desire to make a difference in the realm of gun control was reconfirmed. The Black community has been dealing with gun violence forever, but the gun violence in our communities was not a mainstream topic. The tragedy with Congresswoman

Giffords was national news. Even so, I recognized more than ever that our communities would still be left out, which made me double down to ensure our voices were heard. There was no turning back.

In March of 2012, approximately a year after Congresswoman Gabby Giffords was shot, I sat in my living room holding my son listening in horror with the rest of the world as the news replayed the story of Trayvon Martin. At work, we had been involved already, but the audio was further traumatizing. His story was disheartening, knowing life was stolen from someone so young. No one deserves for their life to be cut short, especially not at the hands of hatred.

Trayvon's mother, Sybrina Fulton, who is my dear sister today, found herself and her family thrust into the public eye while mourning her son's murder and advocating against the unjust act by a coward who took Trayvon's life. He was so young and killed while doing what every teen reserves the right to do, walking to the store to get snacks. There was no way I could organize for Trayvon's case and not see Tarique's face under that hoodie. Trayvon was all of our sons. We were all Sybrinas. The levels of fury that brewed inside me were smothered in anguish.

It wasn't until I was on the front lines fighting for Trayvon that I learned the power of my words. Up until this point, I spoke up in the meetings and at smaller-scale rallies, but never before had I been one of the main team members responsible for calling people to action at a rally. The moment my lips approached the microphone, my words were doused with fury, and it was from that place I spoke.

"We are going to shut this whole thing down. Tear this city up. This time we are not backing down. Today is a new day."

Looking out into the crowd, I could see the helplessness on their faces and the pain in their eyes.

It wasn't until I spoke those words that anyone seemed to feel anything. The random shouts from the men in the far distance, screams of approval from women in agreement, the fist pumps, the stomps and claps in unison, let me know we were alive, in one accord, and ready to fight. Trayvon's life was proof yet again that for the Black community the expression of our outrage was not an option. We could not afford to not fight.

When I stepped offstage, an elder organizer pulled me to the side. Steam was still on my lips.

"Tamika, do you realize what you just did?"

I wasn't sure if I was about to be commended or chastised. I waited for them to confirm.

"If you're not careful, you will be accused of inciting violence.

"If people go out and riot, then there will be blood on our hands."

This conversation made me feel uncomfortable and I questioned whether or not I was off base. Confusion set in. My intent was not to incite violence; it was to call for accountability and justice. Wasn't it my job to be radical? Was I not allowed to be radical because I was a woman? Was I expected to walk on eggshells in public and only speak a certain way in public? The natural thing for me to do is to blame myself. This is often easier than dissecting the actions of others, but this time I knew in my heart that my disposition was valuable. Although this was not my first time being fired up and speaking out against grave injustice, this time there was something different in my heart that came through my voice. In the past when I spoke up, no one critiqued me the way I had been critiqued that day. The more I pondered the words used to chastise me, the more I came to terms with carrying the weight of a new level of responsibility, which gave me a perspective I never considered. There were more eyes and more scrutiny that I would be subjected to. This was a wake-up call.

Don't get me wrong. I am clear that words have power; however, a large part of being in an organization not founded by you means that you take on the history, trauma, lens, and disposition of its leadership. In full transparency, I was in no way trying to incite violence, but it was then I felt like my voice was being censored, and I didn't like it. Nothing I said was wrong, and as far as I was concerned, the tone of my message could have been even stronger. There goes that tugging again. It was time to move.

My words were a testament to my anger. The lack of concern from so many in the country was telling. The discussions surrounding Trayvon's murder and the act of self-defense was triggering for our community. Trayvon's murder taught me that even though we all heard the same audio, America is not experienced through the same lens. It stung. It was a gripping truth that I was forced to sit with and one I was now expected to lead through.

Now, fully settled into my role as executive director at NAN, I allowed myself to fall even deeper in love. There was no longer a question of what we were to each other. We were no longer just dating exclusively. We were partners, doing life together. It was of immense value to be in love with someone who had experienced more life than I and one who took pride in helping me navigate many of the major decisions on the horizon. He was knowledgeable about the movement but also possessed high levels of business acumen. This intrigued me, because I was still learning. Although he was a media executive, Don was well-versed in the interconnectivity of the conversation on economics and Black power. He too was a soldier in the fight, but in a different way than I was. More importantly, he demonstrated levels of emotional intelligence I had yet to realize in my own life. My past traumas in relationships cultivated my approach to the way in which I loved. Differences of opinion were expressed through an argumentative disposition. Debate and indifference to the point of either hostile takeover or surrender were what I had known. Unchecked, the toxicity of who I was threatened who I desired to become. Amidst what would have been one of our first arguments, he stepped extremely close into my personal space such that I could feel his energy, looking directly into my eyes before speaking.

"I don't know about these kids you've been seeing. I'm a grown-ass man. I don't communicate with yelling or bullshit accusations in your head. If we want this to work, we need a better way to communicate."

There were no words worthy of retort at that moment. Instead, my levels of consciousness were elevated. And although his words were powerful, his actions were even stronger. Don didn't believe in carrying a fight from day to day. If we had a disagreement the day before, it was over the next day. Don't get me wrong; I never stopped giving him a piece of my mind if I needed to do so; however, I was thrust into a space of doing the deep internal work necessary to be with him. My prior reactions in relationships were knee-jerk, but with Don I took the time to examine scenarios and the root of his intentions, as well as my own, before responding. This disposition educated me not only personally, but also professionally. Once the relationship evolved, we connected more with those who were important to us. He initiated a relationship with Tarique and also escorted both of us to the various events I attended for work. Don was special in that he had his own company to run and affairs to attend to, but he always demonstrated a genuine interest in the things that were unfolding for me. At times I think he got a kick out of watching the phases of my life moving so quickly and knowing he had a hand in how and why I showed up the way I did. He reinvented my responses to the people, places, and things of the world, how I dressed, and even how I spoke. I was a diamond in the rough and he polished me.

"When you walk in the room, be the big bitch," he would say.

He taught me to fight with my mind instead of my ego or my fists.

With him, I had the liberty to live what we now refer to as a soft life. He coached me through understanding the difference between exerting my power in the world and at home. Don became my safe space. He understood the weight of a big job and that I had worked hard to get there, so by no means was I willing to fuck it up. He could advise me in ways that someone who had only experienced the same amount of life I had could not. It's one thing to have a mentor you can confide in outside your home, but it's another to have them in your bed. Even though we did not do the same work, we shared the same passion and worked for the same reasons. His goals were Black equity, justice for Black people, and bringing Black people to the forefront. Don was also a prolific story-teller who believed in taking control of Black narratives. Due in part to my relationship with Don and that I had worked my fingers to the bone at NAN, I began to question what else the world could offer me, and I offer it. Don was and still is my shelter from the storm.

AS TOLD THROUGH DON'S EYES

I was instantly drawn to Tamika's passion. She was beautiful and more importantly, she was smart. Tamika was without question one of the hardest working women I had ever met. Her fire for the work she did and the impact she wanted to make was infectious. I admired her from afar. The more I learned about her, the more I wanted to know. It did not take long for my admiration to evolve into affection.

In every room she walked into, she brought a lot to the table. I watched her be appointed as the Executive Director at NAN. I also watched her make history while leading as one of the Co-Founders of the Women's March where millions of people around the world gathered in protest. Her work was proof of the fact that she was ambitious which was beyond impressive.

The hard truth is that not everyone is happy about your success. There was a group of people who started attacking her because of her positioning in the march. They attempted to dig up things about her past and use affiliations against her, particularly in relation to the annual Savior's Day led by Minister Farrakhan. Her attendance at that event dated back as far as when she was ten years old attending with her parents.

Even though they tried to destroy her character, she still managed to emerge with guns blazing. As someone who loves Tamika, I can't say that it is easy to watch her work as hard as she does while navigating the dangerous landscape of activism. We live in a time when maliciousness is at an all-time high. The proud boys and gatekeepers act without reason. There are even fools out here attacking politicians. The blessing is that she had a team of people around her. Her family is also a tremendous source of strength. Over the years, I too have become an intricate member of her village. Together, we raised her son Tarique and worked to give him the best education possible. As with any young man, the rearing process is not without struggle. When I reflect upon the fact that Tarique is now a great father himself, I can't help but think that we did a pretty good job. Today, I believe he also recognizes that we always tried to do what was right by and for him. Recently, Tarique called me very late one night to say that he appreciated everything I had done over the years. Oftentimes you don't hear from your kids until much later. To know the impact of the efforts made brought me great joy.

At the beginning of our relationship, Tamika benefited greatly from the years I had already lived. There were experiences I had and trials and tribulations I conquered. Therefore I knew how to navigate them. There was also the presence of wisdom that only time can award. There were moments in both her personal and professional life that I could see coming a mile away. My goal was to be there for her and to navigate them with her.

The older I got, the more patience I developed as I watched her aspire to greatness and overcome tremendous adversity. Admittedly, there were times when we had disagreements, not to the point of breaking up, it was just me imposing some of what I learned through experience.

We came to know without question that we had each other's backs. It was an unspoken pact. Regardless of anything that could happen, we vowed to move forward together. The hardships were proof that we loved one another. When you face difficult times in a relationship, it is easy to leave. Love is the glue that reminds and encourages you to work together.

Tamika was also a tremendous foundation for me as I solidified my legacy. As the Founder and CEO of the premier multicultural advertising agency in the country, I had my work cut out for me. Tamika kept me informed about what was happening in the country on several fronts. She had the capacity to shed light on the grassroots community, ideas, trends, and concerns that needed to be addressed. She was also instrumental in supporting me while I was dealing with the African-American community from the top-level marketing perspective. Tamika's insight was critical market research that proved to be invaluable. She helped me to remain focused on what consumers wanted. After I synthesized what she taught me, my company reached new heights in the creation of vehicles for communication with the masses.

So much of our relationship has involved a balance of personal and professional support from one another. It was as if we provided each other with the best of both worlds. In this space, the stakes regarding what has been required of each of us to perform in our professions have remained high. Over time, operating at extreme levels can be difficult. Even so, our goal was to create our own version of a fairy tale. The hard truth is that not every fairy tale has a perfect ending. My career, the business I built with my bare hands from the ground up, and my ambition were front and center from the day Tamika and I met. Managing over 200 employees is not for the faint of heart. Tamika weathered it all. What I failed to realize was how burned out I was becoming while burning the candle at both ends. Our relationship has surpassed so many barriers over the years, my career and her career being two of them. When time lapsed, and life happened I got sidetracked with closing the company. The pandemic forced me to relocate to the south to care for my mother, who is now 100 years old. Today, there is no formal title on our love, it is just love. Unconditional love.

In full transparency, I don't think anyone says the words "I love you" as much as they should. My desire is to reinforce to Tamika how much she is loved by me. Logically speaking, Tamika will outlast me. I am more than twenty-five years her senior. There will never be a time when I don't do all that I can to make life good for Tamika. I promise to do so when I am here and when I am not.

In the words of Jay and Bey, "Who wants that perfect love story anyway?"

CHAPTER 12

CLOSER

After working with the premier civil rights non-profit organization for over thirteen years, having served in various roles, and now as the executive director, I believed I had witnessed tragedy at every level, but I was gravely wrong. It wasn't until I helped a mother, Shianne Norman, bury her baby that I was forced to come to grips with the reality that there were no limits to murder and gun violence. Not one of us was safe. Not even our babies.

Lloyd Christopher Morgan Jr. was only four years old when he was killed in a crossfire during a memorial basketball game in the Bronx. July 22 is a day when children and families should be enjoying New York in summer. Lloyd and the other hundred-plus people at the park were robbed of their chance to do so when three guys began shooting. The purpose of the gathering was to pay tribute to another victim of violence who was stabbed to death two years prior. Go figure.

The morning I learned of Lloyd's death, I was in my office and the news left me dumbfounded. I remember stopping to pray for his family and asking God why? Why didn't this baby get to grow up?

Shianne and I became friends, with me sometimes taking calls at 4:00 a.m. or anytime she needed me. I knew all too well that grief does not keep track of time, nor does healing.

Five months later, the nation cried along with President Obama while he spoke at a press conference confirming the horror of Sandy Hook Elementary School. We watched our country bury twenty babies between the ages of six and seven and six adults dead at the hands of a person with a Bushmaster rifle. December 14, 2012, will forever be chronicled as an unjust bloodbath in America.

On January 21, 2013, at 11:55 a.m. Eastern Time, President Barack

Obama delivered his Second Inaugural Address. The speech was 2,137 words long and took fifteen minutes to deliver.

"America's possibilities are limitless," he said. *"For we possess all the qualities that this world without boundaries demands: youth and drive; diversity and openness; an endless capacity for risk and a gift for reinvention. My fellow Americans, we are made for this moment, and we will seize it—so long as we seize it together."*

As President Obama spoke, I stood in my living room, listening intently. It was a Monday and I had resolved to view the address at home before getting dressed to go into the office. It was the level of hope he so eloquently inspired that I wanted to soak up like a sponge. I needed it and I needed to be able to exchange it with my staff as we continued to navigate our arduous line of work. When the address was over, I turned the TV off and sat on the couch. By the time I showered, the phrase "seize it together" stayed with me. Even as I left the house, I replayed it over and over again in my mind. To me, "seize it together" meant that we needed all hands on deck to bring about real change. And although, at that time, President Obama had not been all that I wanted or believed he could be for Black America, I appreciated the idea of seizing the moment together. For me, it didn't mean just one of us or that politics alone could eradicate injustice. I was clear that seizing the moment meant that it would take hands from every walk of life, from people in the streets to people in the suites, to get the job done.

That day, hope filled my lungs once again as my driver took me to work. When I arrived at the building, I stood outside staring up at the sun. Although it was cold, the air felt different outside. It was lighter. Crisper. Much like the first appointment of President Obama, that day was proof progress was possible. The prospect of it was enough to keep me and so many others at NAN on the battlefield for change. There wasn't anyone or anything that could have stolen the joy I felt, and at the office the nods with gentle smiles confirmed the same.

Eight days after the country witnessed the second inauguration of the first Black president, the high of hope came to an abrupt end, reminding anyone who had forgotten about the reality of the war of gun violence on our hands. The reminder came in the format of the breaking news of the murder of fifteen-year-old Hadiya Pendleton making its rounds. Hadiya, from Chicago, was shot and killed a week after performing at President

Obama's inauguration. It was a devastation that was becoming all too common. It seemed as if there were murders happening on a daily basis.

The gun violence continued across the country, and there were countless examples of destruction, which meant there were no days off for me. Even if they had been available, I didn't want them. As I saw it, if there was murder, then there was work for me to be doing and anything less than that was unacceptable. The good thing for me was that I could work in Don's Florida estate in front of the pool or in our California king bed, or in our customized dual office, which made the ten-hour workdays more bearable. Don was an advocate of work/life balance. There were days that he would come upstairs and say "Stop, let's go to dinner, right now," or I would hear him turn up the music, pop a bottle of champagne, and jump into the pool. This was an attribute I always appreciated in him.

Before that, in New York, Chicago, and other places, there was lots of gun violence very similar to what we are experiencing now. The Obama administration was trying to come up with crusaders to change gun laws. There were scores of activists in the fight against gun violence, doing the work on the ground. The National Rifle Association (NRA) and other gun lobbyists were against President Obama's efforts. In response and opposition, Vice President Joe Biden rounded up leaders in the gun violence space. The groundwork was laid for the establishment of a task force. The continuous string of tragedies made the issue of gun violence a hot-button issue. For me, it was my life and my life's work. To be considered by the highest level of an administration as someone on the front lines for this work was an honor.

The day that I received an official letter from Joe Biden's office, inviting me to the task force, I was surprised. It was coordinated by the White House Office of Public Engagement. After reading the letter, I sat thinking to myself, Wow, there are people out there who value my input. It was a very refreshing feeling, one that made me want to work harder. That same day while visiting with my mom and dad I told them about being slated for the task force.

"I've been invited to work on a task force under the leadership of Vice President Biden," I announced.

"Good job," my mom said as they nodded in agreement together while sitting at the kitchen table. Dad was eating peanuts he shelled, and Mom continued, hopefully they will get something done.

Before I could even finish the story of how the process happened, Mom was already on the phone with Aunt Ola Mae. When I left, I distinctly remember telling them that we were likely not supposed to be disclosing this information, but I don't think they listened. They were proud, as they had been on the front lines of the battles for my life all the times I disobeyed and disrespected the purpose I was now fulfilling.

As always when the opportunity comes your way, there will be mixed feelings. There were some who were happy for me and others who likely felt that I was selling out. They didn't trust the government at all. People didn't necessarily like Joe Biden. He was still seen as the Crime Bill dude. Although I did not disagree, I chose to focus on being surrounded by far more support than not. There will always be internal politics to maneuver, but I learned so many strategies while at NAN that I was prepared. More importantly, I believed myself to be worthy of the extension of the invitation based on the work I had done with gun violence.

There is so much to learn in these roles. Although some might assume that you instinctively know everything, oftentimes, we are learning as we go along. I had the hope of someone who was young and ready to get to work. I began to learn the ins and outs of government and the political scene. I was walking into a task force believing that if all the key players are aligned, then we should be able to make real change happen. I learned that alignment alone was not enough. There were other factors at play—lobbying being one of them.

There is money in lobbying. The gun companies make billions of dollars. They want to protect their entities, no matter the cost to society. When attempts are made to shut them down or to restrict their rights they have to have a power that is strong enough to push back and win. These lobbyists work very closely with the NRA.

I learned about lobbying, one of the most powerful functions in government.

When I'm really in my conspiracy theorist bag, I often think about how hard the NRA and its members go to protect a right that has harmed and even killed too many to name. This is not just about the right to bear arms, but oftentimes they are unhinged in their advocacy. I discovered this to be the case after the NRA distributed a national ad targeting me, attempting to demonize my support for the preservation of safety.

It is my belief that some of these folks fear a potential return on their crimes against Black people. It is possible they fear that we may one day turn on them. They keep their weapons, because they believe there will come a time when they have to maintain the position of power. The country is browning. Latinos are the fastest-growing race in our society. Maybe it's not a conspiracy at all. They have to fight and they don't care if babies die in the process.

In the first Task Force meeting they were talking about how they would tackle these factors. There were so many on the outside who felt like I should not work with the administration. There are some people who, no matter what you tell them, will not work with the government and that's cool too.

Up to this point, I witnessed many styles of leadership, such that I was well-versed in what it looked like to take ownership of a cause. There were leaders who protested verbally and physically to get their points across. Then there were those who were militant, subscribing to the belief that less talk and more action was necessary. And then there were those who were more conservative and fought their battles through formal documents and intentions set on legislative change. There were leaders who only did their best work organizing government. They all mattered, but the key was being able to navigate the terrain of all of the environments. The traction I saw produced took place inside government and outside at the grassroots levels in the community. Furthermore, my observations taught me that there was power in negotiation. Daily, I sharpened my ability to do so. I was sharpening my skills in every single setting.

The other unspoken factor is effective communication with those who have taken up causes before you. Regardless of age, there are always people who deemed it necessary to work on a cause before another person decided it needed to be done. Those people have intel that is of extreme importance. I've witnessed new leaders come straight off the street who don't want to listen to anyone because they somehow believe they have all the answers. And the ones who label everyone else as a sellout because they have convinced themselves that everyone besides them is working for the man.

Until you have matriculated through the levels of activism, you have no idea how real power is established. And whether you believe you've studied the history and made yourself aware of the issues at hand, there is so much happening that you may not know. I caution anyone who believes that leadership that has the power to evoke change happens in the absence of strategy and collaboration. It does not.

Real power is established when a person has an acquired understanding of the intricacies of the systems and institutions they are fighting to dismantle, the effects they have on the people, places, and things they endeavor to protect, and the key players, funding, and human capital necessary to bring about said change. An understanding of this magnitude is not formed overnight.

Posting "fuck the system" on your social media page alone is not enough to implement change. And that's not to say that one action has no impact. It is to acknowledge the depths of time, talent, and treasure necessary to attempt to win the war. A war will not be won in isolation.

Do you want to create change? You will need protestors with the loudest mouths who can make people uncomfortable in the face of injustice. You will need voters who show up early and stay late at the polls. Those who vow to do everything possible to get others to the ballot box. You have to understand economics and the mind-set of an entrepreneur with a skill set capable of bootstrapping financial resources.

My matriculation through the levels of activism at a time when civil rights leaders were transitioning and passing the baton afforded me a front-row seat to the who, what, when, where, and why of it all. Equipped with this knowledge, I was empowered to determine what derivative my leadership style could be.

Although it was an honor to be considered for the Task Force, the element of excitement died quickly. I naively believed that we were going to do something earth shattering, but the challenge of fighting against special interest groups was crippling. We worked and we organized, but in the end we were unable to pass meaningful gun control legislation. There was still much work to be done. Too many lives were still on the line. I was to be aligning with people who felt as strongly about the alleviation of gun violence as I did. My goal was to roll my sleeves up for another battle.

CHAPTER 13

UNITY

The morning of November 9, 2016, I could feel myself drowning. Watching the country prepare to transition leadership from the first Black president to an aspiring dictator who rode to the White House on a campaign that plainly promoted inequality, separation, violence, and fear throughout the nation was crippling. And with every fiber of my being, I blamed myself. Had I not done enough to stop this vicious cycle? Had I not gotten enough people to the polls? Had I not believed in real change enough? Although we worked our fingers to the bone in an effort to do so, the results told a different story. A version that confirmed I had not spoken out enough, mobilized enough, educated enough, or organized enough. Maybe it was me who wasn't enough. With all the speculation surrounding the accuracy of the outcome, and the alleged stealing of the election, had we not created enough of a landslide to quell the questions that plagued the results?

For me, the affliction of the election was icing on the cake. Whether the masses knew the history of hatred spewed at the hands of the man elected or not.

The words "**BRING BACK THE DEATH PENALTY. BRING BACK OUR POLICE**" kept replaying in my mind. Those words, plastered in bold print across the pages of several prominent newspapers in my hometown of New York, were his doing. It wasn't his first time inciting hate. I was reminded on this morning of his call for the reinstatement of the death penalty in hopes of having the Central Park Five executed for the crime they were wrongfully imprisoned for, the alleged assault and rape of a woman in Central Park in 1989. Today we know with certainty that these young Black men, unquestionably innocent, had their futures compromised by bad actors seeking blood. (Thanks to the good sis Ava DuVernay and so many others who contributed to shedding light on their stories.) The idea that anyone would be audacious enough to call for the deaths of innocent children is deeply jarring. It is even more unsettling to consider that we live in a country where so many are easily provoked and willing to rally behind such a vicious cause. Even after they were exonerated several years later, Trump went on record stating that he still did not believe them. And now this man would be president.

It wasn't exactly a depression I felt. It was sorrow. And somehow, the same sense of loss that devoured me when Jason was killed inched into the crevices of my heart. It was broken. I mourned for Black and brown folks and members of the LGBTQIA+ communities. I mourned for immigrants, especially Mexicans, who were his direct target. I mourned for those incarcerated for crimes they didn't commit and for those who might never realize justice. I mourned for those killed at the hands of gun violence and police brutality. Moreover, I mourned for the hope lost. And as the mother of a Black son, I feared that history would find a way to repeat itself, especially with the country in the hands of someone whose objective was destruction. I also feared that history would repeat itself even within my family. The prospect of it all was too much to bear. And I was not alone. As I wallowed in anguish, my phone rang without end—calls from fellow organizers and confidants in need of answers. I had none. After lying still in silence for over an hour, I finally picked up. Without opening my eyes long enough to identify the caller, I answered.

"Hello?"

"Ms. Mallory, this is Janice from Tarique's school. Would you have a moment to speak to me?"

"Is Tarique ok?" I interrupted.

"Yes. He is safe. I just needed to speak with you about the completion of his work and his attendance at school. Over the last few weeks, we've had several assignments missing, and he has not been present. I'm afraid this is affecting his overall grade in some of his classes. I wanted to get in front of it before the semester ends."

I had been laser focused on organizing and alleviating systemic barriers and helping people gain access to the ballot box. I had worked to preserve opportunities for young Black men across the country. And now I was faced with a very personal failing. Had I done so much for others that I compromised the attention to detail needed to parent my own son? And if so, I now questioned whether my actions had been in vain, as the man I was so vehemently against had won the election, and my family was now in crisis. In a moment Tarique's whole life—our life—flashed before my eyes, past and feared future. His birth, his joys, his pains, the family that had closed ranks to keep him safe, and now the renewed potential for him to end up like any one of the five boys in Central Park, victimized for the color of his skin. Made an example of for political gain. All these things made me consider the times I was laser focused on work. Dashing out of the house while leaving him with my mother and father to do my job. My brain attempted to quantify the countless hours dedicated to supporting and gathering resources for families affected by gun violence and other social justice concerns, and the hardship of being Black in America. It had all been done for the greater good, but what about my own seed? It was petrifying to consider that I was failing the one Black man I was raising in a country that didn't have his best interest at heart.

By the time Tarique got home that afternoon, I was livid. Before he could close the door behind him, once he was inside the house, I unleashed rage.

"What the hell, Tarique!"

My mind raced, and the anger mounted. We had spoken before about having the school call me for him not doing the right thing.

"Ma. What are you talking about? What's wrong with you?"

"The school called and said you're not turning in your homework. Why the hell would you not be turning in your homework, Tarique? School is your responsibility."

"I have it under control," he replied. His response, fury, was a mirror of mine.

"That's bullshit. Ain't no way you got it under control and they called me. Shit's outta hand."

"You don't have to worry about me. I know what's going on in my life. Maybe you need to worry about what's going on in yours."

There was an air of disrespect that he let loose in the atmosphere, and I was not having it.

"What the fuck did you just say to me?"

He stood up taller, pushed his chest out, took a deep breath, and exhaled so hard I could see his nostrils flare before he spoke again.

"I said. You need to worry about what is going on in your own life."

He spoke so harshly, it felt like he cursed me out. Before I knew it, I charged across the room. My arms were flailing, and I got into his face, placing the tip of my nail at his temple.

"Get out. Get out. Get out!" I screamed, picking up a trinket from a shelf.

I was at the point of no return. Don came from wherever he was in the house, wedging himself between the open space separating Tarique and me. He had a way of waiting before acting, but never too long to allow for words and actions that could be indefinitely damaging. I repeated the words so many times it was as if I were in a trance. I could feel the heat from inside my body. The tears streaming down my face burned. My breathing was stirred. Tarique snatched his bookbag from the floor by the front door and left. He slammed the door so hard it rattled the walls and a framed piece of art fell and shattered. Kneeling on the floor, placing my hands on my head, I screamed in terror. The only thing that stopped me from yelling out again was the phone in my hand. It had gone off again in the middle of my exchange with Tarique, but I ignored it. Now, unsure of Tarique's whereabouts, I stood up to gain my composure and prepared to answer. Before I could say hello, a familiar voice began speaking. Michael Skolnik was a colleague in the movement. He was also my friend.

"Tamika. Yo. It's crazy out here. Let me conference in Carmen."

Carmen Perez, who was CEO of The Gathering for Justice, an organization founded by Harry Belafonte, in which I was a board member.

Although I lifted my eyebrow in agreement, I didn't immediately respond.

"I don't know if you have seen the Million Women's March advertisement yet."

"Yes, I did see it, but that name is not a good idea," I warned. "That march was twenty years prior in Philadelphia, led by Black women."

After a prolonged silence, I stood up straight against the wall. I was still out of breath.

"You're right. I have one of the women involved on the other line and I was hoping I could connect you. They clearly have issues and need help organizing," he said.

For the sake of this story, we'll refer to her as Karen. Trust me, the name is befitting.

"We're willing to take the call. That's all I can promise."

Michael thanked me for my time and connected me to Karen. After a brief exchange of pleasantries, Karen, Carmen Perez, and I agreed to meet the next day, along with other organizers that were involved. One of the women was Bob Bland. When I hung up the phone, I closed my eyes, bowed my head, and took a cleansing breath before returning to the aftermath of the mess that had just taken place in my home. My child was gone. My child's father was gone. The country that we'd been trying to make a reality felt like it was gone now too.

The lump in my throat was monstrous, and the tears welling in the rims of my eyes were even bigger. The only thing I could be certain of at the moment was that my heart would never allow me to give up on fighting for equality. The face I saw every time I dared to organize, speak, volunteer, and even pray was Tarique's. Everything I had done to make the world a better place was so that he could be whatever he dared to be and so that our people could be free from the same oppression and senseless violence that had taken his father's life and so many others without cause. The moment was surreal. There I was, being offered one of the biggest and potentially most impactful opportunities of my career as an activist to bring people together, and my heart was torn apart. How could I oversee peace on native soil and yet be at war with the seed produced from my body?

At that moment, I made up my mind once again to fight. I knew that freedom was no longer a given. It would have to be strategically taken. I stood up and raced to my room, tearing it apart in search of a binder that I developed over the course of several years, specifically for organizing major marches in Washington, DC. It's a binder that I imagine someone like Bayard Rustin put to work for the triumphant March on Washington in 1963. And it's the kind of binder I bet Donald Trump wishes he had put together for any of his underwhelming gatherings in DC over the last decade. It had been tucked away for a time like this one. Before I jumped back into working, I called my sister Sharon, and she informed me that she was on the phone with Tarique. This gave me a sense of reassurance. After I retrieved the binder, my phone rang again. This time it was my mother.

"He's here. He's safe."

Those were the only words I needed to hear. My mother knew Tarique and me well enough to know that we both needed her, and like clockwork she was there. Knowing that my mom had him freed me to go all in.

As I was hanging up with my mother, my sister Sharon called me back with the same reassurance. As always, they were our greatest protectors.

Just as I prepared to hang up the phone with Sharon, Linda Sarsour was calling. Linda Sarsour is an internationally known Palestinian activist and leader and organizer in the Black liberation movement. Carmen, Linda, and I were a triple threat. Linda was popping mad shit by the time I answered the phone. I had already observed her tweets firing off at white women about voting for Trump—more than fifty percent.

"They should have marched to the polls," she said.

I informed Linda that there was a meeting with the march organizers arranged for the next day and that we would reconvene to discuss what happened afterwards. Linda was out of town. Carmen and I decided to take the lead for now.

———

A series of meetings took place. The first was small, but it was still a whirlwind. The second meeting grew to include many more volunteers. This time, we brought our people with us. There were also young, middle-aged, and older volunteers, many of whom came from Hillary Clinton's campaign, who had quickly come together to help with the march. That day, I also learned that Bob Bland, one of the original organizers of the Women's March, was meeting many of these folks for the first time, like me. Although she was a day or two ahead of me, there were a few others who had been involved prior to her arrival. The organizational system established prior to my arrival denoted seniority based on time of arrival at the assembly.

Hours passed as we talked about the possibilities of working together. Our next, far larger conversation took the form of a group call where we were all introduced to another Karen. A Karen. Let's just call her Karen #2. Karen #2 made it clear that she was not in need of leadership. Instead, she spent her time rattling off a list of glorified administrative duties for us, the "others," to attend to. Let me be clear, there is nothing wrong with administrative duties. I do them every day. I had done them all in the early stages of my career. However, I was now at a point where I understood my capabilities and how to best be of service. I had honed my skills as an organizer and a strategist. The tasks she suggested were not in accordance with those roles, and further fueled my friend Linda's anger. Linda immediately recognized the potential of whom we might be dealing with and that not everyone involved had pure intentions. The movement being proposed now was steeped in appropriation. Linda knew that Karen #2 was aware that her desires to take control of this march did not match up with her ability to actually get people out into the streets to form a substantial protest against Trump. Karen #2's constituency could not assemble the support they needed alone, so her objective was to exploit us to her own ends. While on the call with both Karens, I did what I do extremely well. Luckily, my time at NAN had taught me to read the room and devise a plan accordingly. When it comes to the fight against injustice, there is no time to waste resources. Linda, Carmen, and I had entered an agreement that if we were to participate, we would come to the table with a set of our own terms. That night, over the phone, we strategized. Our asks included them changing the name of the march and naming us, including Bob, as the four co-chairs, with no additional tiers to be added. We would not be used for our communities' investment and then set to the side.

Notwithstanding how hard I was prepared to fight, I would be reminded of the fact that I was viewed as lesser than by many. Even though I was the highest-ranking Black woman in the march structure, it was apparent that the assumption was we were there to shuffle papers and execute administrative tasks.

Questionable comments rang out, like, "We don't need all of those ideas," "We just need to know if you can order a stage," and "We just need you to invite Hillary Rodham Clinton to speak," revealing what they thought about our capabilities. In spite of it all, I knew that I was beyond worthy of serving as more than just a Black face.

From the moment I left that first meeting, I knew the Women's March of 2017 would be the largest professional undertaking of my life to that point. I locked arms with Bob Bland, Linda Sarsour, and Carmen Perez and a host of other super smart people and we got to work.

Now, Mysonne, an activist whom I had been mentoring in the movement, and Nantasha Williams, who worked in the New York State Legislature and is now a New York City councilperson, would be at my side as I took responsibility for rallying Black women and activists to our cause.

Had I been a C-Suite executive vying for the corner office, I might have celebrated the position, but I wasn't. Early in life, I learned that activism is as much about important victories as it is about the freedom to dream of a better world that will likely take decades to realize as well as those you may never see in your lifetime. It is hard to quantify victories when the people you are fighting for and with remain oppressed. To move the world forward required proactive action at all times, and it was my perspective that only with head down and eyes trained forward could I remember that my work was never done. Could never be done.

There was also an entire team of individuals on my side who were not eating properly or getting enough rest. Less time was spent with our families and loved ones and our personal lives were compromised. But anything less would have left this huge undertaking in disaster. There were too many irons in the fire. We could not leave things unattended.

Not long into the process of organization, issues began to mount in every direction. One of the first major bombs was when it was suggested that Hillary Clinton be the keynote speaker. For those who were fresh off her campaign, there was a heightened sense of excitement as they saw it as one way to right a wrong—an honorary moment of praise. The march could have been one of her first appearances after conceding the election. But there was no way I could sit in silence knowing that our first public moment would sideline the voices of the Black and brown women I knew to be most impacted by Trump's rise and who would be most important in sustaining momentum for the long term. To have Hillary Clinton, from a marketing perspective, would have been huge for some. In my conversations with Don, as a marketing expert, we discussed the potency of the impact. However, I understood the members of the march who were angered by the proposition. Many of our Black and brown organizers had very serious political issues with the Clintons. I must admit that I was very young during the Clinton administration and hadn't paid much attention to her work but was forced to quickly get up to speed. We were outnumbered, but we never wavered.

This was a tough decision. Some women cried, and others were verbally aggressive towards us. Some gave reasons why we, as women, should be standing together and fighting back. Many spoke about how Hillary had been a beacon for progression.

We discussed in depth her silence on significant racial justice issues. Although some refused to consider it silence, we were wise enough to demonstrate that the barometer for silence was relatively high, considering the power she had. We discussed her foreign policy history. As the girls say, we had receipts. Our goal was not to engage or incite another debate about Hillary or Trump; it was to ensure that the march was not derailed with raw nerves and emotional score settling. We wanted to keep the issues of the march at the center, which meant the speakers needed to reflect a wide spectrum of voices. We remained vigilant in maintaining the integrity of what we wanted the world to see. I left that meeting exhausted in a way that none of the white women there could understand. What I was not prepared for was the turbulent road ahead, this time grappling with my own sisters.

The Black Lives Matter DC chapter penned a letter that was ten pages in length, filled with historical context and accompanied by two addenda, accusing us of disregarding them amidst our efforts to host the march in their city. Although the letter was meant only for our eyes, there were several others copied on the email, meaning that news of the letter spread like wildfire. One of our many concerns was that this information would be leaked to the general public and media, causing further separation in the ranks of the march. Addressing the contents of the letter became our immediate focus. Here is an excerpt:

Dear ____

We submit this letter to you on behalf of Black Lives Matter DC, an official chapter of the Black Lives Matter Global Network. We also bring with us the voices and experiences of our comrades including other Black Lives Matter Chapters such as Vancouver, in DC and across the country. Our message would not be complete with[out] them. Together we represent Black, non-Black POC, and ally organizers in DC who continue to suffer harm as a result of the Women's March's actions in DC and/or as the result of public statements or comments.

We acknowledge that the structure, board and staff composition of your organization has shifted since our earlier engagement. Despite those changes, we believe that our concerns and statements are still valid and important to name and that reparations are owed and overdue. While some of what we share may be difficult to hear, we believe radical honesty is necessary if we hope to engage in a way that moves towards a more transformative future.

The upcoming March has certainly reignited the long list of issues and unrepaired harm within the DC movement community and DC residents more broadly. For us to learn about the March on Facebook was incredibly disheartening as there has been no attempts to address the ways the Women's March has harmed DC.

In this moment, the way we move through this world matters. We must be able to practice accountability while simultaneously eradicating white supremacy and the advancing women's—especially Black women's—liberation. Being intentional about naming our values and holding ourselves and each other to these values is critical in the fight for justice and liberation.

The values that drive our work within BLM DC shape and guide this letter. These values include addressing harm in ways that do not cause harm, knowing that no one is disposable, understanding people do not show up fully formed and therefore should be given grace and room to grow, understanding the value and power [of] narrative and narrative creation, and the practice of releasing things that no longer serve us.

This letter comes after repeated private and public attempts to call you in. It is a communal attempt to call you in with loving direct communication. This is coming from representatives of the communities the Women's March says it stands in solidarity with telling you that your model of solidarity has been short-sighted, anti-Black, and transactional in ways that consistently perpetuate harm. This is unacceptable.

DC is more than Congress and the White House. It is more than the DOJ and the National Mall. For large mobilizations that come into the District, this means holding the reality of DC as both the nation's capital, the center of empire, a necessary place for national protests, and home to real life human beings with important local issues. Local DC is a domestic colony and the actions of national organizers have to recognize that.

Large mobilizations like the Women's March that have been the poster children for this resistance in the media have inspired hope and action in the hearts and minds of hundreds of communities across the country. As crucial and important as these mobilizations are, we have to acknowledge the years of organizing that made these flashpoints possible. Specifically, the Uprisings in Ferguson lit a fire of resistance and liberation that has been tended by movements from the Movement for Black Lives to Standing Rock.

Each of these movements has not only changed the narrative but changed the sense of what's possible, developed new analysis for how freedom can be built in the current moment and built the critical connections and infrastructure that made other flashpoints possible. Yet these movements receive pennies on the dollar to what the Women's March can raise in a few days.

This is in part due to the fact that the people building these transformative movements are not seeking inclusion in a burning house. Beneath the cries of "stop killing us" are deeper calls for reparations, redistribution of wealth, not simply "help." Yet instead of grappling with these deeper issues, liberal America tends to pour the energy and anxiety that these calls for justice arouse in it into more immediate concerns with easier fixes like respecting [white] women.

Here in DC, these unstrategic mass mobilizations distract from local organizing, often overlook the Black people who actually live here and even result in tougher laws against demonstration being passed locally.

What indigenous folks in Standing Rock called settler activism— folks parachuting in, using resources, extracting their hope, inspiration, and transformation and moving on—is leaving the very communities that made these moments possible destitute. This short-sighted and extractive way of going about change mirrors the white supremacist and capitalist mindset we are all struggling against.

Going to Washington for us was the most direct means to protest against the federal government. But what we had failed to consider was the local community of organizers, some grassroots and some below the root, that should have been acknowledged and involved in the planning process.

The organizers of the BLM chapter stated that in addition to local issues in need of attention (including care for the unhoused and the matter of DC statehood), they believed the Women's March had not yet adopted a strong enough agenda to meet the needs of Black women. This of course struck at my heart. Part of me wishes that they would have contacted me directly to have a conversation. I did not want to be at odds with Black women in public. Like Momma always said, "Keep house business in the house." But ultimately, this snag in the plans was for the better. Many of us had become consumed in technical tasks like securing permits and designing visuals while we'd contended with so many of the macro-level issues we'd come together to address from the start. And now I was battling what felt like my entire community who felt betrayed by my involvement.

I am the first to acknowledge that it is impossible to wrap your hands around everything, everyone, and every issue amidst the construction of a movement as big as the Women's March. And while it is not an excuse for why some organizers could have felt left out, it is a truth that cannot be denied. The other truth is that there are blind spots that are, at times, inevitable until they are discovered. My internal critique, of both myself and our team, was that we should have known to prioritize inclusivity from the start. We were thinking nationally and we left out the local people. We had put forth a gallant effort to make contact with the grassroots activists we knew, but truth be told, we were operating at a level too far removed from the Black grassroots in the local DC community. That was on us. My critique of them was their tone and assumption that we were intentionally disrespecting their city. We were not.

When we decide to call out our own people publicly, we fuel the enemy's attack. I was already being castigated. An attack from Black women organizers only made it worse. The letter from BLM DC, in summary, said that the Women's March ain't shit LOL. Although I am sharing this story with humor, it is not funny—a signal to the outside world that we had become consumed by infighting rather than action.

And whether we choose to acknowledge it or not, for Black and brown people, when one of us is assaulted, it results in an ambush of all of us. We become target practice because the world already views us as open season.

A Zoom call that followed confirmed our worst fears. The DC group explicitly told us of their intention to jump onstage and shut the march down. NeeNee Tay was one of the most vocal leaders at that time. They went on to confirm that they would not permit us to host anything in their territory unless a list of demands was met. To be clear, we weren't the kind of people who would allow our efforts to be shut down. Although members of our coalition were scared to death, where I'm from we're cut differently. My initial reaction was to fight. The one thing this whole experience taught me was to stop and think and to respond with humility. The simple act of listening transitioned an attempted hostile takeover into an amicable alliance and mutual protection as NeeNee Tay became invested in our shared values and struggle.

Freedom had not yet been realized by any of us, which meant we all had work to do. We were called, not qualified. And because we were called, the universe qualified us to carry out a mission far greater than ourselves. We would take a stage that afforded the whole world a front-row seat to an uprising against the perils of a man who meant the country more harm than good. With our bare hands, we intended to do everything in our power to stop it.

Today I call NeeNee Tay my sister and friend. She is now the co-conductor of Harriet's Wildest Dreams, a Black-led community defense organization. NeeNee and I saw each other. We recognized ourselves as strong women with good hearts vowing to give all of ourselves to eradicate ill of our community.

Although we managed to navigate the letter, Pandora's box had already been opened. The momentum of the anti-march message grew into a resounding chorus as my participation became a top-tier criticism.

In an effort to turn the tide, the decision was made to host a candid offline discussion about the issues presented. In the Women's March, difficult exchanges were dubbed courageous conversations by Carmen. This format denoted that it was a safe zone to interchange ideas and feelings free of judgment and that those involved were committed to listening to one another.

I could sense that my past as an organizer had earned a false perception of my motivations and commitment. Reflecting on the time leading up to this moment, I had been referred to as a problem. My career had been rooted in more traditional practices, which meant that many saw me as too conservative for their goals. There was an imaginary line drawn in the sand between those who had come from legacy organizations and "new" leaders. The perception was that I was either out for the spotlight or not real enough to be radical and about the business of progress and change. I was the one who took meetings with the White House. For some I was too liberal and for others too bougie. All I knew was that I had a fire inside me for justice that the unwarranted opinions of others alone didn't have the power to put out.

———

Once it was determined that each of the co-chairs would be permitted to give an address at the 2017 Women's March, my mind raced as I attempted to answer the questions inside my head and heart. What was I going to say? What was I going to talk about? Should I assume the responsibility for creating a kumbaya moment or something different? Would I speak about the things that would make me accepted and favorable to white women or was I brave enough to shake the table? Considering there would be so many at the march who did not know who I was, what would their introduction to me be? There were many who did not know me at all, and others who did and did not consider me a radical advocate for justice. This was the first time they were going to encounter me and me them.

On top of the swarming questions, there was also the pressure of time. There was too much at stake for me to allow anything to stand in the way of the words to be delivered to the people.

As the days left to prepare dwindled, my pastor called me for a candid conversation.

"Tamika, you have a big responsibility to deliver a powerful message," he said.

He never talked for the sake of talking. I knew he shared the same perspective about the magnitude of what he perceived this speech to be.

"You have a message that is supposed to be God's words and not yours. The only way you can deliver a message from God is that you may be in sync with what God wants you to say."

His words settled in my soul. The night before the speech, I had my friends come in and pray with me. I stopped taking any other visitors. I was using the time to not only study my words but also study my spirit. After preparing the first draft, I enlisted the guidance of Elder Kirsten John Foy and Reverend Stephen Green, two of my friends who are also preachers, to come in and review my speech from a more spiritual perspective. The third draft was revised by a professional speechwriter. My vision was to go straight to the heart of the critique and address the issues at hand.

Madonna, Dr. Angela Davis, and Alicia Keys among others were powerful presences slated to speak on the program. I was in tremendous company. They put me in a prime-time spot where media was going live and covering that moment. My name had been the focal point of so many conversations around the involvement of Black women in the march. It felt as if everything from negative to positive and mid-critique of the Women's March was coming for Linda, Carmen, and me. It was a hefty price to pay. I worked from my bedroom with the lights off. Somehow, turning the lights on made the task feel ever more impossible. Nantasha often accompanied me in the dark at a desk nearby with a desk light as fear of rejection, sleep deprivation, and the workings of my heart and my mind shifted into overdrive. The bags under my eyes were large enough to have been assigned their own area code.

I literally felt the stress pulsating inside my body. And on the outside, we were dealing with looming bomb threats and hatred from the avid Trump supporters preparing for his inauguration. Our meetings in the basement of the Watergate Hotel were purposed to review final details for execution but instead were primarily focused on safety precautions. The hotel maintained a locked-down status in an effort to keep guests safe. Meanwhile, my mind replayed all the faces of those who had come to me lobbying for their issues to be represented in my speech. I grappled with whether or not to use the term "people of color" and how to be intersectional, while also ensuring that the interests of Black women were heard. The only peace I discovered was in a little bottle filled with pills—Xanax shared by a trusted friend who'd seen my head falling beneath the waves of the task ahead of me. I decided to take only half of the suggested dose. The next morning, I realized she was right. I slept better than I had in months, and for the rest, I was thankful as I prepared for the biggest stage I had ever stood on. I wasn't preparing to move a community; I was preparing to move a nation.

JANUARY 21, 2017—WASHINGTON, DC

Thank you so much. I am so proud to stand here with all of you today, to be in service to you. Because this was truly a service opportunity for all of us who work for you. It has been such an honor to work along-side the co-chairs—Bob Bland, Linda Sarsour, and the birthday girl who you just heard from, Carmen Perez.

Today is not a concert. It is not a parade, and it is not a party. Today is an act of resistance.

Now some of you came here to protest one man. I didn't come here for that. I came here to address those of you who say you are of good conscience. To those of you who experienced a feeling of being pow-erless, disparaged, victimized, antagonized, threatened, and abused. To those of you who for the first time felt the pain that my people have felt since they were brought here with chains shackled on our legs.

Today I say to you, welcome to my world. Welcome to our world. I stand here as a Black woman, the descendant of slaves. My ancestors literally nursed our slave masters. Through the blood and tears of my people, we built this country.

America cannot be great without me, you, and all of us who are here today. [Cheers] Today you may be feeling aggrieved but know that this country has been hostile to its people for a long time. For some of you, it is new. For some of us, it is not so new at all.

Today I am marching for Black and brown lives, for Sandra Bland, for Philando Castile, for Tamir Rice, for Aiyana Stanley-Jones, for Eric Garner, for Michael Brown, for Trayvon Martin, and for those nine people who were shot at the Emanuel African Methodist Episcopal Church.

We have a chance, brothers and sisters, to get this thing right. We can do it if women rise up and take this nation back. When you go back home, remember how you felt. What made you—that instinct, that gut, that said, "I gotta get on a bus, a plane, a train, no matter what, to protect my children." That feeling—take it back to wherever it is that you came from today.

You have awoken a new and renewed spirit, and I am so excited to be a part of this with all of you.

But, to be quiet in our whisper, to speak low about it, is not going to get it done. We must be bold, the way you were bold to come here in these large numbers today.

When you feel that we are not taking care of one another properly, put your feelings aside, put your pride aside, and stand up for the most marginalized people in this society. Because if you stand for them, you stand for all.

Dr. King said, "I will not remember the harsh words of my enemies. I will remember the silence of my friends."

God bless you.

———

After the Women's March, I felt a renewed sense of hope about everything. Now back under the same roof, Tarique and I were working on more effective communication to ensure our continued healing. It was now my top priority, in spite of everything that was manifesting in my career, to stop and pay closer attention to his needs. Even though he was intrinsically motivated, I now recognized that he needed a mother, not a community leader. My mother had been saying this all along. My role in his life was not negotiable or interchangeable. My only goal moving forward was to reach down into the depths of my soul and to give him the fullness of a mother's love. I still wasn't the best at it, but damn if I wouldn't try.

There was also a great deal of internal work necessary for me to communicate better. I grew up in an era when whatever a parent says goes. Things were different now. The days of yelling to get your point across were becoming passé. I knew I also had to learn not to be frustrated with his response. Growth required a safe space for expression, even if I didn't always agree, but I maintained no disrespect would be tolerated. This was not the first cycle of my development as a mother and it would not be the last. I stand by the confrontation we were forced to have about his attendance at school that day, and the time apart forced necessary inward reflection for us both. By the time he returned, I recognized that healing for us was not a one-way street. There were dark crevices and difficult places that I too would need to address.

On the work front, I saw opportunity to transform the aftermath of the march into a movement. I discerned that far greater efforts would be necessary to activate more women to work together going forward. My speech was a litmus for such an opportunity. At no point had I shied away from speaking truth to power. I stood boldly in the face of America and shared our concerns for all the world to hear.

Many groups who had not acknowledged or, far worse, had denounced the march's efforts now saw some benefits of allegiance. It was not just my address that lifted the veil of our intentions. It was the collective of who we intentionally passed the microphone to and placed on the platform for the world to see and hear from. Both Carmen and Linda were masters at constructing programming that was collective. People with felonies, mothers who lost children to violent incidents, and sex workers all had a voice and stories to share. Come hell or high water, we were sending a message to the world that this had gone a bit further than your mother's feminist movement.

CHAPTER 14

TIME TODAY

Let's start here with this—context is critical to every discussion and every narrative. Up to this point, I believed that all I'd seen, heard, and done in my career had adequately prepared me for public scrutiny. I was well aware that it came with the territory. By no stretch of the imagination was I a stranger to being ridiculed. The difference was that I was now being introduced to new levels and, dare I say, new devils. From the moment I accepted the role as co-chair of the Women's March, many of my words and actions were taken out of context and served on a platter for public consumption. An unfortunate truth about activism is that when you embark upon a quest to demystify the narratives of marginalized communities and to amplify the voices and stories of those whom the oppressor deems the lesser, a target is placed on your back. There are key players in this warfare who throw rocks of anti-Blackness and hide their hands, further perpetuating the ills of structural racism and violence. Although this strategy of those who seek to be oppressors is not new, it does create new entry points that serve to infiltrate a community of people who have been given countless reasons to be hopeless and to feel unprotected. My only goal in life and activism has been to reinstate hope for those who have lost it and to dismantle systems that threaten our safety. Every effort that I have exerted has been to this end. Even so, not a single person who has walked the face of the earth could have prepared me for the season of physical, emotional, economic, and spiritual warfare I would be up against. The good news is that I lived to tell the story, but Lord knows I was bruised and broken in the process.

The aftermath of the Women's March of 2017 left me feeling exhausted. Quite possibly, I was tired from decades of activism. My soul never got the opportunity to rest as the same issues I had always fought persisted. Violence against Black people continued. The documented and undocumented occurrences of discrimination continued. The lack of the establishment of laws and practices to protect us continued. When I wasn't fighting for us, I was fighting to protect myself from some who looked like me. By then, I had lost count of how many conversations I had with people who felt that what we were doing with the march was too extreme. Was there a limit to how far I should have gone to help protect us? Were there boundaries I should have placed on how big of a stage I was willing to stand on to acknowledge the same injustice that perpetuated violence in our communities?

My grace was in knowing that after all we'd been through, I, along with the village I assembled for Tarique, had nourished him safely through his adolescence and that he would now begin the next chapter of his life at Morehouse College. With Tarique settled, I was back on the battlefield.

––––––

The planning process for the next Women's March was immediate, even if only in theory. There wasn't a time when we didn't consider, as a collective and in our quiet moments, ways to improve, to mobilize more people, to raise more awareness, and to build more allies. During this time, I traveled the country speaking to various groups of people, including a series of fireside chats and intimate conversations in the homes of white women. Even though I was on the road, I could feel myself maturing as a mother and being more attentive towards Tarique, more so than I had been in the past.

While the next march was months away, the pressure from inside and outside the organization continued to mount. More people took issue with our approach and the way we worked, and what we represented. More pockets of people believed they weren't represented enough. There were many Black women who took the stance that they were not a part of the feminist movement. They had no interest in aligning with women who had not been showing up for them in any way, shape, or form. It was Linda who, after much research, alerted everyone that in order for us to really lean in politically, we needed to go into a swing state instead of returning to DC. Las Vegas was the city of choice. In an effort to ground our mission and activism there, we also made the decision to set up shop in the city to return frequently and execute more effectively.

For several weeks, we leaned into heavy political commentary during the Senate elections as we set up residence, with the goal of making the right connections and allies. We faced massive drama, inclusive of many of the same issues we faced in DC. My friend Sheila Collins and her father, Gene Collins, longtime activists and organizers, held our hands. Their reputation preceded them. They were well respected. When I called Sheila to request that they help us to navigate some of the relationships, she didn't hesitate. We also received support from Mrs. Wynn, notably of the Wynn Hotel brand, who emerged as one of the biggest financial supporters of the Women's March in Las Vegas.

Although the concept and execution of the march were not new, the efforts of true intersectionality were still a challenge. There were many silos to reach and bring into the conversation. The act of combining groups of women who never worked on issues outside of their own personal interests proved to be challenging. On January 21, 2018, after much toil, we once again brought a community of many together, this time as a rally focused on fighting for the rights of all women. Scores of women gathered across the country en masse. Efforts to dismantle the rally were unsuccessful. The world had witnessed and could attest to the fact that as a collective and when united, women had the power to create real change in our communities. Seemingly, it had all been worth it. We were making history just one day shy of the US government shutdown. Thousands gathered in Las Vegas, and it was beautiful. My speech that day focused on challenging white women. After a year of working with them, we recognized fundamental lacks pertaining to Black women's needs. We were no longer interested in only dealing with issues that were safe and comfortable for them. Abortion rights being one of them. They were only interested in finding the least confrontational ways to address the issues that involved Black women and other races. As difficult as it may have been, I was well aware that the only way out was through. In this speech, I was unapologetic in my approach and less concerned with people pleasing than I had been the year prior. So much had happened that opened my eyes to the harm that white women can cause to women of color. For me, it was about getting to the heart of the matter: amplification of issues concerning marginalized voices for women, no matter how uncomfortable it made our so-called allies feel.

JANUARY 21, 2018, LAS VEGAS, NEVADA

Ladies and gentlemen, there's much more coming. Just so you know, we have some great performances that will be coming up and we want you all to be here. I know it feels a little cold. I'm actually freezing, but somebody on our team told me to shut up and come out here and say what I'm supposed to say, so let me do that.

Thank you all for being here, first of all. Let me tell you that all of you are the wind beneath our wings. We cannot do this work without each and every one of you who is here today.

I want to give a special shout-out to someone in this crowd. I'm only going to do one, but it's really important that I say something about a Black woman who I called in Nevada and asked her to stand with me to help us make this happen. Her name is Sheila Collins, and I want to say thank you, Sheila, for all that you did. Got to give Sheila a little more love. She got all y'all here. Between her and Debra and all those who worked, we want to say thank you to the Collins family.

In this year since the Women's March on Washington happened, women have continued to win. We continue to win because we continue to organize and to show up. That's what winning is about right now—continuing to show up.

Our voices, though, have to get louder. Most people believe that women are just loud anyway. And that's ok. To hell with it—turn it up. Be louder. Don't worry about that.

But now we cannot just be loud with our mouths. We must be loud with our votes, ladies and gentlemen who are with us. We have very specific work to do. People are counting on us.

You know the names. They've already told you, and you know who's hurting. Even though many of you may turn a blind eye, you know who is hurting in this nation.

Don't come to this rally today and sit here with your pink hat on, saying that you're with us, and you're nowhere to be found when Black people ask you to show up in the streets and defend our lives.

Our job in 2018 is to make good on all the times that you left us out here in the cold. Stand up for me, white woman. Come to my aid. You say you want to be my friend. I don't want to hear it from your mouth; I want to see it when you go to the polls in midterm elections.

We must build an inclusive movement in this country. We have not done it just because we're all here today.

There are women in Nevada who did not feel they were a part of this. They're Black women, and it hurt me to my heart to come here today knowing that many of them stayed home. They didn't stay home because of me—I can't take it personal. They stayed home because they are tired of showing up for you and allowing you to stand on their backs and do nothing to protect our lives.

Black women that came from Africa. Black women. To call Africa a shithole country—Donald Trump, you need to know it only shows your disrespect for women, because Africa is the mother of all civilization.

So we don't come from shithole countries. But Donald Trump, let me tell you something—you are an asshole.

We have the power. We have the power. And with all movements like this one, there's going to be division. Some people are sent to divide. That's their job. They show up to complain that they weren't invited even though they got every email. They knew about the meetings. But they didn't show up because their job is to create division.

Be unswayed, brothers and sisters. Dr. Dorothy Height said, "Women seldom do what we want to do. But we always do what we have to do."

We have to stay together. We have to march together. We have to organize together. We have to mobilize together. And we have to vote together—even when we don't like one another. [Cheering]

We have the power to change every policy and make every elected official work for us. But they cannot see division among us because they will go and do nothing for the people. We must stand up and be loud and be bold.

The same way we were in Alabama. [Cheering] In Alabama, we went there and said, "Hell no." A man who is running around malls, looking at teenagers, chasing little girls around. You can't be a senator in this country. And Black women said, "Hell no. Hell no. Hell no."

But white women, I want you to know that over half of you voted, still, the wrong way. From Emmett Till all the way to today, there is a problem in your community. It is not my job to fix it for you. It is your job to get uninvited from Thanksgiving and Christmas and all the other holidays because I want you to say, "Hell no. Hell no. Hell no."

Ladies and gentlemen who stand with us, and our brothers and sisters and folks who are gender-nonconforming, we see you. [Cheering] Our trans brothers and sisters, we see you. [Cheering] Stop looking for someone else to lead you. Don't look to your left; don't look to your right—look in the damn mirror. You are the leader. It starts with you. Go forward and do what you have to do. When they say, "Get back," we say "Fight back!"

God bless you. Go in peace, and do the work.

When I stepped off the stage, it felt like my heart would jump right out of my chest. It was certain I had ruffled some feathers, but at the time I was not aware of the magnitude. Mysonne and Linda cautioned me that my speech was going to piss a lot of people off. I was prepared for it all; at least I thought I was.

The next day, I was on a plane to the annual Holy Day of the Nation of Islam. The Saviours' Day event earmarks a time when the Honorable Minister Louis Farrakhan issues his national address.

Within forty-eight hours, a damning series of tweets by CNN journalist Jake Tapper sparked outrage around my attendance. It was the first flicker that ignited a forest fire of attacks against me. Tapper tweeted a number of statements by Minister Farrakhan. It was well known to some that there was long-standing tension between the minister and many in the Jewish community. Interestingly enough, I was not aware. This had not been a focus for me or my family.

For many years, my family, so heavily involved in Black empowerment, traveled to every space in New York to meet with other likeminded folks who wanted to see Black people be both free and safe. The Nation of Islam, once led by Malcolm X, was by far one of the most disciplined and dignified organizing spaces in Black America. As a young girl, attending Saviours' Day with my parents I was in awe of the power in the room. The rumbling of strong voices, relentless determination, and the unique laurels of respect exchanged inspired me. As I got older, after the death of my son's father, I began attending on my own. Amidst some of the darkest, most trying moments of my life, there were a number of people and especially the women of the Nation of Islam who created a safe space for me. Their kindness was not something I ever believed myself capable of repaying. I watched the positive impact of the Nation in my family and community. I watched the positive impact of the Nation in my family and community, and their transformation of drug abusers and prostituting mothers into community leaders and pillars of excellence. My family never joined the Nation of Islam; we were Baptist Christians. Although both communities were impactful, committed to faith and spirituality, the two spaces were different. The Nation was more community focused. There was such great emphasis on helping wayward people recenter. It was also notable the amount of men who were a part of the Nation of Islam. Both of these communities were intricate pieces of my development. In full transparency, no other group of people was more impactful in my presence. My family was solely focused on Black empowerment. We never discussed the minister's commentary on Zionism and what he calls powerful Jews.

In the days and months after the march, I found myself in a constant state of defense from the lies and deceit being fed to the public about who I was and what I stood for. I was dealing with the rage of those who desired nothing more than to ignore the issues that were most pressing for Black and brown women. There were some who wanted me to denounce the minister, specifically using *that* term to express my misalignment with him. There was rage from some of my own brothers and sisters who believed I should not under any circumstances denounce or speak against the minister. There was rage of some in the Jewish community, having been introduced to me through Tapper's tweets. There were some in the Jewish community who were sincere in their concerns, which extended beyond my attendance at the Saviours' Day event to what they believe was a lack of involvement of Jewish women in senior leadership of the Women's March. Although I had done national organizing as well as local organizing, many were meeting me for the first time. Therefore, their opinions were based upon the horrific media rush instead of my long-standing work and efforts. It was all a big mess.

The tapestry of the laurels of the Women's March was coming apart at the seams. What I was most in need of was peace, but instead, I was surrounded by war. The only time tranquility was attainable was when I was asleep—deep sleep. I yearned for the type of sleep that I could only achieve with the help of the pills. The more I took, the better I slept. The pills became my escape, and escape became my mission.

———

While I was defending myself against accusations of anti-Semitism, attacks from some within the Black community continued. In addition to these attacks, we were still fighting the issues.

On April 12, 2018, two Black men awaited the arrival of a friend for a business meeting at one of their local Starbucks stores in Philly. After these men were denied access to the restroom, the store manager called the police with a grievance of trespassing, citing that the two men had not made a purchase. By the time their confirmed guest for the meeting arrived, they were in the process of being escorted off the premises in handcuffs. Like the rest of the world, I watched the viral video of the arrest on social media. Although I wish I could have claimed to be in disbelief, I wasn't. Scenarios such as these were why my phone rang constantly and why I never stopped working on the ground. To add insult to injury, Police Commissioner Richard Ross defended the actions of his officers. Starbucks, however, apologized. Not only did the CEO, Kevin Johnson, apologize publicly, but he also requested time from the public to allow the company to reevaluate and regroup. Respectable, right? We thought so. From what I knew, Starbucks had exerted efforts to partner with community leaders. Some of my friends in the anti-violence community in New York were using Starbucks cafés for meetings to do their work. And because we were aware of these efforts, my team was willing to sit back and watch the series of events play out before escalating our protests against Starbucks. The corporation moved forward with creating a task force to review its policies and practices.

By April 2018, they announced the decision to close eight thousand stores in the United States for company-wide implicit bias training and made the curriculum publicly available. They also announced a new Use of the Third Place policy, defining a customer as anyone who enters a Starbucks space regardless of whether or not they make a purchase. It appeared to me they were on the right track to publicly right the wrong and execute a series of preventative measures to ensure this type of injustice didn't happen again. Then the bottom fell out when they announced the members of their advisory committee. All of the entities who were listed on the council were positioned to speak towards the dismantling of injustice, with the exception of one, the ADL (Anti-Defamation League).

Believe it or not, the ADL's politics have been extremely divisive for the Black community. As written in the *Boston Review* years later, in 2024:

> The ADL's calls to action have successfully mobilized public opinion against Black leadership for decades, from the Student Nonviolent Coordinating Committee (SNCC) and Ocean Hill–Brownsville parents in the New York City teacher strikes of 1968, to most recently the Movement for Black Lives and my friend, author, scholar, and TV personality, Marc Lamont Hill.

In 2024 with tensions high around the Israel invasion of Gaza, *The Guardian* pulled out some receipts of its own. Leaked messages from the ADL's internal communications showed an organization struggling to keep employees content while carrying out activities opposed to its progressive messaging to the public.

"The Anti-Defamation League has surveilled leftwing activists and 'regularly tracks, profiles and sends threat assessments of individuals,'"* *The Guardian* reported in July of that year, with the publication adding, "The ADL has come under fire in recent years as it has leveled charges of antisemitism against leftwing Jewish groups, Black Lives Matter, Palestinian rights groups and other organizations critical of Israel. It has increasingly lobbied for federal legislation on antisemitism, some of which critics say is intended to target leftwing Jewish and Palestinian rights groups." One Black woman activist, leaked messages showed, had a file opened and maintained by the ADL as they targeted her for holding "extremist" views, *The Guardian* wrote. "It scared the shit out of me," she said.

The ADL's general conduct grew so out of line that in June 2024 Wikipedia declared it a "generally unreliable" source of information on the Israeli-Palestinian conflict. Why then would we consider the ADL a credible source? I was told by a number of knowledgeable people accusing the Women's March of anti-Semitism and specifically me.

To this end, on April 17, 2018, I tweeted: "#Starbucks is NOT serious about doing right by Black people. #boycottstarbucks."

For clarity, let's consider the issue that happened at Starbucks did

---

*Perkins, Tom. "Internal Memo Reveals Anti-Defamation League Surveillance of Leftwing Activist." *The Guardian*, July 9, 2024. https://www.theguardian.com/us-news/article/2024/jul/08/anti-defamation-league-surveillance.

not involve any other community. The injustice was against two Black men and the Black community. The advisory committee assembled was inclusive of other communities. I would be remiss if I did not say that it feels like every time something happens to Black people, every other community benefits from the solutions established to address our concerns. Perhaps this is something to be proud of: however, we need, want, and deserve specific focus on our issues. While it is honorable that others benefit from our solutions, I do not believe that everyone should be involved in the discussions about how to fix the issues that plague us. We are best suited for this task.

Uncoordinated, I tweeted, Carmen tweeted, and Linda tweeted. These series of tweets were heard collectively. Some of the participants clearly agreed with our views. Although we were not on the task force and did not speak to or communicate with its members, the end result was that the ADL was removed.

While still speaking out and strategizing to ensure the community was aware of Starbucks's misstep, we were in the thick of the planning process for the 2019 Women's March. I was battling with my mind and my body due to the insurmountable stress of my position as co-chair, the anti-Semitism accusations, and an overabundance of microaggressions within our organization, as well as critiques from some in the Black community. The sum of it all attempted to break me. Even after all of the work I personally contributed to the cause and the undeniable impact made as a collective, there were still people and forces who wished to restrict my presence. Some people refused to accept that my attendance at the Saviours' Day event was not equivalent to support for every comment made that day.

Who I was, what I stood for, and the communities I served never wavered. I have always been vocal and consistent in my fight. Never in a million years did I believe that my presence at Saviours' Day would lead people to question my beliefs. Furthermore, I refused to allow people to reduce all of my years in the movement to my attendance at a single event. This event has been a staple over the course of several decades. For the life of me, I could not understand why the world villainized me by association when my work spoke the loudest. There were so many other issues that were far greater than what I could see or understand at the time. The scarlet stain of the anti-Semitic label was placed on my forehead, further fueling the fire and criticism of my role as a co-chair of the Women's March.

Instead of making headlines for the work done for almost two years without ceasing, the world was laser focused on my connection with Minister Farrakhan.

The widespread interest in categorizing me as a hater of the Jewish people attempted to overshadow the work and my true intentions, but there were other motives. My relationship and close proximity to Linda Sarsour, a powerful, unapologetic Palestinian American who very vocally challenges Zionism, made people angry. And my personal trip to Israel and Palestine from which I returned—much like we would later hear from Ta-Nehisi Coates—with concern that the Palestinian people lived in occupied territory.

In my line of work, there is much controversy. It's everywhere and happens all the time. Truth be told, we live in a controversial society. Over the years, I have gained more understanding of the cycle of life. As they say, history repeats itself. Most of the things we see today have happened in one way or another in the past. Equipped with this heightened sense of awareness, I am empowered to take pause and sit back and process events unfolding with more patience and discernment than I had when I was younger. When I speak of "younger," I am not only referring to age. I am also referring to experience.

With increased experience comes increased accountability. Asking myself questions like Who am I? How was I raised? What would make my parents, my family, and even me proud? These questions became the barometer for the actions backing the decisions I made.

In doing so, I have been forced to accept the fact that sometimes taking a stance means upsetting people who have an established set of expectations of me. It is a hard pill to swallow in general, but even more difficult when those people are the ones you love, respect, and care about.

There have been a few times in my life when I took a position on an issue that went against what some members of my community wanted from me. A harsh reality that I live with is that no matter what stance I take, there will be someone, somewhere, who will not be happy. This rings true, particularly when the issue of race is on the table.

My rearing was nestled in a doctrine of taking action and fighting in the face of injustice. The fight is not just something I do; it is a part of who I am. It is not possible for me to witness injustice and sit idly by. Whether that injustice is towards me or someone else, I will not sit on my hand and watch it take place. Action is all I know. This stance is not always welcomed.

In retrospect, the accusations had little to do with people feeling that I was someone who walked around with vitriol in my heart for Jewish people. Nothing could have been further from the truth. What I now understand is the politically motivated intentions that sought to destroy what I represented—change.

From the outside looking in, some might have assumed that my stance was one of neutrality. Those around me had only watched me fight. Fought beside me. Stood behind me. Supported me. Those same people watched in anticipation, waiting for me to fight back. Maybe they felt that not fighting back in some way represented compliance. What no one realized or could understand was that I was exhausted. So much of my time was spent fighting injustice within the Women's March, a layered and complex struggle. One that made the anti-Semitic accusations an even heavier cross to bear. Miz Sofia in *The Color Purple* said it best with her infamous "All my life, I had to fight" line. The wear and tear from years of struggle caught up to me. My scars and wounds from war shone.

I was left to sift through the politics of a tumultuous time that far exceeded my capacity to fight. This war—a Goliath of a battle—was never all about me. Beyond the unjustified attacks and nasty trolling, it was about an undeniable history of hatred, suffering, and pain that both Black and Jewish people have experienced. A history I took no part in creating but one in which I was cast as a leading character. It was as if I were standing in the middle of the Red Sea. However, for me, unlike Moses, it would not part. Eventually it would, but not in this season. The one good thing that came out of all of this was that I learned about a struggle beyond my own.

If I had to do anything differently, I would have resolved to stand still longer. My immediate reaction in the midst of being attacked publicly was to respond publicly. The accusations were all-consuming. I am well aware that we all carry prejudice. Even so, nothing about my intentions was a hate for the Jewish people. It was for this reason I was compelled to speak out to address the concerns of those who genuinely wanted an understanding. As hard as I had fought for Black people, never once had

I done so at the expense or for the demise of another group. This in no way aligns with who I am or the way I was taught to fight in the face of injustice. However, the act of defending myself in an attempt to battle the ridicule revealed much of what I did not know.

My tweet "They crucified Jesus" was the proof.

This phrase is commonly used by Black people as a coping mechanism to get through a difficult time. It is a reminder that not one of us is exempt from public scrutiny and a reminder of sorts to persevere. And although I was going through my own crucifixion, the historical context of my commentary was not something I considered. No matter what my intentions were, it appeared I was continuing down the path of feuding with the Jewish community, attempting to bring up biblical references about how Jesus was killed.

Instead of silencing the critics, my words and actions provided people with an opportunity to misinterpret my disposition further. As they say, patience is a virtue. (In other words, I shouldn't have said shit.) I remember getting a call from a number of women I respect, including Brittany Packnett, Symone Sanders, and Rachel telling me as much. *Please don't Tweet anything else*—that was their collective message.

Not everyone understands the immense scrutiny that transpires when you're in the public eye. It often feels like commentary about your life, particularly criticism, travels at lightning speed. Over the years, I have felt a sense of urgency to respond and to defend my honor. I know that I am not alone. For me, social media not only accelerates this process but also increases the urgency I felt to speak up about the false narrative that was spiraling out of control. At that time, I believed that allowing too much time to pass without a response would have been likened to an unspoken confirmation of the lies. I was raised to defend my honor.

It has taken me years to uncover and process a new truth. One that has reshaped my perspective. Although I can't say there was one particular "aha" moment, I am certain that time, countless hours in therapy, rehab, and my internal drive towards healing have led me to an understanding that the attacks were designed to kill a revived women's movement. This was an attack on the potential impact that could be made as women aligned to fight against sexism, racism, and every other ism that has long unleveled the playing field. The Women's March was the vessel.

I also learned from this process to take more time to listen, learn, and then study so I can respond properly and how to adequately prepare before doing so.

This chapter is closed for me. There may be other people who choose to focus on trying to use this topic to harm me, but I think I got the message that God wanted to teach me through this turmoil. Despite being extremely hurt and continuing to suffer real consequences, I believe I've learned what life needed to put before me. I'm back to doing my work.

CHAPTER 15

CHANGE GONNA COME

By June 2018, I was signing contracts, preparing to lift my voice and speak my truth on a different type of stage. This time, the audience would gather before the big screen. When I was approached by talented director Amy Berg about being a featured story in her documentary about the women's movement, I was reluctant to sign on. Having my life documented on camera was a foreign concept for me. Doing so went against the notion of flying under the radar and remaining discreet. Several people convinced me that my participation was important for the historical reporting. Once the planning for the next Women's March began, I immediately regretted my decision. In fact, I ran from the cameras. I didn't want to film. I didn't want my life on display. Still lacking adequate rest and still fighting to maintain my sanity as the anti-Semitic accusations continued, I was miserable in my own skin. Having cameras in my face for long hours made it all worse.

There was, however, some joy associated with the project when we embarked on a journey to tell the story of the Mallory lineage. The day we took a camera crew to learn about a man we believed to be my ancestor Sheppard Mallory was one I will never forget. In 1861, three Black field hands owned by Confederate Colonel Charles Mallory traveled by water to Fort Monroe in Virginia to negotiate a pathway to freedom for themselves and others who could make it to the fort. Benjamin Franklin Butler, a Commander for the Union, chose not to send them back, but instead to make them contraband, which means they were not completely free, but not enslaved in the traditional fashion. They were considered to be the first three runaway bondsmen.

I beamed with pride as my family members traveled alongside me. That day, we learned what appears to be the history of my father's early family. My heart was broken when I learned that none of the footage from these moments made it into the documentary. Anti-Semitism was front and center again. Let's be clear that I understand and feel that we need to be talking about anti-Semitism, just as we do for all kinds of hate in this world. There is so much of it to fight against. I just wish that my family's story would not have been interrupted from a documentary about my life as it was. It had taken over my storyline. Things got so frustrating with production that I found myself yelling at the top of my lungs over the phone at Amy one day. I was no longer interested in meetings with people whose intentions were not to engage in meaningful dialogue. Their motives were rooted in searching for opportunities to scold me. And there I was, trying to explain myself and my intentions in hopes of attaining an approval I would never get.

Let me acknowledge that Amy is an incredible director. She held no malice in her heart, nor did she carry any ill intention towards me. It was her documentary that was derailed. She too was a victim of the perils of me being labeled anti-Semitic. When Amy first came to me, major Hollywood folks wanted to get behind her project. As far as supporters were concerned, the Women's March was what we all thought would be the greatest story ever told. She was in talks with a major company to bring the doc to the big screen. The more the controversy was amplified, the more doors we watched close. Deals were being canceled left and right. Amy was doing everything in her power to pivot. She was attempting to give the film clarity so that those people who were starting to turn their backs would understand her vision. A Jewish woman, she was spending every day with me. She knew that I did not hate Jews. I suspect because of our conversations she also knew how much I did not understand about anti-Semitism. She was trying throughout the film to make people see Tamika—the person she had met and learned about over the course of many months filming together.

Amy was trying to push me to do more and say more. Her disposition was that I had a real shot to express myself. She also knew that people were following the controversy and would more than likely watch the film. Obviously ratings are important. She tried to create *that* moment. I explained to her on several occasions how demoralizing the situation felt for me, not the film. But it was still hard to convince everyone (including my friends who trusted Amy and saw her vision) that I felt we needed to stick with the original direction.

The filming went with me on a journey to confront the topic. I had loving conversations with a full spectrum of Jewish people—white Jewish people and Black Jewish people. I had a deep fellowship with Black Jews about their sense of dislocation and struggle to find acceptance in the larger Jewish community and was grateful to the rabbis and others willing to have conversations filled with love. Two relationships that developed during this time are Rabbi Barat Ellman and her daughter Sophie Ellman-Galon. Many tough conversations, but we showed one another true compassion.

But there were moments of tension as well. Members of our team attended a series of dinners in Jewish communities, seeking power in counsel. One dinner was attended by thirty rabbis and other Jewish leaders, as well as some Black and brown folks. The evening was tension filled. A male rabbi disrespected me real bad, speaking to me as if I were a thirdhand child—a bastard child. Another rabbi, a woman, stood up in my defense: "You disgust me to speak to her like this."

She went on to call out her colleague and his outrageous behavior towards me. That night, those words stayed with me. She put herself on the line to defend me. And boy, did I need it. Not only did I feel alone in that room, but I was also having to film similar conversations for the documentary. It wasn't until I spoke candidly with Amy, making sure she and the rest of the crew understood that there was no way I could continue to put myself in emotionally hostile situations and remain sane. They had no idea about my addiction and how many pills I had to take to cope with all of this. Their asks were dangerous for my mind and my spirit. I'd imagine there was some part of Amy's spirit that was broken in the process too. She was like a big sister to me. Had she known that I was coping with prescription pills, she would have flipped. From every corner I was being told that I wasn't vulnerable enough. That my face was too hard. Some folks had the nerve to tell me that I had not begged for forgiveness in precisely the right way. I longed for the discovery of hope amidst the trying days. I just couldn't seem to find it. In my mind those people who wished death upon me were louder than those who spoke life into me. There were days I fought to convince myself otherwise, but the proof was unquestionable.

I was convinced I could find salvation back in the arms of my work. I was determined to help Stacey Abrams in her race to become the first Black woman governor in American history. But as I packed to depart a phone call headed me off the cause.

"If you were planning to come to Atlanta for the election, folks in the campaign think you should reconsider."

More than likely, Stacey Abrams was unaware of these conversations. I don't hold any ill will towards her for what happened.

Shocked, I responded.

"I'm not sure what you mean. Are you saying you don't think I should come to Georgia?"

"Yes. You probably should not be seen in the state at all. If by chance Stacey doesn't win, would you want to be the scapegoat as the reason why?" They were specifically concerned about me bringing Linda due to all of the controversy surrounding us at that time.

The question was posed, and in my heart the answer was simple. It was the pain of knowing my integrity was questionable to people I respected. There was a deep sense of anguish in the acknowledgment that the world no longer saw me for my heart and dedication. I was now depicted as a villain. At least, that was the story being told, and my addiction was starting to make me believe that I no longer had the power to change the narrative.

By December, the *New York Times* was reporting that the charges of anti-Semitism overshadowed the Women's March. And by the New Year, nothing had changed.

———

The days leading up to the 2019 Women's March were gloomy. I would say that attempts to be what Don needed were less than stellar, but he was kind and I was thankful that Tarique was now self-sufficient. Any attempts at attaining sleep on my own were a failure. I was now reliant on the pills to get any rest at all. The self-imposed limit of half a Xanax coupled with the daily dosage of Percocet was my new normal.

Mysonne had always acted as a kind of shield for us, and me especially, in the Women's March. He was our protector and the keeper of all our burden. He took care not to position himself in the group's internal politics. He also recognized that the efforts were for women and, therefore, should be carried out by women. Some days I had to remind him. He would be fuming from the mess of it all.

Even though he had not outwardly expressed his disdain for how I had been treated, he was well aware and disgusted. While on the train, headed to Washington, DC, for the march, we sat across from each other. He watched me take calls back-to-back as my facial expressions intensified. In lieu of it all, he tried to get some rest until the sound of frustration in my voice awoke him. I could see his eyebrow raised as he tried to make sense of the conversation.

It was Linda on the other end of the phone expressing the concerns of the other women in the march. As she explained it, they had been attempting to coerce her into asking me to stand alone on the stage at the march to resign in front of the world. The act of isolating and destroying a single member of what had been perceived as a solid unit is a classic tactic of white supremacy. Once you are isolated and you feel like you don't have support, your power is gone. Once you have been broken, the likelihood of your resistance diminishes. It wasn't a discussion I had to have with Mysonne. He recognized immediately what we were witnessing.

"Fuck that. You are not resigning. And you damn sure ain't resigning onstage in front of all those people. As soon as we get there, we're addressing this shit. I sat back long enough, but this is not happening. Not on my watch."

Neither of us could sleep. By the time we arrived in DC, there were two cars waiting to transport us to a scheduled interview. I told Mysonne to ride in the first car so that I could talk with Linda. He didn't listen—immediately. He was a mixture of noticeable emotions ranging from sadness to disappointment that the attack of the enemy we had fought so hard together to overcome was gaining ground. If one of us lost, we all lost. Begrudgingly, he grabbed his belongings and got into the first car while Linda and I reconvened in the second car.

When we closed the doors, it was apparent to me that from the time we spoke to the moment we got into the car, Linda came to recognize the play in motion and that there were people attempting to drive a wedge between us.

"Tamika, I know this doesn't make any sense, but everyone is saying that it's best you be the one to resign."

"Why would I resign alone? Make it make sense. What have I done to deserve this?"

"They are saying that if you don't, we will all be noted as the people responsible for ruining the women's movement of the twenty-first century. It will be our names in the history books noted for destroying the movement. This concerns me, Tamika."

"I understand your concerns. They are valid, Linda. What I don't understand is why I should do this and no one else should be standing beside me."

Linda was shaken. No activist who believes in a cause signs up to ruin history. Sis looked bad—worse than I had ever seen her. I recognized the game. Their only objective was to put as much pressure as they possibly could to break the person closest to me in a desperate attempt to then break me.

Behind the obvious war, the LA network of the Women's March was threatening to pull their support from the national organization. The Women's March as a whole could not afford to take another blow. After disclosing these details, I also reminded Linda of the elephant in the room, my connection to her as a Palestinian woman who was very vocal about the plight of her people. She understood and it further broke her heart. Anti-Semitic labels were being used to weaponize me because of my relationship with her as a Palestinian. She apologized to me for everything. It was a difficult time for us. Instead of focusing on how my resignation was conceived, we instead strategized what we would do next to push back.

Around us, there were operatives promising people that they could make us say things that we had not agreed to say and to do things we had not agreed to do. I needed to call in seasoned reinforcement. Overcome with the grief of the moment, I called my mentor Cora Masters Barry. She was the only person who would know what to say or who had the wherewithal to tell me what to do.

Cora, the wife of the late great Marion Barry, mayor of Washington, DC, was no stranger to the daggers and vitriol that often accompany the light cast on those who serve. She had a front-row seat to abomination at the hands of the media on many occasions despite her husband's incredible yet controversial work as a public figure. She had accompanied me to some of the meetings with the Jewish community and was advising me as things unfolded.

"Hello!" Cora answered the phone already on edge.

She was on alert because every day, there was new shit.

"Tamika, how are you?"

"Not good. Not good at all," I responded.

"What happened now?"

"I just got off the phone with Linda and people have decided I should resign by myself."

I closed my eyes, took another breath, and unleashed the truth about the terror and humiliation to which I had been subjected. My stomach was tied in knots as I recounted the series of events unfolding in the present. I lost it. In a sea of emotions, I was drowning. Cora was a woman of tremendous strength and action. In addition to being a confidante, she was a relentless problem solver. She never played checkers. It was always chess.

"What time will you be here?" she asked before connecting Minyon Moore, a major political strategist and leader. We repeated the short story to Minyon, who was driving at the time. She pulled over to the side of the road. Although I rarely heard her curse up to this point, on that day she joined Cora in disgust with the unfolding of the series of events. They asked me for the name of the hotel and said that they would meet me there. The last words she said before hanging up the phone were music to my soul.

I didn't ask any questions. There was nothing left to say. So much of my life has been spent standing in the line of fire, defusing, dispersing, and fighting for the well-being of others. It's hard to admit that I was a skilled general while on the battlefield for others, but I had not mastered the art of war fighting for myself. This was a Goliath moment and I was uncertain of what the outcome might be. At least when the ladies hung up the phone, I knew a lifeline existed. I exhaled the breath I had been holding since sitting on the train. My mind flashed back to all we had done to establish the Women's March. It had become much of who I was. And I had sacrificed so much for it.

———

By the time we arrived at the office headquarters, at The Mayflower Hotel in Washington, DC, the air in the room was stale. It reeked of evil. The energy was different. The faces that had once been familiar were unrecognizable. The hairs on the back of my neck standing up were confirmation that I was treading unsafe waters. Had they really wanted me to resign? On a public stage in front of the world? Alone? It was bemusing to believe I was being asked to remove myself from a table I had invested blood, sweat, and tears to sit at. To serve at. Unsure of what to do, I said nothing, not to anyone. My eyes were filled with fury, and my mind raced in search of what to do next. Pacing, praying in desperation, gasping for air, I needed to think. I tried not to look at Mysonne, but I could feel him watching me and fuming. There was nowhere for me to scream. No outlet for the release of the frustration now transferred from them to me. It was me against them. Had I not been clear about the dissension before, it was now a glaring reality.

Forty-five minutes or so passed by before Cora called me to meet her at the revolving glass doors. She wasn't alone. She was accompanied by a human arsenal, a group of three well-known leaders. Minyon, and civil rights leader Bishop Leah Daughtry, and Melanie Campbell, convener of the historic Black Women's Roundtable. All four of these women are powerful political strategists in Washington, DC, and across the country. They wafted through the doors like the rapture, bearing straight faces, raised eyebrows, and unapologetic. We embraced. They asked to meet with everyone. We went into a ballroom with a few chairs scattered around. We made a circle with the chairs.

I spoke first.

"I think we all know why we're here. I am being asked to resign tomorrow alone on the stage."

Without hesitation, Cora asked, "Why?"

The silence was an unspoken admission of guilt.

"They believe that it is best for the march and everyone involved if I take responsibility for all of the controversy that we have found ourselves in," I said. They. They. They. If I had a dollar for every time that was said in the room, I'd be rich.

Minyon said, "Who in the hell is *they*?"

One of the culprits was sitting in the room with us. She did not respond immediately.

"Call *they* on the phone," Cora said. "Are *they* here? Bring *they* downstairs."

A backstabber and organizer whom we had hired began to mumble through an explanation mentioning the LA group as a major influence in this decision. She never said that she was the ringleader, but Leah and I looked at each other. Leah asked me, "Is this what I think it is?"

"Yes," I replied. At that moment, it was explicitly clear that I was identifying this person as *they*.

After some back-and-forth, Melanie inserted, firmly, "Look. I left a meeting to come here and say one thing. If Tamika is forced to resign and y'all don't stop mistreating her I will use all the power in my body to shut the Women's March down. Go back and tell *they* to try me."

They got up, grabbed their things, and walked out. On the way out the door Cora leaned back and said, "Give me a call later."

The room was silent. Everybody understood.

Later that day, Leah got a call from a Black woman in the LA network who was attempting to turn her against us. She shut it down quickly and let me know they were more than white women. Some of our own were involved as well.

One day when I am old and gray, I will tell you all who it was. It was so damning that I know our community can't take the blow. She was and still is a jealous . . . I'll leave it there.

After that meeting, the calls for my resignation ceased.

Black women came to my rescue and saved me. Black women built a barricade against the forces who set out to destroy me in front of the world. Had it not been for their efforts, it could have very well ruined my career and legacy.

Carmen was not present in this meeting because she had not arrived in DC yet. She was a new mother and had recently moved to LA with her husband, Jay Jordan. I thank God that we made it out of this difficult moment and that Linda and I were able to save our friendship. Today we're closer than ever.

———

The fallout of the march left me with a whirlwind of emotions. My attempts to stabilize my thoughts failed. The anti-Semitic accusations muted the sound of my real voice. I could no longer hear from myself. I was unsteady in every aspect of life. The winds of scrutiny were turbulent enough to uproot my feet that had once been grounded in purpose. I was now beyond the point of no return while self-medicating not just to sleep, but also to stay calm. The pills became my safe space away from the rest of the world. In them, I found what I believed to be a way to reclaim my power. So you understand the magnitude, I was not just taking a pill here and there. I was now up to fifteen to twenty-five pills per day. I was addicted to the sense of numbness they were producing inside me. What I either didn't know or willingly chose to ignore was that the pills were killing me softly, devouring my internal organs.

The specific feeling that opioids and Xanax give you is likened to heroin. When people think about pills, they classify them differently. And if I'm being completely honest, that hierarchy is often established by the price paid for the drug. The ugly reality is that all of those who are addicted are chasing the same high. In one of my attempts to get help from a psychiatrist, he laughed when I attempted to talk about my drug abuse as if it was better than the next person's.

He said, "It always humors me when my clients believe their addiction is more dignified than others. It's all the same. You are an addict."

My body began to tell me that I needed the pills. There was something about me physically that was off. Brain fog was at an all-time high. I could no longer remember small details, and my mind moved at a slower rate than it once had.

There was no question the pills had a hold on me. I longed for them to quiet my deepest emotions that, if allowed the space to speak, had the power to break me. There are only so many daggers a human body can sustain before collapsing.

I was a high-functioning addict. Maybe not. As I think about it, I wasn't high functioning at all.

Externally, the world was clueless as to what was happening to me. It was as if I were atop a stage, standing before a sea of people who wanted or needed something from me. Although there was a smile on my face, on most days I was paralyzed internally, attempting to bear the brunt of lies, pain, guilt, and deceit. Had I turned around, the bloodstains leaking from the wounds in my back would have been exposed. No one really knew the depth of what I was experiencing. Mysonne and Linda could see the depression drowning me, but they still had no idea of how bad it really was. And there was very little to alert anyone that I was spiraling. The thing that did stand out was my weight. I was getting smaller and smaller. Emotionally I was unavailable and wanted desperately to be alone. All of these elements could have easily been attributed to the obvious stressors of the march, which prevented most from questioning whether or not I was healthy. Even so, my makeup was done and my hair was laid. From the outside looking in, many assumed I was well. I wasn't. In fact, I was at the worst place of my life. In the past, misogyny, imposter syndrome, feelings of a lack of accomplishment, homelessness, failed relationships, the murder of my son's father, and nonstop tragedy knocked at my door, but somehow I had survived it all, without the use of coping mechanisms. Not this time. By summer, I was spending a little over a thousand dollars a week on pills. My savings became an ATM to execute my transactions. The more I used, the less I noticed the slow drain of money from my account. And because Don took care of everything financially, we lacked nothing.

Although my team noticed a slight decline in my bookings due in part to the creep of anti-Semitic talk, there was still a steady flow of requests that kept me booked and busy. If I had to travel to speak, the pills were nonnegotiable. I even had a small attaché case that I kept with me at all times. And if by chance I forgot that case, come hell or high water I was going back to retrieve it. There were times when I missed entire flights when traveling with the team due to forgetting the pills. From the moment I realized that I had left them, I would make up an excuse—any excuse to get back to them. Under no circumstances was I willing to depart without the pills in my possession—I couldn't, because I would get sick. They became as important to me as my cell phone. The way I saw it, I needed both to be fully functional.

If we arrived late at night or early in the morning and there was time to rest before a public appearance, my normal routine was to take some pills, do some reading, and drift off into a deep sleep for as many hours as possible. On most occasions, I would wake up feeling refreshed and ready to handle my business. While out, my mind always drifted off into a longing to return back to my hotel room, where I would lock myself in and repeat the cycle of popping pills, reading, and returning to sleep. It was a cadence that calmed me. Deep in my heart, I knew that my addiction was growing and that I would not be able to live recklessly forever.

I met retired NBA All-Star Jayson Williams back when I was working for NAN, and in this period we just happened to reconnect. While catching up, I learned that he had opened a rehabilitation center in

Florida and was working with other facilities around the country. It was in my mind in that moment that I would have to find a way to ask Jayson for help.

A seed was planted. Jayson had no idea, but it was almost like God sent somebody to help me whom I could trust and I now knew rehab to be a viable option. But at the time I wasn't ready, so I tried something different. Instead of rehab, I decided to treat myself on my own. I went back to the psychiatrist who gave me a prescription for Suboxone with instructions to stay home and break the addiction on my own. The way I saw it, desperate times called for desperate measures. That is, until my curiosity got the better of me. I was Googling the shit out of the prescription in hopes of becoming an instant expert. All roads pointed back to people getting hooked on the very medication that was supposed to help them get off another drug. In my mind, Suboxone was a transfer of one problem to another. I was already fucked up. Why get fucked up on something different?

Instead, I decided to try on my own, cold turkey, but that proved not to work either. It caused unbearable sickness. What was I to do?

So I worked harder to conceal my disposition. My new normal became to wake up, take three and a half pills, and go back to sleep to rest for another hour. Just before falling asleep, I would lie in bed thinking about my day ahead. Then I would get up and gather myself before attending to the tasks at hand. There was never a time I took pills before going to work without sleeping first because they made me drowsy. It was in the hidden burrows of my addiction I learned how much more dangerous it was to keep the people around me in the dark. Instead of leaning and depending on them, the pill bottle became my shelter. Thoughts of suicide live here. Reproduced there. Thrived there.

I kept busy to keep the worst thoughts away. There were times I was so high-strung I would slither into the bed or a quiet place, withdrawn from the world around me, and black out. If I was traveling, my mission was to remain locked away in my hotel suite, with the curtains blocking all signs of daylight. On several occasions, Mysonne's visits were followed by his attempts to get me to get up and get moving.

"You need to open these windows," he would say as he drew the curtains.

Now a master at the art of faking reassurance, I always convinced everyone that all was well, but it wasn't. My self-administered dosage was now in the double digits, and my emotional well-being was severed. When preparing for speeches, I made it a habit of giving myself at least a two-hour window from the time that I had taken the last dose to my scheduled appearance. I knew better than to show up anyway except with what appeared to be the best version of myself. There was also a level of clarity that came along with not having the drugs immediately in my system that I desperately needed to get through the delivery of the speech.

There were times I could hardly catch my breath while standing in front of the mirror, preparing to face the world. While there was constant criticism from social media, news outlets, and even trusted associates and some whom I considered friends, there was an invisible mute about the looming death threats. On many days, I accepted everything that was happening to me as my cross to bear. The question was, how long would my body allow me to do so? After several months of the same song and dance, putting on a happy face to appease the public and the movement, the melody was somber. Standing on the scale in a hotel in Pittsburgh a few hours prior to preparing to deliver a speech revealed that my weight had been reduced to ninety-eight pounds. Not only did it not look sexy, but I didn't feel sexy. The day I discovered that my weight had diminished, I made up my mind to fix it. If no one else was going to know about my addiction, and I was keeping it hidden, then I must also be capable of solving the problem for myself. I knew I needed some serious help, and quickly.

One day I was just crying on the bathroom floor thinking, Maybe this . . . maybe that . . . maybe maybe maybe. There was no one there to save me or throw me a lifeline. The revelation that was hardest to accept as truth was me against me. Maybe I deserved to be sick. Maybe I deserved to die. Maybe the movement didn't need me as much as I thought it had. Maybe I didn't need it. Maybe all the sacrifice was for naught. Could change actually manifest? Were my people ever going to really be free? The wandering of my mind wasn't healing, as I had no resolve.

For at least two hours, I sat in the bellows of my sorrow. The only notion profound enough to peel me from the bathroom floor that day was the consideration that there were leaders who had been killed while doing the work I was yet alive to do. I thought of Dr. King, who never got the opportunity to stop doing the work on his own accord. He had been robbed of that. I thought of Harriet Tubman, who used her mind and her body to set our brothers and sisters who were enslaved free. I thought of Angela Davis, who defied the odds and lifted her voice to speak truth to power about inequality unapologetically. All of these leaders and so many more had one desire, to free the most marginalized in our society. I aspired to the same. That day, those thoughts were enough for me to get up, dust myself off, and try again.

In the days to come, my efforts to deny myself the pills cold turkey failed and matters turned from bad to worse as the residue of the recession caused Don's financial situation to become public knowledge. Leading up to this point and despite the economic crisis, he continued to remain loyal to his word, sustaining hundreds of employees until he couldn't any longer. Things were pretty bad.

For at least two decades, he had been at the helm of employing the best and brightest Black and brown faces in advertising history to ensure proper representation in the media at large. To watch him suffer was unbearable.

The ending of this era was taxing on him. For so many moments of my life, Don was there to lead and guide me with his steady hand of confirmation and direction. I felt terrible that I was only capable of giving him a portion of what he had given to me in the way of emotional support. Still my addiction absorbed so much of my energy. Much of his attention that had in the past been intentioned towards supporting me was now diverted towards sustaining himself.

In Don's care, neither Tarique nor I ever worried about bills being paid or the necessities such as a roof over our heads, clothes on our bodies, food to eat, or love and affection. Now that responsibility primarily belonged to me. Even so, the mounting costs of my addiction were impactful, and I worked like hell to ensure no one knew. In spite of having proven to each other that our bond was unbreakable, all of this stress was wearing on our relationship.

The more I was fighting to maintain my career and save my reputation, the more he was looking towards the hills of settling down into the next phase of life. For decades he served as a culture master and industry leader. And when he was on, he was *on*. Together, we were unstoppable while traveling the world and running our businesses. When he closed the doors to his company it was the first time he could take a rest from the day-to-day hustle, and I think he liked how it felt not to be so stressed about the well-being of so many others and not have to rip and run every day. He began to settle into a new normal of late mornings and conference call–free days. On the contrary, my days were about strategizing and figuring out next steps. I was becoming increasingly difficult to communicate with. We were ships in passing.

And underneath the sea of emotions, my addiction was floating, causing me to be more agitated than usual. Instead of making a decision to end the relationship, we just allowed it to be. Now living in separate places, we talk whenever we want. We love each other dearly. We support each other fiercely. Neither of us was upset with the other. We are family forever. Grown folks.

CHAPTER 16

LUCID DREAMS

Restless days were now my norm. I didn't desire to die, nor did I have the capacity to continue the life unfolding.

During my first interactions with Jayson, he allowed me to speak in hypotheticals even though he knew better.

"What if a person is taking pills, not like hard drugs or anything? Just pills. What would you do?"

He answered my questions and answered with the knowledge he gleaned from personal experience. Jayson was on a mission to help others.

By my third call—a cryptic one—his disposition had changed.

There was no way for me to fathom the circumstance being any worse than it was. While on the phone with Jayson, I looked at myself in the mirror. I knew right then and there that it could definitely get worse.

"Listen. It doesn't get better. It's a dark hole, and it just gets deeper and deeper.

"Meek, do you drive?"

Without me answering, he continued, "You'll mess around and have an accident or hurt somebody," he said with conviction in his voice.

Jayson spoke from hard-earned wisdom. A wisdom that almost cost him everything. It was apparent that he had done things he wished he could take back and he saw me heading down a similar path. I remained silent. Processing. It was a lot to take in.

"Things like this happen in a split second, and before you know it that's how your crisis becomes public. There's no turning back from that," he warned.

He didn't let up. "You calling me now means you can get in front of it, Meek. Let's deal with it before it deals with you."

I sighed on the other end of the phone. Still not confirming or denying that it was me standing in need of help. He never wavered in his conversation or intent.

"This won't be easy. It's hard as hell, to be honest. People don't understand that overcoming addiction is just as much mental as it is physical, but you can do it."

I could feel the warmth of a tear rolling down the side of my cheek. His words resonated. I knew I was in for the fight of my life. The addiction took up space in places I could have never imagined. It was in my heart and my spirit. I was weak and broken in ways I didn't know I could break.

When the call ended, I buried my face so deep into my pillows that I lost my breath. It was as if I were standing at the altar needing prayer.

I felt exposed, even though the only people who knew were Rachel, Mysonne, the dealers, and now Jayson. He knew then what I know now. An addict will only seek help when they are ready and accountability partners must manage their expectations. It was my call. Not a single person had the authority to decide when the right time for me to go to rehab would be. For those who love people with addictions, patience is a virtue. The harsh reality is that nothing you do will make a difference unless the one who is addicted is ready for change.

After speaking with Jayson, I toiled with the idea of checking myself in. It was easier to mask the inner turmoil from the range of emotions I felt with work. My mind raced with decisions regarding if and how I would tell my parents. What would they think of me? I had disappointed them so many times before. I questioned whether or not I had the guts to do it again. What would Tarique think? While he was away at college, what fear or trauma might this incite? He had spent his entire life dealing with the loss of his father and my decisions. His grandmother died from addiction. He was aware of what drugs could do. Would he somehow equate my need for rehabilitation with another form of loss? Instead, I turned back to the thing I knew best, organizing. The calls, text messages, emails, and constant influx of DMs about injustice and violence against Black people didn't stop because I had my own shit going on. No one knew, and I'd venture to say that if they did, most wouldn't care, but it would have made for really good gossip. This was a life that chose me, but now I was choosing it over me.

Eventually, I disclosed to Linda what was happening. I shared with a close-knit few my decision to actively make preparations to go to rehab. Linda was devastated. We had been through so many difficult moments together, and if there was anyone who understood the trauma I experienced at the hands of the Women's March alone, it was her. I needed support because I was scared.

Now my biggest anxiety was telling my parents. However, I knew that if anything were to happen to me and I did not disclose my whereabouts it would be devastating. The last thing I wanted to do was cause them more pain. Professionally, I felt I owed the team full disclosure as our work together would not cease. The people we served would still have a need regardless of whether I was in rehab or not, and my only goal was for our work to continue seamlessly regardless of my physical location.

Rachel in partnership with Jayson was instrumental in getting me to rehab. Not only would she get me there, but she would prove to be my support system for the three weeks leading up. Rachel could understand more intricately than most because she had triumphed over her own struggles.

The night before I was to depart for the airport, it was Rachel who talked me through. That night before I went to bed, I got on my knees and asked God just to help me no longer need the pills every minute of the day. It was me kneeling before him, negotiating on my behalf. My only ask was for God to set me free. Free from the pills. Free from the anti-Semitic vitriol. Free from the bondage of my mind, convincing me that I was not there enough for Tarique. In my heart, I believed that if God set me free, I could do the rest.

————

Not only had Rachel been my emotional support, but she also helped me to think logically in preparation for rehab. She reminded me only to take what I needed and to leave anything of material value behind. She also reminded me to take one day at a time. Rachel made sure I was focused and that my mind was in the right place. Two weeks prior, she encouraged me to cut back on the number of pills I was taking so that my rehabilitation process would be easier. Without Rachel coaching me, I might have reneged on going—I swear I would have, but she was there, holding me accountable. It was because of both Rachel and Jayson and the rest of my close-knit crew that I knew I wasn't alone as I prepared for what was ahead.

The next morning, Rachel caught her flight and I caught mine. She met me at a hotel in Ohio, the state where the facility was located. It was surreal to think that I was leaving behind everyone and everything

I knew. The thought of not being able to contact my son or my parents. The thought of not being able to talk to my family, scroll on social media, or talk to my friends or to monitor what other people were doing with the work was devastating. Maybe it was knowing that I was there because of my own doing that haunted me. It was all too overwhelming as I attempted to lay my head on the pillow to sleep.

As Rachel drifted off, she spoke to me.

"I wish that I could go through this with you, T Mal, but I can't." She always had all of these variations of nicknames for me. "You've gotta do this on your own and I know you can," she said.

She was so peaceful. Tranquility represented growth. Her system was clear. She had not had a drink in a few years. I was proud and simultaneously envious of her. I wanted so desperately to be able to do the same. That night, as I watched her fall asleep, I was thinking to myself, God, I want that kind of peace.

Whether she knew it or not, she motivated me to face my fears and move forward with my decision to report to rehab the next morning.

––––––

The night hours crept by until the morning sun forced its way into the hotel room through the window, and it felt as if I was in mourning. Perhaps I was. Maybe I was mourning the loss of life as I knew it. I was clear about the heavy weight of addiction I was carrying. It needed to be killed, but deep down, I was nervous there were pieces of me that would be irretrievable. I guess there was a need for some things to die in me. The tears rolling down my face were remnants of pain—war wounds.

That morning, I was dead silent. Rachel didn't say much either, but she left me with this powerful affirmation.

"This is going to be so great for you, Mika Mal. Trust me when I tell you that you are stronger than you know. You will return with complete victory. I just know you will."

As we stood outside in the brisk wind, watching as a white pickup truck approached, reality sank in. Within a matter of seconds, I must have thought of a million ways to rescind my decision to get in once the truck stopped. None of them were good enough. The gripping reality was that there was a space at rehab with my name on it and my only option was to get myself there. Rachel's nod was confirmation. There was no turning back. Once we were inside the truck, there were a few random pleasantries exchanged. The driver was kind and nonjudgmental. From the looks of things, he had his own story and his own cross to bear. Even so, neither of us was interested in anything more at the moment. It felt somber. After we pulled off, he reached for the handle on the side of his door and cracked the window. He didn't ask if we minded. I peered at him out of the corners of my eyes.

"Ain't this some shit here," I said under my breath.

The irony that a white man was responsible for taking my Black ass to rehab was all but comical. The air forcing its way into the truck skimmed the shaggy pieces of brunette hair dangling from under his tattered red baseball cap with a big white *O* embroidered on the front. When I looked at him, it occurred to me how easily the *O* could have been replaced with "MAGA," but who was I to judge? He very well may have been completely the opposite. I was facing my own set of problems. His black and red plaid shirt and rugged jeans might have been enough to keep him warm, but not me. I took the black leather bomber I had worn and used it as a makeshift blanket. Rachel peered over at me with a faint smile. For the remainder of the twenty-minute drive, I sat not in anticipation, just silence. If I was uncomfortable, at that moment my definition of the word would be put to the test in more ways than one in the days to come.

———

For some reason, I imagined it to be a medical facility. It was not. When I exited the truck, I nodded my head in gratitude to the driver, grabbed my luggage from the back, and stood waiting for Rachel to get out. There was no way in hell I was going in without her. I was uneasy about the massive American flag flying outside of the house. That can mean different things to different people.

Prior to my arrival, I confirmed the alias I would use to enter the facility. I stood on one side of the door as Tamika D. Mallory, and as I entered the threshold I knew I was leaving parts of her behind. There was no grand welcome committee or staff to escort me to my hotel room as if I was preparing for a big speech. Instead, I was greeted by Sarah, one of the staffers. The only words that needed to be delivered were the ones I would need to speak internally to convince myself to stay.

She was kind but matter-of-fact. We began our exchange with a tour. The open floor plan allowed you to see the living room, kitchen, and dining area at once. The facility resembled a normal home. The usual brown area rug, brown couches, beige walls, with a few random painted flowers in frames were all there. In some spaces, there were murals of affirmative words reminding us that life was not over. One spoke to my soul. It read:

Some people pray for easy lives, others pray for strength to endure the challenging ones.

The house had five bedrooms and an oversized kitchen adjacent to a living room. In addition to a room designated for the medical staff, there was a basement with a lock on the door where the food and medical supplies were kept. As a self-proclaimed germaphobe, my immediate inclination was to question where I would be sleeping. Outside of when we bunked together on long marches, I had never shared living quarters with anyone if it was not arranged. There was a voice in my head telling me to remain calm and suck up whatever the circumstance might be. I knew it wasn't going to be the Four Seasons or even a good Marriott. On the first day, my mind was directed towards getting through the process, whatever it was to be. All I could think about was getting back to a place mentally and physically where I no longer needed the pills to function.

Once the tour of the facility was over, they requested I take everything out of my bag. Rachel helped me while joking about the house dog we'd seen in passing during the tour. She knew damn well that I didn't mess with dogs and I definitely didn't want them messing with me. That was another reason for me to get right back in the truck, but the driver was no longer waiting for me. After about thirty minutes, it was time for her to say goodbye. Inside, I was screaming at the top of my lungs, *Don't leave me here!*, but no sound came out. She gave me a hug, squeezing tightly to affirm that although I was alone in the facility, I was not alone in the world.

After I had been there less than an hour, it was apparent to me that the staff was all white. The next day, I learned that there was a Black nurse practitioner who came around from time to time. I was immediately given several pills in a small plastic container and a bottle of water before being interrogated about the last time I consumed pills on my own. I was unsure of what would happen to my body when I took the pills, but I was desperate to try anything. Throughout the course of my life, I have been in difficult situations, ones that were more challenging than what I believed I had the capacity to withstand, but I managed to overcome them with my mind. At that moment, I closed my eyes and prayed that God would grant me mental endurance for what I was up against. I had to let go completely. I no longer had control over the situation I was in. It was literally *me versus me.*

For the remainder of the day, the pendulum of emotions continued to swing from one extreme to the next. One minute, I felt like Rocky standing at the bottom of the steps, preparing for the battle of my life, and the next, I was fighting back the tears from welling up in the rims of my eyes amidst deep loneliness. I was facing the reality that I was addicted not only to pills but also to my connections to the people, places, and things of the world that I could often access with my phone, which I no longer had. It was difficult not to be able to call or text my family to find out about what was happening with them or to tell them about the things that were happening to me.

Later that evening, I was escorted to the room where I was to sleep. There were two other women assigned as my roommates. One was Jen, and the other was Madison. We casually greeted one another, but no one was up for fake exchanges. We knew we were there because we were fucked up and trying to do something about it, not necessarily to make friends. On the first night, I was too zooted from the pills they gave me to be troubled that I was sleeping in a new place and away from my comfort zone. Although I felt shaky from the medication, I didn't get the stomach cramps like I had when I attempted to detox on my own. The fidgeting was not as bad, but the weakness was not something they could do anything about. I had clammy feet and clammy hands. I was uneasy and doped up at times. My mind was in a haze. Even so, they forced me to move around and would wake me up in the middle of the night to take more medicine and to drink water to avoid dehydration.

The hours after each dose were somewhat of a blur. I'm sure, at some point, I was given food. However, the act of eating paled in comparison to recognizing that I was there to stay. That night and the nights thereafter were agonizing. The reality of circumstance began to set in. Everything I had known was disrupted. Never had I been immersed in an environment with people I didn't know, with no access to those who loved and cared for me. That went against everything.

For the days we were assigned to the same room, our headboards were facing the same direction, which provided an opportunity for us to exchange in the quiet moments. Madison told me about her family and the life she knew before addiction. She was a frail, talkative brunette with piercing blue eyes and a tremor. When her knee wasn't in motion, she was either rocking from side to side or swaying from left to right. She never sat still and almost always chain-smoked. All she talked about was getting back on the street. We discovered commonality over silly things like hating the food and the chores we were assigned to do in the house. Often, we completed ours together. Chores were a part of the treatment program and efforts to build community and to keep us going. It was Madison who taught me about some of the more serious types of pills that existed and how much of an investment her parents had been making to get her sober. Madison was now in rehab for the fourth time. She told me the program was upwards of $80,000. Had it not been for my relationship with Jayson, I would not have been there. It was all too telling about the haves and have-nots when it comes to addiction. The cost alone helped me to understand why I was the only Black or brown face in the program. Unfortunately, Madison's parents' attempts to rid her of the drugs didn't appear to be working. By the end of the week, she disclosed to me that she was planning her escape and had already managed to contact someone from the outside to come and pick her up.

Although the dosages of medicines the medical staff administered to me daily kept me in a state of wooziness, I offered up words of encouragement as often as I could. The words I exhaled were the same ones I would have wanted someone to breathe into me: "We can do this. We can get cleaned up. I know we can."

It fell on deaf ears. Madison eventually left.

There has never been a question in my mind that words have power, and I hung on to them for dear life in that place, replaying that phrase over and over in my mind until it became the subconscious whisper that pushed me forward.

After two weeks, I had a better understanding of their internal programming and how the system worked. If you demonstrated a certain level of progress within a certain amount of time, you were transitioned to a different living arrangement. My process began in a room with two roommates. My next transition was into a community-based arrangement with seven other women in the room. At no point in my life had I lived with that many people. It was humbling. My adult life up to then had been one of luxury to me, and the choice to live with someone in my adult years had always been mine. It wasn't any longer. All I could do was respect that they made sure the space was clean.

At night, there always seemed to be someone who had trouble sleeping, and since there were no limitations on your movement in the house, you could get up anytime you felt the need. The kitchen and refrigerator were always open, and food was available to eat. The immediate grounds outside were also an option, and some walked them at night. The guard dog who remained on watch became my barrier. He scared the fuck out of me, so I remained in the house for the most part. And on the nights when he roamed inside the house, all attempts to leave my room came to a halt. On some occasions, I could hear the quiet terror from people crying, agonizing. The pleas for help tugged on my heartstrings. When addiction leaves your body, there is nothing that anyone else can do about it. The battle is yours and yours alone. The treatment I underwent was more gradual and less violent, likely because of the type of addiction I was there to overcome.

Initially, my regimen consisted of approximately six to seven detox pills a day. In my second phase, I was down to four or five. And so on.

———

I had been pulling myself out of dark places for many years prior to rehab. My son's father Jason's death had been one of those dark moments. It was me who stood tall even while bludgeoned emotionally and spiritually by threats and attacks on my character and the very essence of my being. Now, with me finally in a room alone, my only option was to confront the raw emotions I'd been numbing. I was forced to admit on my hands and knees that it wasn't the world that was killing me. It was by my own hands. It was by my own doing that I was an addict and an assailant to the bounty of my life. In my heart, I knew succumbing would mean evil won.

The more I unpacked the grim realities, the more grief I felt. It burned like acid. And in that space, I began to realize that I was addicted to more than drugs and people, but also to affliction. The work of attempting to mend people, places, and things that were irreparable had also become my fix. Inside me lived an obsession with righting the wrongs of the torrential terrain of injustice. The hope that I held in my heart for Black and brown people to be treated with the fairness of humanity consumed me.

My body was deteriorating, and my soul withered along with it. Some would have deemed this time in my life as a fall from grace. It was true that I had witnessed the mountaintops of bringing the masses together and on many occasions realizing change that defied the odds in the name of justice. But after countless years of fighting on the front lines of the war against oppression, at a premier civil rights organization and once leading millions as co-chair and co-founder of the Women's March to protest sexism, bigotry, fascism, and inequity, I was left to pick up the pieces of a shattered season. Years of tearing off parts of myself to lend support to others had stripped me of my armor. I was no longer covered. I'd lost my ability to cope with the constant criticism, daggers, and distress of activism. Even the relationship with the love of my life had become strained. I'd replaced faith and the pursuit of purpose with an addiction to prescription pills. The only way out was through.

In rehab I was buried in loneliness, however in these quiet moments, I began to hear from God again. I sat with him, and allowed myself to be consoled by his word and promises. In his arms, I began to heal from all of the things that landed me there in the first place. I was also forced to confront myself and ask hard questions, some of which made me examine the role I played in my own destruction. This was also the beginning of my therapy journey. It was in this space I reconnected with my why and reason for existence. It was almost as if I was being introduced to myself for the very first time.

For me, walking into a room filled with people whom I'd never met before and whom I would likely never see again removed the pressure of the need to say the right things. Instead, I was free to speak my truths without apology. In the beginning, I was so out of it from the medicine they gave me that I didn't have the capacity to care about what was going on with anyone except me.

The group therapy sessions were hosted at the dining table in front of a whiteboard in the kitchen. Extra chairs were brought in to accommodate more people. We didn't sit in a circle like you see people in rehab doing on TV. This atmosphere was more relaxed. People sat around the dining table, living room, and countertops in the kitchen. The only expectation was honesty. Bone-chilling honesty. We were expected to be honest with the therapist and, most importantly, honest with ourselves. That day was my first of many sessions with a counselor named Mike. He entered the room wearing a pair of blue jeans, a white button-down shirt, and a pair of white sneakers. He spoke calmly.

"Today, we're going to examine a few simple questions. During our time together, I don't want you to think about anything else. Try not to let your mind wander. Stay focused on this single question. After I ask the question, I'm going to give you some time to think about it, and then we're going to take turns sharing our thoughts out loud."

Leaning over in my chair with my hands on my knees, I waited for him to ask the question. In my mind, there wasn't anything he could ask that I couldn't answer with ease and the honesty they expected from us. I was wrong.

"Why are you here?—Tia," he said, looking in my direction.

Tia was my alias.

"The rule in therapy is that the newest person to arrive here at the house shares first," he said, waiting for me to respond.

Rehab wasn't like a class where when the teacher called on you, everyone turned around to watch for your answer. No one even moved or batted an eye. They all sat with their own thoughts. Everyone had their own crosses to bear.

It feels illogical to take the drugs they give you to wean you off the drugs that you were on when you got there. To be required to sit in session and be emotionally transparent in addition to complying with the physical requests was overwhelming and, quite frankly, scary. Based upon our recovery process, I was so out of it. Most of us were in pain, weak, and in a daze.

"To get clean. To be sober," I replied.

Mike's silence while he was still looking in my direction gave me the impression he wanted more from my answer. The truth was that I had no idea.

"Hmm," he said under his breath while squinting his eyes. He wasn't letting me off the hook. No one else in the room spoke, confirming that until I answered with deeper insight, we would not move on. I attempted once more.

"Death is all around me. I can't eat and I can't sleep without the pills. I'm having panic attacks and things are just out of control."

It was hard to get those words out, but once I had, a blanket of freedom covered me. The more I spoke, the more the others in the room disappeared. They were shrinking into their own thoughts and feelings. It was almost like I was there having a conversation with myself.

"I don't want to die, but I'm afraid of living the way I have been. I'm afraid of failing. I'm afraid of letting people who count on me down."

I peered back at Mike, fighting tears, attempting to salvage what was left of the shell of protection I built all of the years prior. My life was defined by building an exterior that did not allow for vulnerability in the presence of strangers. This was not just about emotions; it was also about safety. Mike's subtle nods were confirmation that my revelation was aligned with what was requested of me. He continued with his line of questioning.

"Tomorrow, you should be prepared to answer a few questions," he said. "Who do you love and what are you doing about it?"

My mind was already drifting when Mike repeated the question. I closed my eyes. All I could see was my son Tarique's face. A stream of tears exploded into a waterfall. I sat up in my chair breathing deeply, attempting to stop myself from crying. The deeper into thought I drifted, the more hopelessness I felt. Knowing that I was in rehab and not outside to help anyone made me feel worse. I clearly had not taken heed to their advisement to stay present in the room. There was nothing I could do except sit with those emotions. They hurt like hell. What quickly recentered my thoughts was the transition of the session to the stories of the others.

The next day, when it was my turn, I was still not ready. I almost wished he had allowed me to answer the day before because it was heavy on my mind all night. What I managed to reply was simple, but it was my truth.

"I love my son and we are working on our relationship. I also want to make a difference in the world, but I'm not doing such a good job at it right now while being in here." Those words were all I had to give at the moment. All I knew was that I desperately wanted to heal and repair my volatile relationship with Tarique. Although we had grown over the years, it still needed work.

Mike interjected. "That's ok. You're here. Getting better. Give yourself credit for that.

"I heard you say you like to help people, but how are you showing up for yourself?" he asked.

Even though I was officially enrolled under an alias, Mike knew who I was and about the work I was involved in.

"I don't want you to answer that right now. I just want you to sit with it. When we meet again for your individual session, we will discuss more. Great job today. Who's next?"

Had I ever fought for myself? There are no words to describe the level of frustration that washed over me when he asked that question.

Although I had fights in the street and too many brawls with Jason, Tarique's dad, I wondered if those instances could be classified as fighting to save myself. Those fights were sometimes provocation, but I don't know that I have ever fought to *save myself*. The only instance I could recall was as a child, in elementary school, fighting against discrimination as a Black girl in a heavily Latino environment with a number of white faculty members who made up most of the school's leadership. Back then, I learned that fighting against people with authority was an uphill battle. I couldn't answer even if Mike intended for me to do so. I wasn't sure. That night, I tossed and turned in bed so much that instead of sleeping, I sat up anxiously waiting for the next medicine call. The more I thought, I could not, for the life of me, recount a single time I had fought for myself.

I considered the fights I'd had at work a few times—and how my voice had been drowned out by the louder or more articulate "voices" so often. And then there were the times I fought in the Women's March. We saw how that ultimately worked out. I was at a loss.

The next day when I met Mike for therapy, he was the only other person present. The private therapy session provided me the chance to unload the chamber of my emotions until I had nothing left to say.

Mike asked me if it was ok to use my real name and I agreed. It honestly felt good because I had been faking my identity over the last few days, which made me even more uncomfortable during the process.

"Tamika, I appreciate the honesty you displayed on the first day when you said you didn't know why you were here in rehab. I want to encourage you to continue to allow transparency to be your guide in this safe space and out in the world. I'm proud of what you are trying to do. You will be ok. Believe me when I say there is life after addiction. The last thing I want you to remember is that it is ok to not be in control."

I nodded my head and I cried as he continued.

"You must understand that there are some people who are born with an unexplainable calling to help other people. And for people like this, like you, there is something inside that will not allow you to sit back and do nothing in the presence of suffering. There are just some people who are lovers of humanity," he said.

"Most of the time, these are people who don't do such a good job at taking care of themselves. Thinking about their own needs, wants, and desires sometimes feels selfish, so they put themselves last and others first. Could this be the case with you?"

He was spot-on. I sat there torn up inside, pulled between the celebration of a new reality discovered and the destruction of the rose-colored glasses I convinced myself to wear each day.

In rehab, I was forced to accept that I was at war on two fronts: one with the world for the cause of injustice, and another with myself. It was there I learned to wave the flag of caution, pain, fear, and all the things I had been hiding. That day I learned that speaking up is the only way to sustain. I learned the act of vulnerability and acknowledgment of the war within must become a daily practice, and this was to be a lifelong journey, not a destination.

There was no noise from the outside world to distract me from confronting the hard truth I could no longer deny. The only person available to hear from me was God. When I arrived at the facility, I was laser focused on getting through the program. I needed to be set free from the chains of addiction. This was no longer the case. I was gaining clarity as I began coming off my medications. My mind began to fill with all the thoughts and feelings I'd gotten away from for some time. I was coming into myself again. Paralyzed by the guilt of not being there for my son, I felt a deep sense of sadness. There were times when his voice echoed in my ears saying, *Mommy, I'm with you.* Those words replayed over and over again, just like the night I told him I was leaving Darrin. My clarity of thoughts was a sign I was getting better. I was no longer sitting on my own in a stupor. I felt like God intentionally quieted my spirit so that I could hear from him and make promises to him I would not break. One of them was to never pick up those pills again. Although I did not have the answers regarding every aspect of my life, I was crystal clear on that.

————

In my heart, I knew that my time at rehab had come to an end. Cleansing my body and mind from the drugs was just the first part of the treatment plan. The second part involved me going to a farm for more internal work. The decision to stay was something I grappled with, but because I no longer needed the pills, I saw no reason to remain in a foreign place. I was hell-bent on leaving. I needed to be home. I needed to be comforted by the ones who knew my heart and cared deeply about me. Making the decision to contact Jayson was not easy, but necessary. I requested a private phone call.

He picked up on the first ring.

"I'm out of this place," I proclaimed.

"No, no, not yet," he pleaded.

I kept it a thousand with him.

"Listen, my brother. I gotta get back to my world. I'm out here with these white folks and I don't feel comfortable. There is even a guy who is subliminally trying to let me know he knew who I was. I have to get out of here, bro."

He attempted to convince me otherwise, but I kept building my case.

"Look, Jayson, I've accomplished something major out here. I'm off the pills. I don't need them. I don't want them. I just need to get back to the folks that hold me down."

His silence on the other end of the phone spoke volumes. He had likely seen too many who believed themselves ready to return to life outside the facility only to backslide. Who would want something like that on their hands? I was *sure* that would not be the case for me. That day, I refused to take no for an answer. Jayson and I continued the conversation until we reached an agreement that I would consider transferring to a recovery home he owned based in Florida. He described it as more of a wellness center than a rehabilitation facility. To move the conversation forward, I agreed that I would consider it, but it also became obvious that the decision to walk away from rehab was not solely mine to make.

The staff is trained and committed to convincing you to stay. After I spoke in depth with Jayson, the staff on the ground at the facility were who I needed to tackle next. As I understand it, leaving that quickly is not healthy, but for me, staying had the potential to harm me even more. The next day was spent in a web of meetings. I began at the bottom and worked my way up through each member of the medical staff in the house. In communication with everyone from the doctor to the social workers and the management and everyone at every level, kept trying to encourage me to reconsider. To no avail.

Let me say this here. I do not suggest anyone leave rehab early. It's probably better to try to stick it out, do the work, and follow the advice of the professionals there to help. But I personally did not feel physically safe in that space. As a public figure, I was aware that my presence had become a point of discussion among the staff and that it seemed to be only a matter of time before my location and identity were revealed. And even if these things were just in my mind, I made a decision I felt was best for me at that time. And thank God I've not ever had to look back.

After almost a full day of my persistent pleas, they eventually agreed to allow me to return to New York. The condition was that I would be given a prescription and some time at home, followed by a return to the facility. Neither they nor I believed I was coming back. My mind had left long before my body. And although I was present physically, there was not a single person who could have kept me there. The most profound lesson gleaned from rehab was that whatever you aren't changing you are choosing. There was no part of me that was willing to choose being bound by anyone or anything any longer. As I saw it, freedom was mine for the taking. I've been off those damn pills ever since and I declare, I'm never going back.

CHAPTER 17

AIN'T GONNA LET NOBODY TURN ME 'ROUND

My last night was spent with the sweet smell of a small victory. Nonetheless, I knew that the fight in front of me would prove to be just as daunting as the one I was leaving behind. The only difference would be that the process could now take place on familiar grounds, in my home, versus in the middle of nowhere around people I knew nothing about. The act of packing was cathartic in many ways. It took me way longer than it should have, as my body was very weak. It was then that I noticed the impact of the weight loss, which had gotten even worse by this point, as I grappled with placing my empty duffel bag on the bed. Bent over and riddled with weakness, I placed my belongings in one by one. Since I had fought tooth and nail to leave the program, there was no way I could request help from the staff. My entire argument for leaving was based on me affirming that I could take it from there.

Now I needed to be responsible for getting myself home. By the time I finished and made it to bed that night, the persistent fever that plagued my body was back, and I went from hot to cold.

This time, there was no one waiting to assist me with my bag like there had been when I arrived when Rachel and I were picked up from the hotel. They gave me back my phone and I called an Uber to drive me to the airport. With my head hung low, I struggled to keep my eyes open. It was the sound of the driver's voice that alerted me that we arrived at the airport, which meant that unbeknownst to me, I was out cold for the entire fifty-minute drive. As I lifted my head from the window to look towards the airport doors, it was as if I'd lost my ability to focus. Wiping the drool from the corner of my mouth, I mustered up enough energy to lift the lock and pull the door's handle to exit. Barely standing at the back of the car, my body ached and wavered in the wind as I waited for the driver to place my luggage on the ground. He lowered the trunk before saying, "Have a safe flight, ma'am."

"You too," I replied while turning to face the entry doors of the airport.

In a haze, I hadn't stopped to consider that he was not preparing to board a flight. It was me who was leaving the state. I pulled together whatever strength I had. I didn't care that walking was a struggle. I didn't care that I looked like hell. I didn't care if someone saw me that day, disheveled. Instead, I held on knowing I was returning to my familiar arms, and that gave me the strength I needed to walk to the gate. Everything from boarding the flight to landing at La Guardia was a blur. All I know is that when we touched the ground, I had a text on my phone from my parents that they were waiting for me. It was fuel for my soul.

The blurred vision of my parents in the distance, standing outside for me with open arms, was all I needed. All I could think about at the moment were the countless sacrifices they had made over the years, mostly in response to my choices. Despite it all, they had never given up on me. Their unconditional love sparked the fire that burned within me to get sober and stay sober. Leaving rehab, I was certain that God had broken my need for the pills. And for that I was grateful. Although my body was fractured and wounded, I gathered myself to walk towards them with some dignity.

When I got to the car, I was fatigued and could hardly walk. Even so, we shared some pleasantries.

"I made you some vegetable soup," Mom said.

Her words were the perfect way to melt the ice between us. I was beyond nervous about how to re-engage. Although I had been gone almost three weeks, everything was different—I was different. My mom has always had these ways of showing her love. Her soup was one of them. All the women in my family who were influenced by Grandmother Pauline Mallory have their own version of vegetable soup. In our family, this dish was not just sustenance but a source of healing and something that brought us together. If people are coming to your house, this meal was a nonnegotiable. No matter the season, summer, winter, spring, or fall, the soup is customary. Over the years of my life, I've watched my grandmother make it from scratch. It has been that very recipe that saved us from the harsh winters and flu seasons in New York, and it was saving me now, upon my return home. That night, I had only about four spoonfuls, mostly broth, before turning over and going to sleep. When I finally awoke, it felt like days passed, although it was likely about five or so hours. At the facility, they wake you every few hours to make you eat and administer medicines. My guess is they wanted to break the deep levels of sleep that the medicines induced and to ensure you took your meds before sickness from withdrawal set in. Now with me at home, and with my family not fully aware of every medical step taken, no one woke me.

———

When I did get up, a blurred vision of Don's silhouette was there, waiting, watching over me. We didn't talk much, and whatever words were spoken escaped me. All I know is that he stroked my forehead, gave me a few more spoonfuls of soup and a kiss on the cheek, and I was back asleep again. By the third day, I hadn't showered. The only time I'd moved from the bed was to pee. And there were times that the bathroom seemed too far out of reach when I just held it. The minuscule energy I had to make it through the airport had now left. And although my mind was working, my body didn't have the capacity to keep up. People in my immediate family and circle were in and out of the house. Some coming to peek in on me and keeping me company. Sometimes I was so out of it that they would just spend time with Don. From time to time, I could hear familiar voices, and my heart smiled as they confirmed I was loved. I could not engage. Beyond that, I didn't want anyone to ask me the most obvious question: *How are you doing?* I wasn't doing. Period. Shame overshadowed everything else. One day I heard a familiar voice. It was raspy and euphoric. As it drew closer, I knew it was my friend, multifaceted entrepreneur and executive Yandy Smith-Harris. She swarmed into the room unapologetically. Without a knock, she opened the door.

"Tamika. Girl. I know you are not in here still in this bed."

A silent grin was all I had to offer. And it was all she needed to know she had my full consent to take charge at that moment.

"Sis, we've got to get you up from here," she said while peeling my body away from the bed. "When was the last time you had a shower?"

"Hmm. I didn't," I mumbled under my breath.

Without hesitation, she said, "Well, you will today, Mama."

She asked no further questions. Instead, she made me get up and allowed me to rest on her shoulder as she assumed the weight of my body, transitioning me into the bathroom. She placed me to sit on the toilet to wait for her as she turned on the water. Although I hadn't had a shower, I had forced myself to take hoe baths because, in addition to everything else, I got my period. And while the shower was running, I could hear her searching through the drawers. When she returned, she checked the water and helped me into the shower. It was there that she prayed over me, helped me wash myself, and cleansed my wounds from the world. I ugly cried. Her hands restored me, and her sisterhood filled the holes in my heart. And even if, for only a moment, all was right in the world. There is something special about the ancestral spirit of a Black woman to heal another Black woman. The shower was what I needed. With me feeling a little more like myself, we changed the sheets on my bed together. When I laid my head on the pillows I noticed a glimmer of light. Yandy must have brought it with her. This time, when I closed my eyes, I'm certain there was a smile on my face. I'm sure Don was thankful that I had taken a real shower.

AS TOLD THROUGH YANDY'S EYES

Throughout my friendship with Tamika, there have been naysayers and those who have questioned the bond that we shared. My interest has never been in quieting them. They have their own insecurities and triggers for which I have no remedy. I also recognize that not a single person in the world other than Tamika is enlightened to the intricacies of what I now know to be a sisterhood in spirit and in truth. Life has shown me in more ways than I can count that people who lack genuine, unshakable connections in their lives will cease to recognize them as they take shape in the lives of others. More importantly, life has taught me that there are those who will establish their own narratives, and it has not been, nor will it ever be, my place to convince them otherwise. Instead, I vowed over a decade ago to be my sister's keeper. It is my belief that Tamika is one of the wonders of the world and worthy of preservation.

My first encounter with Tamika was while working on a campaign for Obamacare. I was intrigued. Her unprecedented levels of commitment to activism were not ones I had encountered. To see someone who looked like me and was of a similar age who led the charge for widespread change and equality with the strength of a lioness was not only inspirational but heart stirring. The sound of her voice was thunderous when she spoke. Most profoundly, she maintained a presence with people that told the true story of her dedication. She was a leader who walked among the people. My admiration for her was immediate.

If she desired that deeply to see others be signed up for health care, then my mind led me to believe she was someone worth knowing. After one of the meetings, I made the decision to approach her.

Directly and intentionally, I said, "I want to get to know you. This is my number. My company hosts events all the time. You have to come out."

That gesture led to me inviting her to various events that I believed might be of interest to her. At the time, my platform was now directly correlated to the *Love & Hip Hop* franchise. Although I had several ventures and managed several artists before that time, the world now knew Yandy from the show. When you are a personality on TV, your platform increases in ways inconceivable and your access to people grows. However, I often questioned if there was more assigned to me by God to use the platform.

Tamika was a part of the more. There were rooms that I was in that were void of her activism. From my perspective, activists were not normally at events hosted by VH1 or industry parties, but I was there, and I knew with certainty that the people in those rooms needed to hear what she had to say. What I had not known then was that I too would be a recipient of her favor in the same way.

On the brink of unforeseeable personal turmoil, Tamika proved to be a bridge over troubled water not only for me but also for my family when we learned of my husband's pending incarceration. At no point in my life had I known to prepare for the type of judgment and scrutiny we would face. The penalty of persecution came from those who smiled in our faces and those who threw daggers behind our backs. In that season, I learned that not everyone in your circle is meant to remain there for a lifetime. There is merit in recognizing that some people are only for a season. Tamika, on the other hand, proved to be an all-weather friend.

Before meeting her, I had very little knowledge of the criminal justice system or its historically heinous track record of wrongful convictions of

Black men. Activism was not my world, nor was it the world of anyone in my family. The necessary action to fight against injustice and inequality was foreign to me. When the grim reaper of unjust conviction knocked at my door, I immediately understood the impact. It threatened the very fibers of my family. Tamika taught me how to understand a system that was never established to protect us. I learned through research that the percentage of Black men who are found guilty at a federal trial is in the ninetieth percentile. My husband's sentence was eight years. Out of those eight years, he was required to serve five. What I found to be most heart-wrenching was that he was not guilty.

The pain of idly watching a piece of your heart personified in human form being torn away from you and accepting it is indescribable. Accepting my husband's absence at the hands of misuse of a system meant to protect us did not sit well with my soul. Moreover, I was now in the process of establishing a plan to care for my husband's oldest son. At the time, little Mendeecees was around eight or so years old. Like most youth that age, he loved to wear hoodies, until they became an international symbol representing the acceptance of hatred for Black men and boys in America. I too sat in my living room and watched as the terror consumed my body during Trayvon Martin's public execution. The anxiety of knowing that we lived in a world where even my best efforts to protect the Black men in my life could fall short was tormenting.

The reality was that America was ok with a husband, father, and friend being torn away from his family and community for a crime he didn't commit and a little brown boy's life being stolen as he was innocently getting candy from the corner store.

Consumed with guilt, pain, and despair, I leaned heavily on Tamika to help me attain a clear vision of the world in which we lived and, more importantly, how to take action in it. The closer the time got for my husband to turn himself in, the more the whispers transformed into roars. Some proclaimed I thought I was better than the people around me, and others accused my husband of being a drug dealer. It was all slander being accepted as reality. My faith was shattered, and my ability to hope was compromised. Tamika was the only person who could understand and, more importantly, discern and lead. When I reached a breaking point, I called her. Instead of a speech or long-drawn-out exchange, our conversation was straight and to the point.

"I got you," she said.

At the time, I didn't know exactly what she meant, but I would soon learn.

"And now that you have your own source of understanding of this broken system, I want you to express what you feel with the world verbally," she urged.

In my head, I thought I was too broken to find the words that would adequately describe the hardship my family faced. Not only was Tamika encouraging me to lift my voice in front of audiences I knew, but also those I didn't. She began inviting me into spaces to create awareness the same way I had invited her to do the same.

When I expressed to her that I wasn't getting invited to these rooms, she replied, "Well, here's your invite. These rooms need your voice."

She constantly emphasized the importance of people like me being vocal, while insisting that the movement needed soldiers from all walks of life. Tamika knew that if I became vocal about the injustice happening right under my roof, the face of advocacy could be further evolved. She granted me a pass to speak freely in a space that would have never considered passing the microphone to me. Since I was on *Love & Hip Hop*, the brand was often demonized. We were actively fighting not to be canceled by many, but I knew our voices were yet worthy.

Even so, there were times I worried that if I was unaware or ceased to use the appropriate vernacular, I wouldn't be taken seriously or, far worse, heard. Tamika continuously eased those concerns, urging me to be myself and to speak truth to power. Both she and I laughed often about the shared insecurity, wondering whether or not we had the right words for the room. It was in this space that I realized activism to be a part of my purpose. It was the reason God granted me the influence garnered from being in the public eye for so many years prior. God placed me near Tamika to show me what activism in motion looked like. He allowed me to witness the fearlessness necessary to advocate for real change, had me near her, and this is what she does. I did not feel as though any of this was a coincidence. For me, activism became a source of healing. To know I wasn't just sitting back and letting the justice system dictate my life and that I was speaking out against injustice was the wind beneath my wings to keep going.

Tamika stood on the front lines for justice more times than I could count, fueled by history's scorn, heritage, and the series of events that transpired in her own life. Now I was standing on the front lines with her, motivated by my own need for activism fueled by my personal pain. What the world witnessed was a beautiful collision of two seemingly different worlds. A look beneath the surface revealed a myriad of similarities. We were far more alike than different. The energy exchanged and mutual understanding enveloped an unbreakable bond.

As we fought together, we grew together. Now, on the other side of the system, I witnessed Tamika's work and sacrifice in a totally different light. I had a front-row seat to the intricacies of her life and, more importantly, her internal struggles that resulted from the unspeakable pressure to be who she is. The outside world knew her to be powerful, resilient, and unbreakable, and she was all of those things, yet I now recognized she was human. There were moments when she questioned if she was doing enough to save us. And times when she felt she was not speaking enough, working alongside allies enough, writing enough, or spreading enough awareness. It was puzzling to me as her work never ceased. She woke up working, making phone calls, and taking meetings to form alliances. She went to sleep working, writing emails, and posting to keep the public aware of the injustices unfolding in the world around us. Witnessing her in this way made me love her even more. There was so much relatability. I was able to pull strength from her because she gave me a new fight. She gave me something to think about other than the fact that I was now a single mom, a role I had not believed myself to have signed up to do. Tamika's life was proof of the fact that I still had work to do. If she experienced tragedy and still woke up and put on a strong face to fight, then I too had the substance within me to take bookings and leave my baby with my mama and find someone to help my son be a young man. At the same time, I was trying to be an entertainer and maintain my status in that industry. Not once did Tamika bring up the headlines from the blogs or what they were saying about my family or my role on the show. She never made me question whether or not I was good enough for the movement, because she was the first to recognize that I too was fulfilling my purpose in that space. She did not make me feel like I did not belong in those spaces of activism. She made me feel like I was exactly where I was supposed to be, to reach those people too. With Tamika's encouragement, I realized that it didn't matter that I wasn't ready to get on the mic to speak out against injustice. Instead, she put me on the spot to speak up and made me realize I too was fighting against the breakdown of Black women. I too can be a voice for people who are like me. The people who are not considered role models and those not labeled as activists. My story was an example of the fact that it was possible to make it through. Her faith in me was empowering, and at that moment the sentiment I needed most was to be empowered. The closer Tamika and I became, the more I realized that she was the strong friend who needed to be checked on.

When I realized just how much she had been internalizing the torment from the Women's March, my heart ached for her. There were critics who said she wasn't Black enough, not vocal enough about Black issues and the plight of the Black woman, and others who deemed her not enough in general to lead such a magnificent charge. There were critics who expressed their disdain for her decision to attend the Nation of Islam's Saviours' Day. Unfortunately, society has always found a way to dehumanize Black women. From the moment we walked through the point of no return at the slave dungeons, America's assault on Black women has been woven into the fabric of our existence in this country. The attacks have always been centered around breaking down, belittling, and the removal of power from Black women. Nothing has changed. I've seen our husbands and the patriarchs of our families taken time and time again. I grew up in the projects and witnessed Black women denied Section 8 if a man was present in the house helping to raise the kids. I was too young to understand the intricacies and lasting effects of the absence of men in our homes, but today I recognize that our family units are incomplete without them. Tamika was a voice and forceful hand that ensured the violence and affliction that riddled our communities stopped. The attacks on her life, sanity, well-being, and disposition were abundantly clear. Not only were the attacks verbal but also financial. We watched her bookings dwindle away. We watched her speaking engagements at colleges, many of which were historically Black, cease. They called to say they were no longer interested in having her speak on their campuses. How could this have been the case when she was fighting for Black children and Black families? It was baffling to watch those who had been supporters turn their backs on her due in part to a false narrative being fed to the world. The outpouring of rejection and lack of support were hurtful to her. And although the public could not visibly see her wounds, I witnessed them. My only goal was to become the source of strength for her that she unquestionably became for me. No matter what the road ahead looked or felt like, I made a decision that I was going with her. Although in a different arena, I knew the pain of having your narrative be controlled all too well. Not on my watch. I had every intention to stick beside her. There was no limit to what I was willing to do to help her. Whether financially, emotionally, or physically, our journey had brought us full circle, and our bond was unbreakable.

When Tamika hit what I believe to be her lowest space, her body began literally breaking down. I witnessed moments when her knees ached and her legs stopped working. There were times when her back was hurting to the point of loss of mobility. Eventually, she opened up to me about the pills she had been taking and their adverse effects. By the time she confided in me, she had made the decision to go to rehab. Her concerns about being separated from everyone she knew and everything she loved were valid. It hurt me that I could not go with her or be there to assist her. It was agonizing in many ways because it felt like I was being refused the opportunity to be for her what she had been for me. And because of those factors, there was no single person, place, or thing that could stop me from being by her side when she returned home. After I made a call to Latoya Bond, who was managing both of us at the time, to request to be with Tamika, she made the necessary arrangements.

The first day I arrived, Tamika was in great pain. She was crying and weak. All I could do was be by her side and remind her that the pain would not last forever. I can remember physically carrying her to the bathroom, disrobing her, and washing her from head to toe. She needed to feel human again after such an arduous process. And while I washed her, I simultaneously prayed over her for a breakthrough. I prayed for her healing and full restoration. We were both vulnerable at the moment, as I had never washed an adult. Even so, there was no way I would allow my hands, heart, mind, or intentions to fail me. To fail her. She needed, wanted, and deserved to be cleansed from the residue of the pain the world inflicted. Not only did I bathe her, but I also changed her linen. For some reason, in my mind the act of doing so represented new beginnings.

Afterward, I lay in the bed beside her and we talked about nothing and everything. Although I had never grown up with brothers or sisters, there was no question that Tamika was now mine. The world had fought to take her joy away, and I was fighting in my own way to ensure it was restored. It was not only me who needed Tamika at her best. It was all of us. It amazed me that God packaged so much power into such a tiny frame. Her gift to challenge the world's darkness with light was like nothing I had ever seen. My heart was convinced that, in time, she would be back on her feet, fighting and restoring hope in the crevices of the world where it ceased to exist. She would return to bearing the weight of the world on her shoulders and standing tall for those whose legs failed them. She was the personification of the movement. Tamika D. Mallory represented the great hope of our people, which I was ready, willing, and able to defend. What neither of us could have known at the time was that God was preparing her for a powerful rebirth. She was, in fact, becoming the greatest version of herself. And every event leading up to that moment that set her back would prove to be an intricate part of the setup for her unprecedented success. Together, we learned that this unspeakable joy that rests inside the souls of Black people was not given to us by the world. Therefore, the world had no power to take it away.

—YANDY SMITH-HARRIS

CHAPTER 18

DON'T SHOOT

Sometimes less is more. If I had learned nothing else from my time at rehab, I was crystal clear I could not survive spiritually, mentally, or even physically if I did not find a way to simplify every aspect of my life. That meant how I lived, how I loved, and, most importantly, how I perceived myself in the world. I resolved to regain control of my thoughts, and granted myself permission to dictate my actions from that moment forward.

After finishing the last of the medication I was given in the program, I woke up on a Saturday morning with an urge to cleanse my house of every other medicine in my possession, with the exception of a bottle of Imodium I was advised to take for restless legs syndrome. I could now boldly claim victory over my addiction, and that was enough for me. Still slightly groggy, I entered the bathroom, in my pajamas, with internal marching orders to make the medicine cabinet anew. I didn't give a damn about brushing my teeth or washing my face first. All I could focus on was getting every ounce of medicine that inhabited the cabinets out and into the trash where it belonged.

Everything that hurt me was attached to a bottle. In a rage, I picked up a bottle filled with anger and torpedoed it into the trash can. I snatched a bottle labeled emptiness, opened its top, and poured the contents into the toilet. I took hold of bottles labeled inadequate and insufficient and threw them towards the wall. And the bottles bearing the labels fear, guilt, and loneliness were destroyed as I hurled them into the garbage where they belonged. By the time I was done, I was panting and sweating and my hair was disheveled. It didn't matter. Standing in front of the mirror for the first time in a long time, I had the courage to face myself. It had been forever and a day since I recognized the reflection staring back at me. And let me tell you something, she was a bad bitch. Right then and there, I knew there was not a single word that could be uttered that would prove powerful enough to break me like this ever again. Not words spoken by the news reporters. Not words spoken by naysayers. Not doubts whispered by some in my family. Not cautionary talk from some of my friends. Not even the innermost thoughts I verbalized to myself. No one. That day, I declared that if someone's opinion was of no value to me, their words had no power to take up residence in my head rent-free. This is not to say that I don't have real feelings that can be hurt, but never again would I allow anyone or anything to do to me what addiction had done.

About a week later, I was preparing for my first therapy session outside of rehab. Although I knew the power of therapy, it had not been a route I chose for my mental wellness, a decision that could have contributed to my breakdown in the first place. Considering I had fought so hard to convince the team at the rehabilitation center to allow me to leave early, I followed their recommendation to be seen by a psychiatrist, who would have the power to monitor me mentally and physically should additional support or prescriptions be needed. Begrudgingly, I accepted the help. I had no intent to threaten all of the work done to rehabilitate myself.

In preparation for the first session, I replayed so many thoughts in my head. More so, I questioned how I had gotten to the level of breakdown powerful enough to threaten my life. There was no question the emotional work necessary for my recovery would be a marathon, not a sprint. I also directed my attention towards getting rid of the physical pain that accompanied my addiction.

The visit was much different from what I imagined. I quickly learned that my time would be spent arriving at my own conclusions and awakenings. Through simple conversation, I was led to discover that I was responsible for overseeing the levels of anxiety I experienced. That ball was in my court. Although a hard truth, the energy exchanged around and through me was managed by me. I was also held liable for addressing the triggers in my life and the ways in which they manifested. What I had not known before my session was that the anxiety I experienced often presented itself through physical symptoms. Mannerisms ranging from easy agitation to claustrophobia or lack of being present at the moment or hearing those in my presence were symptoms that people who did not know me intimately could not have identified. When I left therapy, I had a new prescription that could not be housed in a bottle—peace. The greater question for me became how, in my line of work, I would manage to maintain it. And even though I didn't have the answers, I was confident that in time I would discover them. I began carving out several moments of each day to sit quietly. No phone. No TV. No noise. I was also taking naps strategically and listening to my body when I felt tired. Sleep was still something I struggled with, but I worked at it.

In the weeks to come, I could feel the benefits of the rest, and I was noticeably healing. I slightly changed my diet to include more balance. So much of what I consumed was a result of convenience, as I was always on the road and never at home long enough to enjoy home-cooked meals. More conversations on the phone with people who brought me joy, like my sister Sharon, my hilarious godsister Nadine, and my mother, to talk about nothing and everything became a source of healing. Together, we laughed about stupid things that weren't important, yet they were entertaining. We exchanged war stories and found fun in just being. I needed that. And then there was Tarique, who was navigating the world now for the first time on his own in college and as a Black man in America. He represented one of the populations I vowed to protect with my entire heart and soul. Whenever I spoke to him about the things happening in his life, it allowed me to forget about what was happening in my own. Hearing his voice meant that nothing else mattered. There was peace in the immersion into the lives of others and away from the struggle and strife of the movement.

After almost two full weeks of recovery at home, and away from work, the phone calls began again. As I understood it, the need for my work never left. It was I who needed to leave to save myself. Now, with what I felt to be a solid lifeline in place, I prepared to roll up my sleeves and get back to what I was born to do. Even though my mind felt ready, my body and my heart said otherwise.

———

For me, the break from work also meant a break from social media. I was out of the loop about much of what was unfolding in the world around me. The anxiety from the open floodgates of reports, updates, and DMs about the injustices of society was somewhat silenced. The day I logged back in, I was immediately overwhelmed. Not only was my feed inundated with normal internet drama, but my direct messages were swarmed with posts referencing the Metropolitan Detention Center in Brooklyn, New York. It was the image of a viral video of the prisoners banging on the walls with their cups that tugged on my heartstrings. It wasn't that I put my healing on hold, but rather on hiatus. There was yet work in our community to be done. Immediately, I called Linda, Mysonne and Angelo Pinto—an attorney and one of our movement colleagues—and we spent the remainder of the day strategizing to identify resources to do what we always did—activate. Although we had not formally established an entity of our own, we worked collectively.

Before that day, there had been ongoing informal discussions surrounding leaving the Women's March and establishing an organization representing us Black and brown folks that grew from whispers to roars. We clearly did not want to establish anything that only made space for women in leadership. We also welcomed the presence of our brothers as leaders as well. One of the takeaways we gathered from the Women's March was that movements established to benefit Black and brown people should not be void of the voices of men. Let me be clear, there is nothing wrong with women-led organizations, however for what we are passionate about, a model excluding men does not serve the purpose. Both Mysonne and Angelo were proof that the contributions of Black men are of too much value to be denied. Linda, Angelo, Mysonne, and I were movements by ourselves, but a mighty force when we worked together. The notion of two men, an attorney, an artist who happened to be formerly incarcerated, two women, a Palestinian Muslim, and me, aligning in the fight against injustice was quite possibly, to some, a far cry. Not to us. We were covering a lot of ground with the diversity in our leadership. While it may be true we did not have every part of our strategy figured out, we had what was most important—the will to fight as a collective.

The next morning, on what was noted as the historically coldest time of the year, we stood outside of the Metropolitan Detention Center in Brooklyn, New York, in solidarity with the imprisoned fighting for basic rights. They had been denied access to blankets and necessities to live.

From a lack of food to utilities, their means to survive were compromised. To make matters worse, a fire in the jail was also reported, further placing them in harm's way. We created a snowstorm of awareness. Our efforts garnered support from a myriad of people, including Jay-Z, who paid for an RV and groceries that allowed us to rest overnight at the site of the protest. Linda, Mysonne, Angelo, and I were on one accord, so much so that some believed we had already established our own organization. And those who knew we had not were vying for us to do so. Dr. Jamila T. Davis was one of them. She joined us at the detention center to show her support. She was so happy to get us alone for a pep talk. Dr. Davis is an author, activist, and professor, and had been incarcerated for almost a decade. She sought out a partnership with us. Dr. Davis was brilliant. She possessed an ability to spot talent from a mile away. She also had a way of activating people wanting to take action in the movement. I welcomed her into our circle with open arms. She knew firsthand there was a need for Linda, Mysonne, Angelo, and me to create a formal structure for the organizing we were already doing.

"You all need your own organization. It's time," she said.

Eventually, she helped Shaheim Harrison, one of the dopest graphic designers ever, to design what would become the official logo for Until Freedom, a name Mysonne—a master of marketing ideas—came up with. Something quick, catchy, and meaningful.

I credit Dr. Davis's encouragement as one of the motivating factors for why Until Freedom exists today. Dr. Davis eventually went on to found the multimedia entity called Black Women's Lives Matter. It has been a huge success, and a testament to the brilliance I always believed she had. She refused to wait for mainstream media to give steam to the stories and voices that she felt needed to be heard, devising a cancel-proof machine for media consumption.

———

While outside the detention center, we were in constant communication with elected officials who were ready, willing, and able to assist not behind the scenes but on the front lines. In New York City and many other cities across the nation, an elected official can visit a jail at any time to make an assessment. Their efforts included executing spot checks, which were wellness checks on certain individuals whose loved ones were concerned. On the ground, family members were telling us the names of their loved ones whom they believed to be in danger. Those were the names I shared with the elected officials. The longer we remained on the ground at the facility, the more families began showing up and living outside with us. We were all adamant about not leaving until we knew for certain that those on the inside were safe and the basic human needs of the imprisoned were addressed. The severity of the living conditions was both jarring and apparent. These guys were clinging to gates and jumping up the walls to be able to communicate with their families, and they were banging cups on the wall so people could hear them.

The protest was amplified when a young man inside, who happened to speak with his mother, saw her from the window. They were yelling back and forth in an attempt to communicate. His words were a piercing cry for help.

"It's cold in here, Mom."

Those words spoken from a child's mouth to a mother's ears are without question enough to rattle a soul. Overcome with emotion, she charged the gates, trying to enter the building. The desperation in the air was shared by many, and crowds surged into the building after her. Once they were inside, the guards Maced everyone who dared enter. Yandy was one of them. After years of organizing and protesting, you learn a thing or two about dealing with Mace. The fat in milk deactivates the compounds in the Mace. We knew this to be true, because Palestinian protesters shared the tip over Twitter with activists during the Michael Brown protests in St. Louis, Missouri. And thank God we had milk on hand, much of which was donated by supporters. It wasn't long before photos and videos of the incident began circulating on social media. I was reminded of the lack of sensitivity that some display in the face of torment and injustice. What's far worse is that there are times when these acts are committed by people who look like you.

DJ Funkmaster Flex on Hot 97 in New York posted a tweet that read: "The way that they just have the milk sitting around. This is such a gimmick." He was accusing us of having milk at the protest site in a staged effort.

His post agitated me, and I responded: "It's not that we had milk ready for someone to get Maced. The milk came from the groceries that we bought because we slept in the historically coldest weather outside and that milk was for coffee and breakfast and cereal."

Needless to say, he never responded. Instead of being quick to criticize our people, perhaps we should take the time to ask for clarification. As a people, we have been forced to lay a foundation with the bricks thrown by others, even at times when the hand closely mirrors our own.

———————

As my life was getting back on track, I got a call one day from a woman who was producing a series about celebrities and their mothers. The request was for us to film a TV pilot in Atlanta. Upon our departure from New York, I was still weak and fighting to regain a fraction of the weight lost while in rehab. When we arrived at the studios, there were whispers about my appearance. One of the producers made mention of it to me directly by saying that I didn't quite look like myself. It is likely that no one noticed the drastic changes in my appearance when we were at the detention center. Due to the extreme cold temperatures, we were all wearing several layers of clothing. Even so, there was no one unaware of what I had been through. They recognized the Women's March, coupled with years of activism, was enough for anyone to have been tired. They did not know about rehab. We were given very little information about the show's full scope or what would be required of us. The visibility was welcome as I attempted to reconstruct the building blocks of my career after their dismantling. While on set, I received a call that forever changed me.

"Tamika, I tried calling your mom but couldn't get her. It's Aunt Ola Mae. Y'all need to get here."

Although we had known for quite some time that she was ill, there is nothing more humbling than the call that reminds you death is certain. Both cancer and dementia had been taking a toll on her quality of life for the past three years. She deserved to be free of her pain, but it hurt nonetheless. My cousin Raven Norwood, who is still my personal support system whenever I'm in Atlanta and my go-to person, to hang out with, was on set with me. Together, we decided that the next day we would leave Georgia and drive to Monroeville, Alabama. Over the years, we'd received a few *you need to come now* calls, but somehow, hearing it about Aunt Ola Mae hit me differently. After notifying the producers, I spent the next hour filming the remainder of my segment. My heart was thankful that God positioned us to get to her sooner. The next day, we made the four-hour drive. When we arrived at the hospital, to our surprise, Aunt Ola was in a better state than she was when I received the call.

Laying eyes on Aunt Ola warmed my heart. It was the first time I'd seen her since dementia had taken its toll. She represented courageousness and the fight that was embedded in the DNA of our family. Even so, her body had grown so fragile, the rims of her eyes were heavy, and her breaths faint. She was in good spirits despite it all. Seeing her condition proved she was human, which meant that my mom was human too—a humbling admission. One I'd been forced to reckon with while at rehab. Instead of focusing on her declining condition, I absorbed as much joy as possible with her, my mom, and our other family members over the two days we were there. Together, we reminisced about old times while growing up and I listened to her children recount their childhood. Aunt Ola Mae could not participate much. Before this time, she was the life of the conversation. She was the keeper of the stories. That chapter had ended.

When my mom and I returned to New York, I vowed to be mindful that life is not promised. The notion was further confirmation of my personal battles. Instead of the pills, I was forced to look inward for comfort. Little did we know that just two days later my mom would receive another *you need to come now* phone call. Mom packed up once more, and within a week she went back. Now escorted by my dad, she made the decision to stay longer as my aunt hit another low.

In an attempt to move forward with life, I began allowing a few calls to be placed on my calendar. There was still unfinished business regarding the Women's March that needed to be handled. Taking it slow was not an option. Neither my body nor my mind could handle the same levels of overwhelm that had led to taking the pills in the first place. Time revealed I wasn't as strong as I thought I was. My attention was truant. I lacked focus and productivity. In spite of my best efforts, I couldn't work. My conscience wouldn't allow me to direct my attention towards anything except family. It was a blessing to know that so many family members were gathering around Aunt Ola Mae to love on her as she transitioned, yet there was an emptiness in the pit of my stomach because I wasn't.

At the last minute, on a Friday, I canceled my meetings and caught a flight to Alabama to surprise my folks. She was now at home after having been released from the hospital. Her bedroom was symbolic of so many moments for our family. It was the place where I was scolded as a child when I had not followed directions. It was also a place of praise when I had. (That rang true for all of the cousins.) More importantly, it was a place of healing for me. At that time, I knew that being in her presence could grant me a front-row seat to inspiration.

It was equally important to be physically present to support my cousins as they let go of their mother. My parents were also hurting. Both my mom and dad had grown up under Aunt Ola Mae's guiding hand. Family members were coming from across the nation. Anyone who knew her was coming to see her before she died. Aunt Ola Mae was our balm in Gilead. She had loved so hard that there was not one of us who could deny her impact in our lives. Now, with the tables turned, we resolved to be there to support her. It was a reminder to me that we arrive in this world vulnerable and we leave vulnerable.

My head and my heart needed to be with her and with those who loved me without condition. When I showed up at the entryway of her bedroom, I instantly locked eyes with my mom, who walked over and placed her arms around my neck. My dad followed suit, embracing us both. The closeness was a conversation between us, void of words. In their arms, I knew I was not alone, and they knew that, once again, everything in time would be ok. There was no question that it had been hard to love me. Not because I wasn't lovable but because I had never played the game of life by the rules. I had not been the child who did as I was told. My decisions were led by curiosity and my choices were made by passion without consideration of consequences. And not that they would have ever done anything other than love and support me. It was just that I had not always made it easy. It couldn't have been easy for them amidst the times I ran away from home and overlooked their directives. Despite it all, their mission to teach me what was best and to show me the way had not been in vain. And now, on the heels of my recovery that had likely shaken them to the core once more, they confirmed again I was worth fighting for.

For the remainder of the weekend spent in Alabama, my mom, dad, siblings, aunts, uncles, nieces, and cousins bonded through laughs and conversation. I grew up a little younger than and alongside Aunt Ola Mae's kids. Together, we cared for Aunt Ola Mae. Bathed her. Loved on her. Her house, where we had all been congregating for all of our lives, was filled with rumblings of loud storytelling. The buzz of cousins exchanging opinions about life. If you hadn't known any better, you would have assumed we were all gathered at Big Mama's house, just like in a scene from the movie *Soul Food*. It was as if Aunt Ola Mae was still in control. Even from her hospital bed in her room, she still managed to cement the family together. Aunt Ola Mae was the one who remembered birthdays, anniversaries, and special events. The one who made fighting cousins hug and make up and fighting spouses fall back in love again. She was the one who taught us that even if we fought among ourselves, we were never to let anyone under any circumstances outside of the family harm any one of us. She took no prisoners, and there wasn't a soul who minded. She was tough love personified, and we were all the better for it. She was a praying woman. She knew the Bible better than some pastors. Often, she would approach her own pastor after church to share with him her interpretation.

On Sunday, we gathered near her bed and prayed for Aunt Ola Mae. Although she was limited in speech, she could be heard murmuring scripture: "Lean not to thine own understanding" and "Though he slay me, yet will I trust in him."

Even as she transitioned, she spoke words of praise and power. There was no need to plead with God about Aunt Ola Mae's position in heaven. It was evident from the fruit of her life that she earned her wings long ago. Leaving her proved to be difficult, as I could almost guarantee that it would be the last time I saw her alive.

Even if I had somehow forgotten my own power, the life of my aunt Ola Mae served as a poignant reminder. She was, in many ways, the source of our family's strength. She was the matriarch, the healer, and the hope dealer. Her prolonged sickness was the warning shot, alerting us all that we would soon be forced to navigate the torrential waters of life on our own; however, not a single one of us was ready. My parents remained by her side until the day my mom called to tell me she was gone. After an extensive battle with cancer and dementia, she succumbed. On May 12, 2019, my mom called to tell me that our family had lost the woman who was unquestionably the glue.

When I hung up the phone, I resolved to take with me the memories. Aunt Ola Mae was, without a doubt, sunshine after the rain. The showers of Aunt Ola Mae's life were cleansing for me. Her memory remains a beautiful garden of grace and mercy that continues to follow me.

———

Not only had I lost Aunt Ola Mae, but I also felt as though I was losing myself. My financial disposition went from bad to gruesome as opportunities to speak and paid appearances came to a screeching halt. There is a hidden tax of activism that no one speaks about. A burden so heavy that, if you aren't careful, it can leave you destitute, with little to no resources to support yourself or your family. It's daunting not to be able to pay your bills and torturous when your hands are frozen while your heart yearns to serve and to advocate for the most vulnerable. At this juncture in my life, I was vulnerable in ways I had never been at any other point in my career. I was still fighting to regain my strength. Darkness was all around me. Even when I looked out the window, and even if the sun was shining, it was increasingly difficult for me to see hope.

I needed inspiration again and found it with Linda. She gave me the fuel and permission to allow myself to dream again about getting back to work. During one of our conversations, she introduced me to the work of George Soros, a Jewish Hungarian-American philanthropist who was well known for his contributions to a multitude of causes. She informed me that his organization Open Society Foundations (OSF) had launched a fellowship program that awarded large-sum grants for executing projects they believed to be deserving of funding. For me, applying was a no-brainer. I needed work and I had the perfect program in mind that the Black church needed as well.

The proposal process was arduous. It required a great deal of writing to flush out my ideas fully and to establish the need for my desire to revisit my previous commission to address the loss of connectivity between the Black church and the movement. There was a time when it was more common for activists to work in tandem with pastors to incite change. Somewhere along the way, we lost the threads that wove our value systems and common fight together. Whether we were out in the streets pumping our fists or standing in the pulpit preaching hope, there was a time when we, the majority of us, came together because we were Black.

In those spaces, we were powerful. Times are different now, but I wanted to work towards the restoration of the past. Today the discussion, or should I say omission, of Black churches and their relevance in the movement saddens me.

So many of my friends who are pastors have amazing ministries rooted in social justice. Often those same ties grant them access to the hearts, minds, ears, and souls of our people, therefore I knew what I was working on was possible. My submission to OSF was hopeful about the idea of restoration. Working on the proposal reminded me that better tomorrows do exist. This was the first time I was excited again. Linda was there as a quiet supporter to keep me calm. On most days, the passion and need for change overruled that I didn't have much money and was dealing with so many changes in my life. Sure, I was still being paid from the Women's March, but it wasn't nearly what I was used to. Although I had known better than to place all of my eggs in one basket, the other prospects of bringing in funds had not yet materialized.

Somehow, I believed that God would make a way. And he did. By September, I saw the first glimmer:

> We wish to congratulate you on your acceptance to the 2019 Class of Fellows.

Tears covered my cheeks before I could finish reading the acceptance letter. Sitting in silence, I closed my eyes and gave God thanks in the midst of my sorrow. The lump in my throat was a gathering of all the emotions that stemmed from days of questioning how I was going to make it. God proved once again that when he closes a door he has already prepared a window of opportunity. I was awarded $100,000 to establish and implement the program submitted in the proposal. In spite of the major victory of being accepted as an Open Society Fellow, my hardships were far from over. It's no secret that grant money takes significant time to materialize. This grant was set to pay out in two separate installments of $50,000 each. To some, it might sound like I'm complaining about this investment. I'm not. Most folk would not believe the expenses I carry and the people I support. Financially, I needed to reexamine everything. If I hadn't been ready to face the fallout from the Women's March, I was ready to do so now. After almost seven months of our attempts to turn a blind eye to the consistent flow of defeatist headlines in the news and media and instigators hell-bent on agitating the organizational structure from within, Bob, Linda, Carmen, and I resolved to ignite a series of meetings to discuss our options in-depth.

Everything was weird. The glimmer of hope for the global change I once had was dim at best. This wasn't one of those times when I saw something special and new coming together. This was one of those times when the bottom had literally fallen out. The whispers regarding resignation were still present. Now for all of us, as opposed to the initial request of just mine, the public failed to realize that we held the incorporation documents for the Women's March. No one could force us to leave. We were the founders of the organization. It was Bob's and my names that appeared on the bank account. Despite popular belief, it was Bob Bland and I as co-presidents who held the power to decide who went and who stayed. We were also aware that doing so would come with its own set of consequences. There were now more white women attached to the brand, many of whom believed the organization was theirs in theory.

Some months before, I called a number of women whom I respect and trust to ask their opinion of how to move forward. Dream Hampton was one of them. Dream is a renowned filmmaker, producer, and writer. She told me that I would have to leave the Women's March. At the time, it didn't resonate with me. I was resentful of her telling me to walk away from an entity that I was instrumental in building, but there I was feeling that tugging again, confirming it was, in fact, time for me to leave. Dream, you were right.

Imagine living in a house that you built with your bare hands. There are attributes about it that are sentimental to you. It is likely you have taken the time to discover special rooms in the house that are attached to special feelings. We'd built the Women's March with our bare hands. We had sacrificed so much of ourselves to do so. Not only had we compromised time with our family and friends, but there were also business opportunities left unexplored, sleepless nights, abandonment of pride, exposure to shame, and being subjected to scrutiny. There was not one of us who had not lost a part of ourselves that we could never get back. Pieces that we were more than willing to give, especially when we believed the ascension of the greater good was the return.

But the house, as beautiful as it may have been, was now haunted.

Inhabited by unwelcomed guests. Jealousy, deceit, resentment, spite, suspicion, and even hatred were allowed to have a seat at the dining room table. Love was no longer being served. We could not deny it even if we wanted to. And maybe we were to blame in many ways. Believing that women, regardless of race, had the internal moral compass to unite in the face of perceived and confirmed danger or leadership that did not have our best interest in mind. Perhaps we were too trusting in humanity. None of it mattered. The spirit of toxicity among the members consumed the space and we were depicted as the culprits when, in fact, we were just the opposite.

Our meetings were filled with hot air. There was a myriad of emotions present that had been earned. We could have stayed. However, we were torn on what the right decision was and how to best move forward. If we had made the decision to fight in an effort to prove that the organization belonged to us, the toxic energy would still linger. The decision to leave or stay and rebuild was not an easy one to make and there was much to be considered. There was a discussion of extending our terms and getting rid of everyone inside the organization. There was the consideration of amending the bylaws in an effort to reestablish the organizational structure. We also talked through what a complete exodus would look like. Knowing that I was even remotely considering letting go of an entity in which my name was on the incorporation documents was most difficult.

"Fuck that. We don't have to give up what we built to anybody," I preached.

Linda was extremely vocal while offering another point of view. "Tamika, while I agree with you, at some point we have to start asking ourselves if this fight is really worth it."

Bob chimed in, "I just don't know. We are literally killing ourselves to stay in a place where we're being mistreated. And if we decide to kick every person out of the organization and start from scratch, then what do we have?"

Linda continued, "If we stay with these people and keep trying to work with them, it is going to kill us. The only way is that everyone will have to go immediately."

Carmen had an indescribable look on her face. She too was dealing with the stress of those who did not consider or care about her personal life as a new mother and wife. The poor girl was all messed up.

With the passage of time it had also occurred to us that doing the work of the Women's March had removed us from working directly with the people we believed to be the most vulnerable. Those who shared the same values and goals for which we were called to serve. Over the course of a few weeks, our strategy meetings turned into think tanks as we addressed the real issues we were facing and the real emotions behind them. Our time together allowed us to be vulnerable with one another, and it was necessary.

The more we turned it over, the more we recognized we were in bondage. How could it be possible that you embark upon a quest to free people, yet you are enslaved? The need and want to be free gave us permission to stop caring what anyone had to say. We made the decision together in our late-night conversations, and that was that. Freedom from that situation began to sound good instantly. In the back of my mind, my recovery was also a consideration. Bob and Carmen were unaware of what I had gone through. Linda, on the other hand, was aware, and much of her commentary and pleading for us to consider our options with clear heads versus emotional hearts was in consideration of this fact. Of all the women represented, she knew firsthand how much of a toll the march had taken on me. It took a toll on her as well, having been hospitalized for ulcers from the stress. Carmen was devastated in the aftermath of the march and fighting like hell to regain control of her emotions as her hormones realigned, a battle that was enough in and of itself. She was crying a lot and emotionally drained, but she stayed at the Women's March for a while so that we would have representation.

The final stage of giving myself permission to be free from the grasp of the Women's March came in my pastor's study. He prayed with me and spoke the words that I so desperately needed to hear from him.

"We've been here before. God has brought you through decisions you've made, good and bad," he said. "God brought you through when you left NAN. He brought you through when Tarique's father was murdered. He will bring you through this. Today may be a new challenge, but we serve the same God."

In his presence and before God, I let go. Although I knew my body was sitting on a couch, when I closed my eyes and fell backward it felt as if I were falling from the sky. In that moment, I gave up everything that had weighed me down.

By the time I arrived at what would be one of our final meetings, I was made over from the inside out. My mental switch had flipped from *let's determine how we can save this organization* to *fuck this shit*. With approximately three months to go before our term ended, I resolved to move differently.

Our discussions transitioned towards a strategy for our exit. We considered how to avoid scrutiny from the media while standing in our truths about the unfolding series of events. In retrospect, I recognize that some of my decision-making was based entirely on ego. A rational mind knows that if you dump everyone from an organization and keep going the narrative cannot be favorable. People are apt to be accusatory. Our goal was to avoid further accusations at all costs as well as not to be the scapegoat for the demise of a powerful women's movement. There have already been too many.

Not only was leaving the right choice, but it also proved to be telling. Whatever they are doing now is quite frankly not comparable to what we did. The momentum of the Women's March was never about a brand. It rested on the backs of those who carried it. And now that we are not there, the feeling is not the same. My decision to leave the Women's March was one thing. Life thereafter was another. Perhaps I had not considered all that could unfold in the aftermath. Perhaps there was no way I could think of all the possibilities and ways that life would be different. So much of who I was and even who I aspired to become was tied to the Women's March. My role with the organization wasn't just a job. For me, it was a calling—destiny perhaps. And now it was a tattered memory. A couple of months following our resignation, I woke up early per usual and decided to make a quick run to the grocery store to pick up a few items. Some fresh oranges, a carton of strawberries, and a few gallons of water. Transitioning from the aftermath of the march and everything else that happened, I kept telling myself I would only eat fruits or vegetables until at least noon each day in an effort to be more healthy.

On the way back inside the house from the store, I picked up the mail and tossed it on the coffee table in front of the couch before washing off the fruit and slicing an orange. I took a bottle of water from the refrigerator and drank slowly. After placing the orange slices on top of the strawberries in a bowl and tearing off a few sheets of paper towel, I headed back towards the living room with the fruit in one hand and the water in the other. I plopped down on the couch and sank back into the pillows. My plan was to remain in that same space for the day.

Back inside the privacy of my house, I was brave enough to check my account balance. The balance read, four hundred dollars. It was more than I thought it would be, yet not enough to cover any of the forthcoming bills set to hit at the top of the following week. That four hundred was all I had left to my name. The fucked-up part of it all was that I had done so much to put money into other people's pockets, yet I had nothing to show for it. The Open Society money wasn't set to hit for a while. Sure, I had advocated for many who were less fortunate than me and those living in marginalized communities, but what good was it all if I couldn't sustain myself? What was it all worth? If there were a way for me not to have been mad at God, I would have chosen it, but I was. Why had he called me to do this work? Why had I been chosen to sacrifice so much to, in turn, end up with so little? And by "little" I don't mean the impact. It was there. Proof that I existed in this life was there. Proof that I had made a difference was there. The evidence was embedded in the change, the comfort of the families served, and the hard justice won. Tamika, the activist, was rich, but Tamika, the human, well, that remained to be seen. The financial fallout of the anti-Semitic rhetoric assigned to my name after the Women's March could no longer be denied. There were no requests for me as a speaker. Donations for many of the causes I worked towards had been absorbed.

———

By the first day of December 2019, I was sitting on the side of the bed, agonizing over how I would survive the holiday season. If I had not understood artist Annie Lee's iconic painting *Blue Monday* before, I understood it then. A Black woman in distress, struggling to get out of bed, was the fullness of art imitating life for me. There was not enough money to cover the cost of my bills in the coming month. My car was in jeopardy of being repossessed, and Christmas was an afterthought. The only thing that saved the month of December was the monetary gifts that my friend Lu-Shawn Thompson, Charlamagne tha God, and Amanda Seales sent to me. It was the first time ever that I could not do anything for Tarique. In years past, I made decisions about what I would get him based on several factors. The beauty was that I had the choice. On that day, there was no choice. There were no other options than to be still. And although I spent the holidays with my family, I fell victim to the guilt of consumerism. I had been a cheerful giver. I also hosted parties, and created moments for memories that would last us a lifetime, but this year I did not have the capacity to do so, and it hurt like hell. I was fortunate to be surrounded by love and people who had little to no concern for what I could give. My family has always been more concerned with who I was as a person, a value I have also worked hard to instill in Tarique.

The coming days were much of the same. Calls with Linda to strategize, moments staring out of the window, asking God to intervene, and opening bank statements with negative balances, all while fighting to remind myself that I was worthy.

The climactic moment of questioning myself and possibly even my worth happened at the top of the New Year. On an actual Blue Monday, infamously one of the most depressing days of the year as families struggle to recover from the holidays while awaiting their next paycheck, I sat at the kitchen table with sweaty palms and shaking hands. I was fresh out of options and ideas. I was searching my mind for the words to type in a text message to trusted friends and confidants to ask for help. Everything I had ever requested was to be used to help others. Never in my life had I asked anyone to give me money for personal expenses, but on this day it was a final choice between feast and famine. I was in need of a lifeline.

> Happy New Year, Family. I hope this message finds you relaxing and getting prepared for an amazing year and decade. I usually don't send personal financial appeals. However, many of you always ask how you can help and now is a time when I need you. If you are able to support me by sending any amount large or small, I would be eternally grateful.
>
> [I included all the addresses for Cash App, Venmo, Zelle.]
>
> Love, Tamika

Pressing the send button was even more painful than the process of drafting the message. I hurled the phone towards the bed. I was angry with myself for going through with sending the message. I was embarrassed. I was broken.

Almost immediately, there was a notification. I closed my eyes and inhaled deeply before retrieving the phone from the floor.

Is this you who sent this text?

The reply came from Brian Benjamin, my friend and New York State Senator at the time. It was proof that my plea for help was almost unbelievable. Even those closest to me know I would have never made such a request. I didn't have the bandwidth to reply at the moment. I sat with my head held down and the phone still in my hands. Within the hour, almost everyone responded, among them Yusef Salaam of the Central Park Five, Brian, a New York State Senator, and Kim Blackwell, an award-winning brand strategist. I watched my Cash App notifications go off as joyous cascades of tears ran down my face. There were just two people on the list who did not give. One who is also in the movement responded to say they too were having financial issues. I stopped immediately to pray for them as I prayed for myself.

The other person didn't respond at all, which was further humiliating. Knowing that someone knew my personal business, and didn't acknowledge it in my eyes, meant it would likely become afternoon gossip. The hard truth here is that not every season of life is a winning season. Admittedly, 2019 was one of the worst years of my life. Death, defeat, and dread were all a part of my journey. I've heard it stated that adversity is among our greatest teachers. There was no question: class was in session.

CHAPTER 19

ALRIGHT

"Let freedom ring." These words, implanted in my heart from years past, embodied the sentiments of my soul. I knew without question that Linda, Mysonne, Angelo, and I needed to get back to work. We also needed to continue brainstorming the blueprint for a collective entity of our own. The poison of white nationalism was persistent. It always has been. There can be no equality in the absence of justice. For my people, the fight has been about the preservation of life and legacy, historically and present day. Just after ringing in the New Year, a phone call from my mother became the voice of reason.

"Tamika, you've been down. It's time to put on your big girl panties," she urged.

That was one of many true statements she made on that call. It was one of the realest conversations we had before her stroke. She was right—about everything. Not only was I attempting to recover from personal financial hardship but I was also grappling with a number of stories about injustice happening across the country I was being made aware of, and at the time I just didn't have the capacity to engage. Not mentally. Not physically. Not financially. One of those stories was about Parchman Prison. It was a facility built in the early 1900s and fashioned to operate similarly to a traditional plantation. From the looks of things they had succeeded. Parchman Prison was the next resounding alarm, alerting Linda, Mysonne, Angelo, and me that there was more work to be done. A closer look into the conditions revealed an abundance of mold in the cells, floods, mass violence, bloody walls, and even a video of a man hanging in a cell. People were dying. It was a true crisis.

On January 4, 2020, an ongoing group text that had been silent over the holidays between Linda, Angelo, Mysonne, and me was reengaged.

"I just want to see if this thing is still working," Angelo texted.

"Testing 1 . . . 2 . . . 3," Linda replied.

"Welcome back," Mysonne added.

Their messages were symbolic that it was time to get back to work.

A day later, I responded. Instead of jovial greetings, I sent a series of photos depicting dead bodies of imprisoned men who had been tortured and traumatized. It was horrific proof that Parchman Prison was in a state of emergency. Within days, we heard from our longtime colleague in Jackson, Mississippi, Rukia Lumumba of the Mississippi Prison Reform Coalition, sister of Jackson mayor Chokwe Antar Lumumba and daughter to their father and respected human rights leader Chokwe Lumumba Sr. She was supporting our work with the Metropolitan Detention Center in Brooklyn from afar and wanted to collaborate to bring some of that energy down south. Her group was determined to gain national attention about the atrocities happening at Parchman Prison. She asked us to come.

My response to Rukia's call for collaboration was without hesitation: "We're on the way."

But I knew we had no money or resources to travel or to fight the government in Mississippi. And we were still developing Until Freedom. Future board chair Monique Idlett hosted in her Florida home as we put the new organization on paper. After much consideration, I thought about an entity that had vowed to support us previously in the past: Roc Nation. Although we had received support from Roc Nation during our work at the detention center, there had been no formal communication up to this point. In 2019, Jay-Z entered a partnership with the NFL to enhance the halftime show and to amplify social justice causes. There were mounting tensions between the NFL and the general public due to a fallout with Colin Kaepernick. Three years prior, in 2016, Colin launched his protest of the national anthem, choosing to kneel during a game while calling attention to the continued killing of Black men by law enforcement. Many were boycotting the NFL at this time. Colin was mercilessly attacked for his protest, and I, among others, organized to support his First Amendment rights. We were just as angry with the NFL. We even collaborated with a number of groups and individuals to hold a rally outside their headquarters, where thousands of people gathered in his defense.

Recognizing the announcement of Jay's partnership with the NFL, I posted the following on Instagram:

Tell Jay-Z to call me please.

There were people who assumed that I wanted to join the chorus of those condemning Jay for working with the NFL. Some people even commented, "Who the hell do you think you are? Jay ain't calling you." Leave it to the internet haters. In my next book I will write about the *online know-it-alls*. There were others who affirmed that I was one of the people Jay needed to be in touch with. The assumptions and accusations about Jay's intentions with the NFL were all over the place. Contrary to what everyone else thought and said, I have learned to do my own research. I also wanted to do what I felt had not been done for me amidst the public attacks on the Women's March. I wanted to gain understanding from Jay directly rather than making condemning statements from afar, and since his partnership with the NFL was to support social justice efforts, we wanted to be on his radar.

Within minutes of making the post, I received a text message from a friend who was sending the number for someone in Jay's camp. Then, Charlamagne called me. We spoke briefly. He said he saw my post and liked the idea of me working with Roc Nation. He suggested I speak with Desiree Perez, who ran all of Jay's affairs and has since been named CEO of Roc Nation. When the right people are involved, movement can happen—just that fast. A meeting was arranged, and in a matter of hours, I was strategizing our first steps. It was a testament to who Jay really is and how he moves. Since Charlamagne was already good friends with Mysonne, it was a natural instinct for him to vouch for our work. It was Mysonne who had introduced me to Charlamagne in the first place, and Jay was no stranger to Mysonne himself. They met each other through the music industry prior to Mysonne's wrongful seven-year prison term.

Still, my observations of the NFL's efforts to address injustice were marred by mixed emotions, and I expressed those feelings in subsequent meetings with the Roc Nation team. They never required me to be silent in exchange for their partnership. Colin, on the other hand, was someone whom I had always supported. It is admirable that he did not hesitate to stand firmly on his beliefs, even in the absence of the support of many. As I sit with it now, I wish that his brave stance had been more connected with the larger movement. There was no question that Colin did his part, but I will always wonder what could have happened if there was more of a connection between the energy Colin's courage generated and the movement at large. When it was announced that Jay partnered with the NFL to tackle social justice issues, many, including myself, feared the NFL would move past accountability. Black people had no reason to trust the NFL. If allyship had been so important to the league, why hadn't they offered more support to Colin? Although I didn't have all the answers, I listened to Desiree and Jay talk about their plan to establish a space for many stakeholders, lawyers, and activists doing grassroots work to come together as a collective while helping all of us scale up the power of our impact.

Weeks later, we sat down with Desiree in person. She had a vested interest in not only helping *us* access the capital we needed to move our organization forward and put our work in action but also in curating a viable plan to stabilize the work of many other groups. This coalition came to be known as the United Justice Coalition (UJC). UJC is led by a beautiful sister named Dania Diaz, who is the director of philanthropy at Roc Nation. Off the bat, I could see Dania was passionate about social justice. Working with the Roc Nation team gave us a sense of independence. They operated beyond the whims of the media attacks we had faced and above the organized targeting of our funding and sponsorships. They were not moved by the negative energy of people who were just plain jealous. Earning their support and counsel was a significant turning point for Until Freedom. As God would have it, we didn't have to do much to convince Desiree's team to support us on Parchman. Roc Nation was already involved and aware of what was happening. We combined our efforts in advocacy work; they funded the legal team of professionals, and we harnessed our efforts towards exposing the true conditions of the prison and forcing some changes. As a result, the nation was finally aware of the ills of Parchman Prison. Let's be very clear, there's still much work to be done to close Parchman Prison for good, but our involvement helped to inject a major dose of energy towards that goal.

In addition to our being on the ground in Mississippi, we were also working with Desiree behind the scenes to get our business affairs in order for Until Freedom. She helped us assemble an annual budget, tighten up the narrative about our organization, and create a target list of potential supporters. These simple acts empowered us to streamline our efforts and to get clear about who we could best serve and how.

In spite of the significant work done and access gained to a new set of resources, our attempt to tackle the Parchman Prison crisis was not easy. When we arrived, some of the local organizers were not welcoming. They wanted us to go back to where we had come from. There were others who were grateful we showed up. There's always a hidden concern that the work of local activists will be overshadowed for the personal gain of outsiders. This is the same scenario that played out in Washington, DC, with the Women's March. The truth is that many people were doing the work to close Parchman long before we were ever made aware of the injustice. Their movement was long-standing and arduous. Many lived in the community and had the harsh conditions directly impact relatives inside, which meant their own lives as well. The local organizers were already in the process of planning their own march. Some of those who were appreciative of our support began to give us some of the details. One of the problems was funding, as is the case with all grassroots efforts. We joined forces to gather the resources to help pay the expenses, while bringing in additional participants, who expanded the reach of their efforts. Roc Nation put boots on the ground and embedded themselves in the community. They paid invoices and heard the concerns directly from the people. Jay and Desiree put up a billboard that publicly exposed the ills of Parchman to everyone who might have not been aware up to that point. It was not a good look for Governor Tate Reeves. Jay even helped produce a film for the A&E Network called *Exposing Parchman,* which was nominated for an Emmy Award.

As an organizer, it was a dream come true to watch a tapestry of time, talent, and treasure be woven together to create impact. The increased awareness meant increased accountability. The result was an announcement by the Department of Justice that deemed the practices at Parchman Prison unconstitutional. A lawsuit was filed on behalf of a number of incarcerated folks and the prison was finally forced to make *some* changes. Parchman is an ongoing fight—one I would not deem a victory until the facility is demolished. The fight against white supremacy and slavery by another name (thank you, Douglas Blackmon) is one step at a time—one day at a time.

In an era when so many others were hesitant to work with me and actively blocked me from spaces, Jay and Desiree embraced our work. I will always love and appreciate them for this, among many reasons. Until Freedom was now a brand-new entity with viable support. Together, we proved we were ready to work. And there was plenty of it.

Progress was being made on all fronts. Not only was my work with Until Freedom in motion, but my acceptance as a grantee for the Open Society Soros Equality Fellowship manifested into a trip to Puerto Rico to meet with other recipients. The last two days while there, I extended an invitation for Linda to fly out to join me with the goal of strategizing and locking in on the next steps for Until Freedom. We spent the day securing all of the digital real estate for the name. From Facebook to Instagram and the URL. They were all available. It was at that moment we knew the name Mysonne suggested was right all along. That afternoon, we made our way to the beach to debrief. I can remember Linda carving the words "Until Freedom" in the sand with a stick. The sun's glimmer was all the confirmation I needed that we were heading in the right direction.

The trip to Puerto Rico earmarked a public announcement of the fellows. During this time, whenever my name was mentioned in conjunction with a public announcement, controversy seemed to follow. The internet started buzzing again, accusing me of taking money from a man with an alleged hidden agenda. This was a far-right talking point by people who endeavored to discredit our movement. Let them tell it, he and I were conspiring. While I am thankful for his investment in a project that I believed was necessary then and still necessary now to revitalizing the movement, there were no ulterior motives or agendas. The truth is that I've never met George Soros himself. In fact, most of the people who worked with me throughout the process of my application review were Black and brown people I knew from the movement. Unfortunately, there are times when Black folks pick up the narratives of the very people they claim to be fighting against and use it to disparage their own. If George Soros's agenda is to allow people like me to come up with ideas and fund them with no strings attached, no commitment to a further agenda whatsoever, then I'm all for it. No representatives from the Open

Society Foundation interfered with our work after we submitted for the fellowship. It was a black-and-white process. I am certain this was the case for other fellows as well. Unfortunately, there are people who like to create a narrative that George Soros is some kind of mythical being pulling the strings on society from afar, which is just not true. I haven't found anyone who can give me clear information to prove that he is a big bad wolf, and my instincts are that I never will.

———

By the close of January 2020, the Open Society Foundation Fellowship grant was funded, and I was in execution mode. My first order of business was reaching out to pastors within my immediate network to get them on board for the new initiative. The response was overwhelming. This meant so much to me coming out of a time when I felt people were skeptical about working with me. Even if it was just in my mind, I was feeling isolated. It was good to have friends reaffirm me. There were several of my ministerial buddies who were excited to see how they could support me. Lo and behold, this was the project and platform to do so. Bishop Rudolph McKissick, who is one of my best friends in the whole wide world, of Jacksonville, Florida, agreed to be a co-chair of this new project. This was huge. He knew everyone. He was well loved and supported by many. He was also a strong voice for social justice in Florida.

For a little over a month, I spent time researching other pastors who supported social justice as a part of their mission. The whole point of this project was to engage new voices. It was bothersome to me that I heard so many young activists complaining that they did not feel welcomed in the church, and I was determined to bridge the gap. My experiences were totally different, which was why I was so passionate about restoring the connection. These same young people communicated their lack of access to resources to run their operations, such as working internet access and tech such as printers and monitors, at a large scale or their lack of adequate places to meet. It was troubling. This was one of the very problems I wanted to solve by connecting churches with the people and advocates who did not have accessibility. My foundational learning was that the church was the home of the movement. We were seeing less of that in the wake of the BLM explosion. Over the years, pastors and elected officials began working closer together. Some of them, rightfully so, began to focus more on their professional ambitions. I believe that this caused a rift between the church and movement. There were more who were beginning to believe that the church was no longer the common meeting place for the movement. I am one who appreciates the personal and professional growth of everyone, including pastors, activists, and any other leader, but I have always believed there must be a way to include real social justice concerns in all of our ministries. Some activists felt like pastors were selling out. I didn't see that as the case. The divide has played out before our eyes. Moreover, the LGBTQIA+ community, who were very vocal in the BLM movement, felt less and less welcomed. My goal was to push against the idea that we could not join forces. I was taking calls, traveling to large church meetings and conventions, and constructing a plan. At the same time, the news was beginning to report on a mysterious virus that plagued Wuhan, China. There were even whispers of travel precautions being implemented. We were on the brink of a global crisis.

ACROSS THE LINE

By February, the World Health Organization announced the official name for the disease that was causing the 2019 novel coronavirus outbreak: CORONAVIRUS DISEASE AKA COVID-19. A month later, the United States declared a public health emergency, and restrictions on travel were tightened. There was still no way of knowing the magnitude of the impact of the crisis. It was still too early. That month, I was a member of the host committee for a women's empowerment retreat, alongside Yandy, my manager, Latoya Bond, and several other influential women, to be hosted in Mexico. On the tenth day of March, I extended my time to remain in Mexico for a few additional days to strategize how I would pivot in the implementation of the programming with the churches considering the impacts of COVID-19 and to figure out the rest of my life. I went to the spa and vibed alone. My goal was to be quiet and process my thoughts. In my heart, I could feel that something big was happening, but I had no way of knowing what that might be. All I knew was that I had to be ready. And by "ready," I mean quiet enough to hear from the creator about what my assignment might be. At every other point in my life, he always directed me and ordered my steps. This time was no different.

Although I was already missing the girls with whom I'd spent time reconnecting at the retreat, I was thankful to have time to hear from myself. There was peace in the quiet. My body of work, the impact made, and rehab were proof that I had come too far to turn around, but the question of where I was headed in life remained. By the time I made it to the water, I pleaded with God for a sign and for answers about how to move forward. The movement and sound of God's creations have a way of making you stop to appreciate *Him*. As I walked closer to the shore, I closed my eyes and allowed the sand to fill the crevices of my toes. The gusts of wind were in sync with the waves, and by the time I could feel the water sweeping over my feet I was overtaken by the presence of peace, I knew God was with me. Instead of speaking to me, he stood beside me. If I had learned one thing in rehab, it was that a quiet mind was the pathway to answers. Enlightenment and direction were exactly what I was in search of while trying to conceptualize the impact Linda, Mysonne, Angelo, and I could have now as a formal collective. The words "Until Freedom" continued to ring in my mind. I turned them over, dissecting their meaning and examining how they would take shape in our work. Where there is confirmation, there is power.

Eventually, I walked back to the resort to have lunch. While seated, I could hear my phone vibrating on the table. I hadn't even noticed that this was the second missed call from my sister Sharon. Just as I attempted to call her back, she was calling again. I was smiling and excited to tell her about my mental progress. My sister is my biggest cheerleader. Sharon was extremely worried considering all I had been through. This was my moment to ease her concern.

"Hey, kid, what's up?" I answered, grinning from ear to ear.

"It's Mom. She had a stroke. It's not good," Sharon said.

A numbness came over me that removed my ability to speak. "I don't have much more. I'm on the way there. I'll call you back when I know." She hung up. I could hear her rushing. My body felt faint.

The tips of my fingers were numb as I began searching on my phone for flights while tears streamed down my face. Considering that it was late afternoon, there were no flights out that night. It was torture knowing there was nothing I could do immediately to help Mom. The ongoing news from the CDC warning of a global crisis didn't help. All I could do was dial the numbers of every family member possible to gather bits and pieces of information. Venturing back towards the resort, I was inconsolable. There was not one familiar person at the resort. Strangers stopped me in my tracks, attempting to help me. Nothing could be done. When I returned to my room, I booked a 6:00 a.m. flight for the next morning. Instead of sleeping, I spent the night pacing and praying and calling everyone for hours. When I wasn't pacing, I sat slumped over at the edge of the bed, counting the minutes until it was time for me to depart. One of the staff members at the hotel checked on me frequently throughout the night. She also arranged a car free of charge to take me to the airport.

The plane ride was grueling. In an effort to make the time go faster, I purchased the onboard Wi-Fi and began scrolling on social media. As I was scrolling, I noticed a post from my father that was completely out of character. To this day, he only shares birthdays and history lessons. This post was jarring. It read:

Please pray for us. My wife had a stroke. It's not looking good.

Pressing a sweater into my face, I wailed. My levels of anxiety soared to see his silent plea for help while flying. In retrospect, I now know that no one was telling me exactly what was happening. They were vague about her condition because they didn't want me to worry, since I had been so far away. None of it worked. I was out of my mind. It was only by the grace of God the lady sitting next to me was sound asleep, or she too would have been exposed to the horror unleashed in my seat.

———

Times of need allow us to see who we can count on. The minister of Mosque No. 7 in Harlem, Brother Hafeez Muhammad (May God rest his soul, he later died from complications with COVID-19), and my Brother Hasaun Muhammad arranged to have a car ready to pick me up and take me from the airport straight to the hospital. I needed them more than ever. While I was en route, the warnings from the CDC reinforced the need for adequate precautions against the COVID-19 virus. No one was safe. It occurred to me that after traveling internationally I could not visit my mom without taking a shower. Going home before going to the hospital struck a chord in me. I didn't want to take any chances in spreading the virus, but I also felt deeply dislocated when it all added up in my mind.

When I arrived at the hospital, I stopped at the entrance, closed my eyes, and took a breath so deep it made me light-headed. I was prepared for the worst and prayed to God for the best. When I reached my mother's room, I was forced to accept the fact that it was the worst. At no point in my life had I ever seen her compromised in such a way. Neither she nor my dad had ever been anything other than images of strength. Mom was unresponsive and in a medically induced coma. Although she was breathing, she looked absent from her body. My saving grace at the moment and welcomed distraction was the people in the room. It was filled to capacity with a revolving door of visitors. Family members, friends, and elected officials who were now trusted loved ones didn't just call or text. They showed up, even with a looming pandemic and in the face of great uncertainty. Their presence was proof of my parents' work and impact on all those they encountered. The vision of all the faces gathered reinforced the power of a collective and the need for a village. It was going to take one to overcome what my family was facing. In spite of the hope we attempted to maintain for her healing, the doctors' reports told of a different outcome—one that was grim. The medical staff warned that she probably would not improve.

As the visitation settled down, a doctor pulled us into the hallway to deliver even more unsettling news: "Your mother has some impairments that you will not see change anytime soon. Due to the impact of the stroke sustained, she will likely not walk again. She may not eat again, but we are not one hundred percent sure."

The stroke doctor was a white man, and he was accompanied by a fine ass Black doctor who was also a part of the same unit. We turned away from the white doctor and looked at the Black doctor as if to question what the other had to say. His words echoed in my ears. And for a moment, I imagined myself as a bystander, watching the conversation play out. How could my superhero not be wearing her cape? Mom was the strongest person I had ever witnessed in motion. Under no circumstances did she break or fold. Mom was the one who stood ten toes down when outside forces attempted to creep into our home. She was the one who strategized when she and my father attempted to make things happen for our family. It was Mom who locked arms with my father to overcome adversity while raising their children.

Was it possible that my mom, my superhero, was human? All my life, I'd watched her be anything but. In partnership with my father, she made a way out of no way. There was nothing she could not do. The thought of her being confined to the hospital bed was all-consuming. No matter what age you are, you will always be somebody's child. And every child who is blessed to have their parent in their lives remembers the moment they were forced to accept that their parents were real people. This was my moment of reckoning. As I shook my head in disbelief, fighting back tears, all I could hope for was that we were all trapped in a bad dream—a nightmare, one we would soon wake up from. To no avail. Reality continued to sink in when my pastor, Dr. Richardson, arrived. The touch of his hand on my back and the squeeze of my shoulder, the tension in the faces of those gathered around my mother's bed, the intensity without which we held hands to pray, and the inconsolable tears made it all real. This was not a dream, nor would I wake up. It was reality, and my eyes were wide open, forcing me to come to terms that Mom, as I had known her, was in danger of dying. And if she survived, according to the doctor's warnings, nothing about her would ever be the same.

———

I'd like to believe that the pleas we made that day awakened the ancestors. I'd like to believe they heard our voices and interceded. Every day thereafter, Dad, my sister Sharon, and I along with my uncle Alex, Aunt Mary, my aunt Janice (Peanut), and other close family and friends sat together at the hospital, searching for the silver lining. Not one of us gave up hope, but I'd be lying if I said that we were not afraid. The looks on the faces of my family members revealed what they were thinking with their hearts but not saying with their mouths. We did not know if Mom would make it. I clung to the Bible verse that my aunt Ola Mae was stating on her deathbed:

PROVERBS 3:5–6

Trust in the LORD with all your heart and lean not on your own understanding; in all your ways acknowledge him, and he will set your paths straight.

If we were to get to the other side of Mom's condition, we were all going to have to learn how to swim. To the credit of my niece's father, Juan Cotto, and my godsister, Nadine McNeil, they kept us fighting when we were yet weary. They were pushy in the hospital, asking questions and advocating. They never lost sight of our end goal—a full recovery. We prayed alone in our quiet moments and in concert when together.

———

After two full days of torture, we witnessed a miracle. MOM WOKE UP! There was joy in knowing that she defeated the first challenge. Her waking up was confirmation in fact that she was the superhero we had always known her to be. Even though she was awake and noticeably fighting, she was in terrible shape. The journey towards healing would require more willpower and strength than any of us knew we had. Her eyes moved from side to side and she appeared to know we were there in the room with her, but she was not able to talk. It was hard to tell whether or not she desired to speak.

The medical staff continued to deliver blow after blow. It seemed like bad news was all they had to give us. They were adamant that her condition would not improve. On her fifth day in the hospital, the doctors came into the room to provide us with updates. My father, sister, brother Milton, and a few others huddled together to hear their report. The Black doctor was there as well:

> Your mother's condition will continue to decline. Her quality of life will not improve. We're not sure how much time she has left. Our team advises that you take her home to ensure her comfort.

The doctors then began to talk about administering a feeding tube in my mother's stomach. This was all in preparation for her ultimate demise. We all stood there listening to their prognosis. My sister Sharon, standing with her hands on her hips, closed her eyes and inhaled before letting out a long sigh and shifting her weight to one leg. The lines across the top of my father's forehead and raised eyebrows told of his concern. My brother had tears in his eyes. As the doctor spoke, I watched my father peering over at my mother. It was as if they shared some sort of connection that was invisible to the rest of the world, and he was summoning her to get up. As the doctor was speaking, my mom's eyes popped open wide, and she began moving her head. My sister jolted away from the huddle back towards Mom's bed.

"I know, Mom. You're not going to be like this forever. I know, Mom," she repeated, consoling her.

It was at that moment, as a collective, without a single word spoken, that confirmed Voncile Mallory was not done. God was not through with her yet.

There was even a noticeable sense of calm across Mom's face as she recognized we were all clear that she still had life left inside of her and in no way did she intend to give up. Not then. Not ever. The doctors went on to advise that a nutritionist would begin daily visits and that they would be monitoring her to see if a feeding tube was necessary. By that time, we were only partially listening. We had witnessed a miracle. What more could he say that God had not already shown us? Mom's confirmation was all we needed to move forward. We continued to hold out faith that she would be restored. Not a single one of us needed the doctors to tell us who she was. We witnessed her strength through the years.

In the days to come, the nutritionist came by as the doctor stated, but each time the medical staff was amazed at the progress that Mom was making. She defied the odds—so much so that they never got around to administering the feeding tube, citing that she didn't actually need it. Mom's continued healing was enough to keep us sane, but everything around us became increasingly stressful. Dad was physically there but noticeably lost without the person he'd spent every day of the last fifty-plus years with. On most days, when I arrived at the hospital I found him pacing the hallways just outside her door, stopping only on occasion to peer into the room. When he wasn't pacing, he was sitting in the family waiting room, reading texts from all of the loved ones who had reached out. Now, early mornings that turned into late nights in the hospital were his new normal.

Although I couldn't see his entire face to make out his expressions due to the newly implemented COVID mask mandate, I knew him well enough to recognize the tension in his forehead and eyes. He was distraught. He often looked defeated. Neither me nor my sister Sharon planned to allow the circumstance we were facing to be the way that the story ended. We each leveraged our skill sets to oversee the affairs of both Mom and Dad. Much like my role in the movement, I assumed responsibility for accessing lines of communication with the hospital staff and others who could help us navigate. Medical care is like politics. Who and what you know matters.

One of my closest friends, former New York State Assemblyman Michael Blake's father, had passed away a few years prior. I spent time supporting Michael while his father was in the hospital. He returned the favor by being there with me and my family. He knew administrators in the hospital and connected me with the president. These relationships proved instrumental in the days to come when our requests were greater amidst the COVID-19 crisis. Everything from paperwork to organizing check-ins with Mom's medical team and administrative duties around my mom's care was handled by me. My sister Sharon, who was now an accomplished RN, was able to work with the medical team to manage Mom's health care. This was a herculean task, with our Mom's life literally at her fingertips.

We had to learn about trust funds and how to organize my parents' finances to gain access to the optimum care that they so desperately needed. Even today, we still reflect on how we each stepped up to the plate. God prepared us for a time such as this. My sister and I were on top of Dad's emotional well-being, physical well-being, and sustenance. It was hard to ignore the twilight zone we had entered. The world around us was in shambles. When the TV was on, the words "Breaking News" became the routine as the continued states of emergency were declared. The reports of staggering numbers of people getting sick were unfathomable.

Instead of a safe space for healing, the hospital was now where the apocalypse was televised. People were walking in literally hanging on to the walls. Some gasping for air, others coughing or struggling to walk. Some people were sweating profusely, with looks of fear in their eyes. Death was literally looming around us. However, we didn't see it with our own eyes. There were no COVID victims that we knew of housed in the wing where Mom was. The longer my mom was in the hospital though, the more the awareness of COVID-19 was heightened. As Mom received care from other departments, we noticed they started to dress differently, masked with face shields and in hazmat suits. It wasn't like that when Mom first got there. We were so engulfed in what was happening with her that we were too isolated to make the connection between COVID-19 and the changing world around us.

———

By Mom's second week, the doctors told us that we would need to limit the number of visits to the hospital due to contagion. They were apprehensive about the prospect of us contracting the virus while there or, worse, bringing it in to contaminate others.

On my last day visiting the hospital, I woke up, got dressed, showered, and parked the car on the deck. As I walked to the front entrance, I was met by Ron, a security guard who was now an acquaintance, as I'd seen him every day coming and going.

"Ms. Mallory, before you go up there, I need to tell you something."

"Sure, Ron, what's up?"

"I know you want to see your mother, but y'all can't come back here."

"What do you mean we can't come back here?" I pressed. "My mother is in there fighting for her life. There is no way I can leave her."

"I understand how you feel, Ms. Mallory, and I'm going to let you see your mother today, but you have to make it brief, and you can't come back after today. This is the hospital's order, not mine. It's not safe anymore with COVID. Too many people are dying, and between you and me, they can't figure this shit out."

He came in a little closer to me so that I could hear him clearly behind his mask: "Believe me, you have to get the hell out of here. The hospital is not safe."

We were aware of the mass of COVID-19 victims, but since all our time was spent at the trauma unit and the look on his face, our perception of the danger was not critical enough. With new eyes and heightened awareness, the landscape of the hospital began to look different. His words angered me, but logic kicked in. I realized that he was trying to help me. Prior to his warnings, I had noticed the chorale of coughing. But upon my hearing his warning, it all came into focus. People were coughing up their lungs, and some in the waiting room looked like they were dead. That hospital and our world was different.

I didn't even have time to cry. Seeing Mother with the white gauze wrapped around her head was so hard, but there was so much business that had to be attended to because of her condition. We found out that being someone's spouse does not automatically give you oversight of decisions regarding their life. This is only the case after they die. If the person is alive, an established power of attorney accompanied by the proper paperwork is necessary.

We had never planned for death as a family, only life. After Mom awoke from the coma, we had no power to make some of the very important decisions on her behalf. And although she was awake, her mind was not strong. It was hard for her to process information to make clear decisions for herself. Even getting her to respond to our prompts was a challenge. When the medical staff requested for her to sign papers giving us power over her care, it took a while for her to focus, but she eventually did. The medical staff was adamant about not coercing her into decisions. She had to demonstrate the capacity to answer questions.

"Do you have a blanket on?" one nurse asked.

"Do you realize that you had a stroke?"

Their line of questioning was purposed to demonstrate she could answer real questions, considering her ability to speak and her penmanship were impacted.

———

On some days improvement looked like survival, and on others it looked like communication. There was a moment when I thought my mother was asking me if the nurses were Black. She could barely move her eyes, but she was forcing herself to shift them backward and forward towards the door. I followed her eyes in the direction she was looking, and lo and behold, there was a sign about COVID-19.

"You're asking me if you have COVID."

Her grunting confirmed.

"No, Mom. You don't. You had a stroke."

She turned away, disgruntled. Maybe she did know. Maybe she just wanted me to say it—to make it real. Either way, it was tormenting to accept it as her truth.

That day was difficult, like the days ahead. The country was in a full lockdown, and our family sank deeper into paperwork and estate planning information overload. There was no time to be emotional, only time to execute. My dad was traumatized beyond belief. The only option was for us to step up for him as he had done for us on so many occasions.

For us, the next series of actions would come in the form of a family meeting. The outcome was a unanimous decision to meet with the hospital social workers to request that Dad be allowed to move into the room with Mom. We had been made aware that the hospitals around the country were overloaded, yet we persisted. On the day we met with the social workers, we were relentless in advocating on Mom's behalf. At first, our requests were met with denials, but we did not let up. Eventually, the hospital broke. Instead of denying our requests, they gave us stipulations. Their demand was that if Dad were to move in, he would not be permitted to come back and forth. He would have no access to the cafeteria or any other area of the hospital. They warned that if he were caught walking away from the corridor where her room was stationed he would immediately be put out of the hospital and not permitted to return. He had to stay within steps of Mom's room. The next hurdle to overcome was the lack of access to beds. At that moment, my father spoke words so potent, that the entire room was filled with emotion:

"Don't worry about a bed. If you would just give me some sheets, I will sleep on the floor in that corner over there."

The rims of his eyes were swollen, and his breathing was heavy. It was like nothing I had ever seen before. The magnitude of dedication and passion in his eyes sent literal chills down my spine. There was no way the Black women assigned to Mom's case could deny her access to the one human whose presence alone had the power to heal her. It was a powerful reminder that love serves as a healing salve for the wounded soul. That day when we left the social workers' office, we had been introduced to hope of a different magnitude. Even so, we needed to restructure the support system to ensure Dad had adequate food and remained healthy during his time there. Since we could not enter the hospital due to a statewide mandate, I began breaking the lockdown rules to at least bring him food. The system we put in place was that when we arrived, wearing a mask and gloves, we passed the food off to Ron, the security guard. He then called the nurses, who came down in fully protective gear to retrieve the bags. It was the best that we could do. Over the next few days, Mom showed signs of improvement, but the doctors informed us that her only viable option was to go to a rehabilitation center. By this time, Dad caught up with the state of the world. Mom's safety and his safety were a major concern for all of us. And now the awful realization came that he would not be able to move into the center with her. We didn't have the same connections at her new location as we did at the hospital. Even if we had, the impending COVID-19 outbreak would not have allowed Dad to be with her.

———

Moving Mom into the facility ushered in a new chapter of isolation for her and for us. She thought that we'd abandoned her due to the minuscule contact we were allowed to have. She was confined in many ways. From being in a foreign place to not being mobile, nothing about her quality of life was as she remembered it.

The torturous act of her being tested daily became unbearable. I was calling politicians, administrators, and everyone I could think of to visit my mother. Although most of the nursing staff was kind, they were under immense pressure to protect everyone inside from the treacherous virus that was now responsible for the loss of life en masse and to protect themselves. Mom's condition went from bad to worse after her mind began to flip. All we could do on the outside was lift her in prayer. My sister did everything she could to talk to them, talking to the hospital every day several times a day, speaking nurse-to-nurse. From Mom's perspective, that was not enough. Her response to us was that we should either come visit or cease communication with her altogether. There was no in-between. She believed we were deserting her. To her mind, I was the one in our family who had connections to get things done. Her request for a visit seemed simple. But the world in crisis made it anything but. Mom believed in her heart that I was not trying hard enough. It hurt like hell to know that she had come to my rescue on so many occasions and I could not at that moment come to hers. The more we attempted to explain, the more it sounded like excuses. In her lifetime, she had never seen the world shut down. How could she have imagined it to be her reality? It wasn't real to any of us. When she went into the hospital, the world was fine. She had no way of knowing how things had changed. As her rehabilitation time continued, sometimes she refused to speak with us and even my father. We were no different from the countless other families separated from their loved ones and it hurt like hell.

A MASSIVE COVER-UP

In New York, in spite of the ongoing COVID crisis, Until Freedom never stopped working. Once the mask mandates were implemented, there were cops handing out water to white people in parks downtown who were "social distancing." Uptown was a different story. There were cases of police officers body-slamming and beating up people on the train to get them to wear masks in areas highly concentrated with Black and brown folks. The mayor also decided that protests were not allowed. No gatherings or marches were permitted, but we organized and defied the ban. We held a protest in opposition to the mask mandates, citing the potentially dangerous escalation of interactions between police and already-attacked communities. After our protest, Mayor Bill de Blasio announced that while masks would still be mandatory, they would no longer be enforced by the NYPD. It was a win for Until Freedom and our community at large.

There was yet another ray of hope when the medical staff at the rehab facility informed us that Mom gained enough strength to sit up on her own. She was also speaking a bit more. It was the start of a new beginning. They allowed my dad into the center so he could learn how to care for Mom at home. After almost a month, we were notified that she would be released to come home. Although it was good news, we were being denied every kind of in-home medical accommodation. Dad was afraid that he would not have the capacity to give her what she needed. My sister Sharon and my niece Skylar were lifesavers. Schools were shut down, so they moved in with my parents. My niece became a hands-on support to help them. My sister who was still on the front lines as a first responder at work every day, also became an in-house nurse.

The first few weeks after Mom came home were taxing. I still didn't have much money in my account, but for the most part I needed very little, as the world was practically shut down. People were cooking at home, and when I wasn't doing that I maintained a schedule of helping to prepare meals and handling my parents' paperwork. We couldn't run the risk of my dad getting COVID; therefore, we put forth every effort to keep him and Mom inside. Sometimes Dad cooked in the kitchen with me, and it was nostalgic. The time of togetherness was something that we all treasured even though it was not under the circumstances we would have wished for; we were bonded nonetheless. Just as we settled into our new routine, I received the call about Ahmaud Arbery. After that day, nothing was ever the same.

CHAPTER 20

MERCY

Even with a looming health crisis, Black people were still being terrorized by civil and racially charged environments. On February 23, 2020, Ahmaud Arbery, just twenty-five years old, was murdered while jogging in a neighborhood near Brunswick, Georgia. Like far too many attacks on Black folks that result in the loss of life in this country, Ahmaud's story did not capture public attention until weeks afterward.

When my brothers in the movement activist Shaun King and attorney Lee Merritt began working day and night, more attention was brought to this case. Shaun, an expert and, dare I say, a genius at online organizing and a master fundraiser, used his talent as he has in so many instances to gather intel about the series of events that took place the night Ahmaud was killed. Lee is a well-respected civil rights lawyer. In concert Lee and Shaun created a simulation demonstrating the probable series of events.

The simulation went viral, becoming the initial awakening of the world at large. Later, video of the actual violence emerged, confirming what Black people already knew. Ahmaud was the victim of a horrific hate crime. Shaun and Lee's work would not be in vain.

In composing this book, I reached out to Shaun and Lee to remind me of all the details of Ahmaud's murder and the aftermath. Sadly, for weeks after Ahmaud was killed, several of his childhood friends began emailing Shaun, pleading for help. Although they didn't really have a great deal of information at the time, they were certain of two primary things:

1. It appeared police and prosecutors were friends with Ahmaud's killers.
2. The police had lied to Wanda Cooper, Ahmaud's mother, when they showed up at her house the day Ahmaud was killed. Police

told her that he was killed breaking into homes. She knew that was a lie. Ahmaud's body had been found in the middle of the road, far away from the home they said he entered.

While attempting to bring national attention to her son's case, Ms. Wanda and a group of Ahmaud's friends faced an uphill battle. Media coverage was inundated with pandemic news. They had a difficult time securing help or allyship as the world appeared to be crumbling at the seams due to the health crisis.

RunWithMaud.com was born to inform the masses and to give the community ways to take action on their own. Shaun's posts for Run With Maud helped gather more than three million sign-ups on the site and was a vital bridge between the initial outrage around his death and the national attention that would only really get going when a video of the crime was released on May 5, 2020.

It's almost hard to believe now, but the same week I was grappling with the sense of rage Ahmaud's story ignited within me, I received yet another call about the loss of a Black life.

"Hey, Queen."

"Hey, Ben, what's going on?"

"Tamika, I need you."

It was Benjamin Crump. The pain in his voice sent me into an immediate panic. Attorney Crump was not one to exaggerate for effect. The severity of the situation was apparent.

He went on to explain that there were only a few posts on social media about the case, but not a real movement that matched the level of outcry it deserved. He was speaking in a monotone and there was the presence of an emotion I had not heard before. Something was different.

Let me just take a moment to tell you about the great attorney Benjamin Crump. I am moved to tears while trying to express who he is and his dedication to Black people and fighting for equity and righteousness. He works on cases that connect him to the cause of justice. It might seem obvious, but that is not the case for all civil rights attorneys. There are so many who chase cases based on perceived financial outcomes, but over the many years that I have worked with Ben, I never once knew him to do anything other than fight for what was right. There have been times when I witnessed him waive his legal fees for so many victims and families.

"I'm working on a case that people aren't talking about," he continued. "Here is a young woman from Louisville, Kentucky, that was killed by police in her home. Based upon the local lawyers and the local community, she didn't do anything to deserve this. Her name is Breonna Taylor.

"I know that this COVID stuff is really serious and these last several months have been tough for you, but what happened to her is not right. I need you to do what you do and help me help this family."

I remembered having seen Breonna's face on social media, but the details surrounding the incident had been scarce. What struck me was that in the photo, she was wearing a service uniform. Upon further research, I learned two months had passed since the police raided her home. The narrative being curated was that Breonna had a drug dealer as a boyfriend, and illegal packages were being delivered to her house. The tone and familiar beats to the story gave me pause. I called Ben back immediately.

"Ben, I need you to put me in touch with Breonna's mother. I see what's happening here," I said.

He connected me with Tamika Palmer, Breonna's mother, and her attorneys, Lonita Baker and Sam Aguiar, who had been working on the case since Breonna was first killed.

It became increasingly clear that there was a level of corruption and silencing associated with the case. Lonita reached out to her friend Benjamin Crump to bring in national reinforcement, and boy, did they need it.

The first step was to ensure that Breonna's family knew our intentions were pure. By the time we were introduced to the situation, they had already encountered a number of individuals who were trying to take advantage of their daughter's story. They also encountered people who had given them bad advice.

When you work with families dealing with great tragedy, they don't need another person shoving opinions down their throats and telling them what to do. They don't need people showing up standing on their tippy-toes, trying to be seen in the camera on the nightly news. Believe it or not, I've seen it many times, and I always shake my head and laugh. Instead, families need safe spaces and support. It took a couple of weeks, but eventually, an unbreakable bond developed between the family, the attorneys, and Until Freedom. Through this experience, Lonita and Tamika have become two of my closest friends.

Every day, as more details unfolded, the situation worsened. Nothing could have prepared me for the heart-wrenching details of how the city failed Breonna and her boyfriend, Kenny Walker, a hero who was with her that horrific night. To add insult to injury, the officials who are paid to protect and serve tried to cover up Kenny and Breonna's true story in the aftermath.

It became clear that Breonna's death was not simply a significant and egregious mistake, or even just an act of brutality. It was far worse. Her death was an indisputable murder. Her blood was on the hands of so many people across the state of Kentucky. It was unfathomable. Even as I write the pages of this book, a judge dismissed two felony charges against officers in the case, while trying to blame Kenny for the warning shot he fired that night, which was completely justifiable by Kentucky law. Breonna's mother, sister, and family were just everyday people who were forced to grieve her loss in the public eye and under the scrutiny of the media. They hadn't asked to be drafted into a war against the massive injustice plaguing Black communities. They hadn't asked to be civil rights activists. They hadn't asked for any of this, but they were in the middle of it all.

Days after my first public comments about Breonna, I knew there was no way for me to immerse myself in the case without putting my feet on the ground where she'd lived and had her life stolen from her. I remembered the pictures of Breonna on social media in her service uniform, and Memorial Day was coming up. Until Freedom began planning immediately to hold a vigil in Kentucky to honor her life.

That weekend Linda, Mysonne, Angelo, and I arrived in Kentucky. We met Breonna in her absence through her beautiful family and the people who loved her so much. Looking into their eyes as they shared stories of her life touched our hearts deeply. Breonna's sister Ju'Niyah Palmer took me over to the window of her bedroom, showing that it was her room that sustained the most damage. Seeing the marks from the holes where the bullets entered the room made me sick, because the night Breonna was killed, Ju'Niyah happened to be out of town. It was jarring to know that she too could have been killed if she was at home that night, leaving their mother to mourn the loss of two daughters instead of one.

This case was very personal for us. With every passing day, the similarities between Breonna's life and our lives became more apparent. She was a young woman, just like so many of our nieces and family members, carving a life and career out for herself in a world that never made it easy for people like her. It was hard not to imagine that this could have been any one of us or our families. Although she was friends with a guy who was deeply troubled, her senseless death had nothing to do with her character, her life, her work, or her story. How many of us have had some affiliation to a person who has either been in trouble before, is dealing with trouble now, or who is potentially going to get into trouble in the near future? *Sure, the company we keep matters, but in no way, shape, or form should it determine whether we live or die.* As much as the media attempted to obscure the facts, the local community in Louisville knew the truth about what happened to Breonna. While there, we began learning the details from them.

Being in Kentucky was difficult professionally and even more so personally. My mom was in a rigorous recovery process to regain mobility. There were times I felt guilty for not being in New York. I needed to be at Breonna's mother and sister's sides. I needed to be by Breonna's side, even in her absence. Although she was no longer with us physically, she deserved to have someone speaking up on her behalf. She needed to have her side of the story told. We received a great deal of national media coverage while on the ground in Kentucky, which was the goal, but not without its challenges.

Coming face-to-face with Breonna's murder and fighting for justice while knowing my mother was amidst a fight of her own made me feel conflicted. My dad was left to care for my mother with the help of my sister Sharon, who sacrificed her life to move in with them to assist. And yet, I would soon be alerted to another heinous act against a Black life that required our presence.

As we were standing in the hotel lobby in Kentucky, preparing for check-out and our return to New York, I noticed a grim look on Angelo's face. He was glued to his phone and I could hear a man screaming. As I approached, Angelo turned his screen towards Linda, Mysonne, and me.

"An officer killed a man in Minneapolis while on video and it's now circulating around the world," Angelo said.

————

On May 25, 2020, George Perry Floyd walked into a Minneapolis convenience store to make a purchase and was accused by a clerk of using a fake twenty-dollar bill. When officers were called, they apprehended

George immediately, manhandled him to the ground, and placed him in handcuffs. As he was confined and laid up against the ground, Officer Derek Chauvin then knelt with his knee on George's neck for over nine minutes—NINE MINUTES. Two other police officers, J. Alexander Kueng and Thomas Lane, assisted Chauvin in restraining George while his face was pressed into the pavement. George's heart stopped beating while he was being restrained on the ground.

Instead of flying back to New York, we drove our rental car overnight to Minneapolis. The back-to-back-to-back murders of Ahmaud Arbery, Breonna Taylor, and now George Floyd sent people into even more outrage. Cities were burning in protest—literally. And while I have never condoned violence, I recognized the lack of consideration for Black lives in our country had reached a point that demanded unprecedented action. When I was asked to address the people in Minneapolis, I, like so many others, was sick and tired of being sick and tired. That night, I sat on the phone with my brother, Reverend Mark Thompson, a civil rights legend, all night, figuring out the right words for me to say at a planned press conference the next morning. By the time some in the media began to blame George Floyd for his own death, Mark and I resolved that at the press conference I should just say what was on my heart. We slept on the phone together that night.

We are not responsible for the mental illness that has been inflicted upon our people by the American government, institutions, and those people who are in positions of power. I don't give a damn if they burn down Target, because Target should be on the streets with us calling for the justice that our people deserve. Where was AutoZone at the time when Philando Castile was shot in a car, which is what they actually represent? Where were they?

So, if you are not coming to the people's defense, then don't challenge us when young people and other people are frustrated and instigated by the people you pay—you are paying instigators to be among our people out there, throwing rocks, breaking windows, and burning down buildings. And so young people are responding to that. They are enraged.

And there's an easy way to stop it: Arrest the cops. Charge the cops. Charge all the cops, not just some of them, not just here in Minneapolis. Charge them in every city across America where our people are being murdered. Charge them everywhere. That's the bottom line. Charge the cops. Do your job. Do what you say this country is supposed to be about—the land of the free, for all. It has not been free for Black people, and we are tired.

Don't talk to us about looting. Y'all are the looters. America has looted Black people. America looted the Native Americans when they first came here, so looting is what you do. We learned it from you. We learned violence from you. We learned violence from you. The violence was what we learned from you. So if you want us to do better, then, damn it, you do better.

This speech and these words were the outpouring of rage and frustration from my soul. My heart hurt for us. To recognize the lack of respect and exercise of humanity against us in a country we built on our backs is demoralizing. The onslaught of violence against us is in no way acceptable. And to make matters worse, we were under the leadership of a person who continuously used demeaning language while further agitating hate and violence. All of these factors were in my head and my heart when I spoke. My words were the purest form of the long-standing hurt we have all been forced to feel.

People were calling my speech "the most powerful of a generation" in the wreckage of that spring and summer. I'd gone viral on social media before, and I'd gotten plaudits from the mainstream at times too, but the difference in how people were coming around to my message this time was palpable. This was off-the-cuff, unscripted emotion. The people were ready for it. My face and my words became synonymous with the movement for justice. The work of Until Freedom was the same as it had always been, but now the spotlight on us was different.

Anyone who knows me will tell you that I have never wanted to be "famous," only well respected and notable for my work. All I have ever wanted was to do my part and to be able to see the fruits of my labor in my lifetime. If a viral speech was what it took to declare a state of emergency about the unjust treatment of our people, then so be it. I thank God for that moment. I thank God for giving me the courage to say what needed to be said.

Shortly after the speech, my team received an outpouring of love, support, and new invitations. One special invite came from Jada Pinkett Smith and her production team. The ask was for me to be a guest on her show *Red Table Talk*. This would be my first time on the show for an episode titled "Black America in Crisis."

Recently, I have avoided videos of gore against human beings. I really believe watching video after video in the past was part of the depression that caused my sleep issues. Imagine laying down every night with videos in your head of people being shot, beaten, and screaming for help. It's not healthy. Not only had Angelo showed me the clip of George being murdered, but I was also forced to come face-to-face with it again while filming as it was shared by production. The sounds of George's life being squeezed out of him made me feel like my soul left my body. All I could think about was my son, Tarique, the moment I heard him yelling for his mother. I did my best to keep my composure on the show, but my stomach was in knots. I was already nervous being on this major platform, sitting around the table with cultural icons, with lights and cameras everywhere and high-tech equipment strapped to my back and legs. It felt like I was going to get sick and have to run to the bathroom, but I convinced myself to sit still. The last thing I wanted to do was interrupt the production.

Legendary civil rights leader and activist Dr. Angela Davis joined us, virtually, on the panel that day. Seeing her on the screen as she spoke was so inspiring. She was proof that activists can see change in their lifetimes and also that the fight is never-ending. It was an honor to have been asked to be on the show and to share time and space with Jada, Willow Smith, and Jada's mom, Adrienne Banfield-Norris (Gammy). It was a joy to be in their presence, albeit for unfortunate reasons. The world was in protest and at war. The weight was heavy on all of us that day on set.

After we wrapped the show, Willow asked if I wanted something to eat. I was hesitant to accept her offer because Linda, Angelo, and Mysonne had already been waiting for me for several hours. They joined me on the West Coast to take some fundraising meetings for Until Freedom. I gathered up enough nerve to ask if they could all come over. We were greeted with open arms. Jada was happy to host us. Once everyone arrived, we entered the Smith family's beautiful home on the grounds near the *Red Table* production set. The whole family was present, including Will, Trey, Trish, and later Jaden arrived.

We spent several hours talking about Breonna Taylor, George Floyd,

Until Freedom's aspirations, and our personal dreams. It was a beautiful time together. I'd always had distant connections to the Smith family, but after that visit they became my family.

A common shared sentiment of the conversation was exhaustion. We kept coming back to how difficult it had been to find hope for ourselves amidst the constant turmoil and ways we could translate that hope (if any could be found) to the world. The protest streets and the work we were doing was exhausting. Systemic oppression has the potential to steal your human rights and your happiness. Jada suggested we take some time off and visit with her again in the not so distant future.

A few weeks later, we returned for another visit with Jada and told her of our plan to go back to Kentucky to stay there on the ground for thirty days. Jada was worried, and if I'm being honest, so were we. Even so, we knew this was the only way forward.

This time, we requested Jada's presence in Kentucky for our first major rally and she graciously agreed—but she didn't come alone. She was surrounded by love. Jada was accompanied by her family and my dear sister MC Lyte. Both Jada and Lyte vowed to support Breonna's family and our work towards holding the police accountable. To this day they have remained steadfast in their promise. Rapsody, the artist and my super friend, my brother Common, and Yandy also attended.

Although the plan to double down on our support in Kentucky was coming together, there was only one problem—I hadn't told my parents I was planning to move to Kentucky. Grappling with how to do what needed to be done for Breonna Taylor while simultaneously supporting my family adjusting to our new normal after the stroke that caused severe damage to Mom's brain and body was difficult, to say the least. Mom now needed twenty-four-hour care that involved a lot of physical strength. My dad and sister were on the front lines, leading me to question so many things.

I asked myself, Would the community in Louisville trust us if we weren't there with them? Could Until Freedom be effective if some of us went back to New York? In all my years of experience, I have learned that it is difficult to organize in a community that you are not a part of or present in. If they are to trust you with their well-being, people need to feel your hands and look into your eyes.

The other factor I struggled with was whether or not I would put my elderly parents at risk for COVID if I were commuting back and forth. Relocating full-time to Louisville appeared to be my only option. After I shared my decision with Linda, she also agreed to relocate. We were not the only ones who believed the move to be a good idea; there were others who agreed. Mysonne and Angelo and our mentee, Reverend Stephen Green, who is now pastor of Greater Allen AME Cathedral Church in Queens, New York, was insistent that we get on the ground as soon as possible to start building community in Louisville.

After making up my mind to move forward with a plan in Kentucky, I called my dad to check on him and my mom. Even though my dad doesn't just talk for the sake of talking, he always knows the right things to say to me.

"Tamika, me and Mom miss you, but we don't need you to be here when you should be out there. We know this country is in bad shape. Don't get me wrong, it's tough here too. Mom is depressed, but we're handling it. We've got her. Sharon is here with us. Just call every chance you get. You do what you need to do, and most of all be safe," he said.

In spite of the fact that I had a plan, I don't know how strong I would have been without Dad's words confirming things were handled at home. They freed me from the guilt I was feeling about not being with them. I was needed on the front lines and that was exactly where I was headed.

THE SUMMER OF HELL

That initially planned thirty days in Louisville turned into a period of four months. We went head-on with skeptics and naysayers in the Louisville community. We put deep thought into how we could innovate and elevate our *shared* mission to realize justice for Breonna. Our posture was to show we were collaborators—not intruders.

In Kentucky, we settled in and immediately hired Black businesses for any service we needed. We paid rental fees to almost all of the spaces that we used in the city to host our meetings and to organize. We gave significant donations to grassroots organizations, including some of those who publicly said they didn't like us—they did not hesitate to take our money. We attended many contentious meetings. We immersed ourselves in the community. One of our larger scale efforts was a conference

titled BreonnaCon. The event's intent was to honor Breonna's life while
continuing to amplify awareness of the grave injustice being committed
against her by the state of Kentucky. We also wanted to give the local
community a space to address issues plaguing Louisville and the state
of Kentucky. Not everyone liked the name BreonnaCon. What many
failed to realize was that Breonna's family had been a part of the planning
process the entire time. Tamika Palmer loved the name.

A piece in the *Washington Post* read: "Breonna Taylor deserves better
than memes and barbecues." We had done enough work as individuals
by this point to understand that great tragedy will always produce a
critical mass of opinions. We were in the thick of several highly charged
situations. We recognized that people are free to express themselves as
they please, including critiquing the precise methods of how we worked
towards making progress. Even so, hits against BreonnaCon felt unfair.
We held faith in our intentions, which were pure. We did not allow a
defeatist mentality to slow our momentum.

In addition to the events we'd been organizing, we had set up residences in Louisville and brought in activists from around the country
to join the fight for Breonna. Trae tha Truth, an artist and humanitarian
from Houston, Texas, and one of my besties, was on the ground immediately. He aligned with the community and with us to get the work done.
He would stay for weeks at a time. Although witnessing a major increase
in activity on the ground in Kentucky was beautiful, we also knew that
along with it came momentum from our opponents as well.

Breonna's name had become a flashpoint for the intensified conflicts
over race and gender that made this summer of protest so volatile. We arranged for each of the locations of residence to be equipped with its own
24–7 security team. But even with that, we did feel vulnerable at times.
The looming death threats and the unknown figures passing through our
security footage were proof we needed to keep our eyes wide open and
remain vigilant of our safety at all times. Visceral reactions from folks in
the area who did not want us there were relentless. "White Lives Matter"
shirts and signs were becoming more present in the crowds that sought
to stop us. That slogan was used specifically to taunt and terrorize Black
people nationwide. Many believed *a proclamation of White Lives Matter
was a confirmation that Black lives did not.* The threat felt all-consuming,
in addition to the constant buzz of helicopters and drones that flew over

our residences at various times of the day and night. During our frequent live social media huddles with our followers online, we'd frequently get comments pointing out what they believed to be suspicious figures in the background.

One night the pressure became too much. I was led to confront local authorities, thinking they had been behind the surveillance. To my surprise, they were as confused as we were. I was informed that surveillance had not been authorized by the police department. They suspected the drones were owned and operated by a private party. That night, I sat in the window of our house, worried. Watching. Hoping and praying that no one was coming to harm us—or worse. There was one night when a swarm of at least thirty police cars circled our main residence where Mysonne, Angelo, Linda, and I were staying and then parked on our street. We came outside and sat on the curb in our pajamas, thinking they were about to bum rush us. Our time in Kentucky was complex and challenging and riddled with so much pain that was polarized and concentrated. Despite that pain, the sun never ceased to shine. Somehow amidst the storm clouds, we found hope in the form of rays of sunshine. We managed to use the discovery of joy as our power against the backdrop of pain.

In Louisville, we established so many powerful relationships that have continued to develop and evolve, and for that I am forever grateful. Breonna Taylor was someone's child, sister, and beloved girlfriend. She lost her life through a senseless act of violence. There is not and never will be a justification for what happened to her. And there is nothing that any of us could have done to fill the void of loss to her family, friends, and the community. What we could do was create real moments of real energy that served to honor her life and to memorialize her legacy, while fighting relentlessly in the face of injustice. And yet, we persisted.

An area named Jefferson Square Park was informally renamed Injustice Square Park by the local community and established as headquarters for Breonna and Kenny's defense. There, people gathered and squatted for months and coordinated daily assignments and discussed activities for activism. The Square, as we often referred to it, became home for anyone who wanted to become a part of Breonna's movement. At the Square, not only did we organize day in and day out, but we also established a sense of community. Some people brought food and others danced, sang, painted murals, and recited poetry. This also became one of the places in the city where I learned all the new line dances. I have yet to master the Tamia dance, but I'm halfway there. My hand-eye coordination had not allowed for the rest. There were days when the Square resembled an open court. People sat around talking and tossing out their ideas. Sometimes arguments and even a fistfight or two transpired. Passion for change overflowed in the Square as well as reminders to spring into action. At noon each day, alarms sounded to alert everyone to get into the protest line and to prepare to shut down traffic.

There were so many people and Black-owned businesses, including Black Jockey's Lounge, 1619 The Gathering Place, and the GRÜV, and Cuita Robinson, our personal chef for life, who opened their doors and pools of resources for us. I would be remiss not to mention another business owner who held us down every day: Susan Hershberg, owner of Wiltshire Pantry. I could go on and on with names of our newfound friends and protectors. From Kela, a.k.a. Auntie, to Jamel, a.k.a. Big Baby, to Nicole Hayden—the first person we met when we arrived in Louisville, and Sadiqa Reynolds, who is another one of my dear friends. Sadiqa was the president of the Louisville Urban League and a major supporter. Keturah Herron, who became our homie, was working tirelessly at the ACLU to end no-knock warrants in Kentucky. Her efforts were successful in having a bill passed. Eventually she left the ACLU and became an elected official, who has since been reelected and is now running for higher office. Shameka Parrish-Wright is another activist turned elected official who also held us down during this fight.

Nicole Yates, our super bougie homegirl and political strategist, kept our relationship with the state of Kentucky open.

It is without question there are more names—too many to identify. Too many who made our work doable. Too many who stuck beside us. Too many who encouraged us. Too many whose kindness will never be forgotten.

With the support of much of the local community and heightened attention came mounting pressure to uncover the real truth about Breonna's death—a truth many members of the community had already discovered. There were some who recognized that there was a fly in the buttermilk, as our elders used to say. Something was gravely wrong.

Around this same time, the FBI opened an investigation to conduct research of their own. Our mission was to assist them in obtaining real answers. Due to our community's long-standing unfavorable history with law enforcement, encouraging people to share what they knew proved to be an arduous process. It was our hope that intel from the streets would assist in attaining an indictment against the perpetrators of Breonna's murder.

At the local level, justice for Breonna was now resting in the hands of Daniel Cameron. Cameron was a Black man who won his election as attorney general of Kentucky in December 2019. With strong endorsement and aid from Donald Trump, he had become the first Republican to take the position since 1943, and the first African American ever to hold the office. Cameron was the personification of the saying "all skinfolk ain't kinfolk."

Months went by as we all awaited a decision regarding accountability for Breonna's murder. There are so many things that happen behind the scenes that the general public is not privy to or allowed to witness when tragedy strikes and judicial actions are in motion. To us, it felt like a whole lot of wasted time with no justice and no peace. Breonna's family's attorneys were talking to the attorney general's office regularly, remaining abreast of what was going on during the grand jury process.

The AG's office called on that fateful day, September 23, 2020, to tell the attorneys that the grand jury had made a decision in the case. Attorney Sam Aguiar replied with a simple request: Please do not ask Tamika Palmer to be present for the announcement if there was not going to be an indictment of the officers responsible for her daughter's demise. Ms. Palmer's home was located an hour away from where the announcement was to be made. Who would force a mother to travel that far to be struck again by disrespect levied against her deceased daughter? Daniel Cameron—that's who.

When the decision came in only one of the offending officers was hit with a charge—three counts of "wanton endangerment." This charge confirmed that *an* officer had indeed fired into a wall and *could potentially* have harmed *someone* on the other side of that wall. Factually, no one was charged with anything specific to Breonna's death that day.

The community and several grand jury members were outraged. Some of the jurors came forward to say they waited for evidence to be presented about Breonna's murder specifically, but it never came. They said they were prepared to look at the evidence and indict on behalf of Breonna and Kenny.

No longer could I sit back and watch the city desecrate Breonna's legacy or the family she had left behind to mourn her loss. My patience was running out. I was experiencing the same anger I had when I spoke in Minneapolis after the killing of George Floyd. We all recognized the politics at play. None of it was justification to demean or disrespect Tamika Palmer in the way Daniel Cameron had. When I stepped up to the microphone that day, I decided that if he disrespected her, I was going to disrespect him:

No justice, no peace. No justice, no peace. No justice, no peace, and if there ain't gonna be no justice, there's not gonna be no peace.

I want to read something to you all that I learned of just the day after Daniel Cameron's decision.

It says: "It is a great honor to receive the endorsement of the bipartisan Kentucky Fraternal Order of Police. To the men and women in blue I pledge to be your advocate and your voice every day. When I first got into this race, I did so to bring focus to the public safety challenge of our lifetime, the drug crisis, and there is so much work to be done to fight this epidemic. I am humbled to have this endorsement and as a chief law enforcement officer in Kentucky, I will work every day to make our communities safer and our families and citizens more secure."

That statement is from Daniel Cameron when he received the endorsement of the FOP, one of the most racist organizations that exists in America. I got time today ok, and half of that statement was a lie. Daniel Cameron is not here to protect citizens and to make the state of Kentucky safer, but he was honest about one part, and it's that he is an advocate for police and he is going to be their voice and do whatever is necessary to protect them. So, we learned that he is still a man of his word as it relates to his relationship to the police. He protected the police and it did not matter to him one bit that those same officers could've ran into his Black mama's house and shot her to death. He's more committed to the white supremacy that he is upholding. He mentioned at the press conference, which I thought was quite interesting, that he's a Black man. As I laid and cried and hurt for Tamika Palmer,

Breonna Taylor, Kenny Walker, and Ju'Niyah, who we need to love up on; as I lay there and thought about him saying he's a Black man, I thought about the ships that went in to Fort Monroe and Jamestown with our people on them over four hundred years ago, and how there were also Black men on those ships that were responsible for bringing our people over here. Daniel Cameron is no different than sellout Negroes that sold our people into slavery and helped the white man to capture our people, to abuse them, and to traffic them while our women were raped by savages. That is who you are, Daniel Cameron. You are a coward, you are a sellout, and you were used by the system to harm your own mama, your own Black mama. We have no respect for you. No respect for your Black skin, because all of our skinfolk are not our kinfolk, and you do not belong to Black people at all.

We learned that the same day this announcement was released was the same day in 1955 (which was sixty-five years ago) when Emmett Till was also killed. He was denied justice because the two white men responsible for killing him were let free. Now, I don't know if Daniel Cameron is just stupid or he is very very very clear about history and made a decision to wait six months before coming forward with this announcement; this garbage that we received on the exact same day that Emmett Till's family received the same result. I want you to understand how wicked he is and how wicked this system is.

Attorney Sam Aguiar, and I hope I don't get in trouble for this, but I gotta say it. Attorney Sam Aguiar said he spoke to the attorney general's office and told them, "Do not have Tamika Palmer come all the way to Frankfort, which is an hour drive away, to hear the bad news and have to drive back. Do not do that to her. You can call on the telephone to tell her the bad news," and that wicked man called for her to come there anyway and had this Black mama drive home with her sister and her family at the hearing that they didn't even mention her daughter's name at. How dare you? What kind of man are you? How dare you? And we are not going home. We will make sure that this city is as uncomfortable as it can be, and we intend to travel across the state of Kentucky and make sure that in every corner of this state they know who you are, Daniel Cameron, and who is upholding the system of white supremacy that continues to oppress our people.

The last thing we will say is: Mayor Fischer, don't get it twisted, don't get it twisted. Do not think for one moment that you're going to hide behind a settlement or hide behind reform. We are happy to see that you actually support us, but it must be implemented and we have to make sure that the work is done. But the main thing that matters at this point, you can have the National Guard, the army, the white militia, the whoever you want to have here, LAPD, whoever you want to have, anybody, turn them loose, but until you fire those cops, until your investigation returns the results that the police officers who murdered (they said they were mad at me for using the language "murder"; I said what I said, they murdered Breonna Taylor), and until those officers are fired from this department, I promise you we will continue to make these streets hot.

Last thing I want to tell you all is that, one, Breonna Taylor has brought us together and we will never be separated, and number two, we are prepared to fight until our own death if it is necessary. Not just for her but for every single little Breonna Taylor that is watching us. Not for what Dr. King did, not for what Coretta Scott King did, not for what those did in the past. They want to know what this generation is going to do to stand for freedom and justice, and I'm telling you, we didn't come to play. God bless you.

How could it have been that the officers who fired over twenty shots, six of them hitting and killing Breonna, were found to have acted justly? Those were the words Cameron used when he described the malicious attack on Breonna. As a human being, how could you stand behind cowardice of this level? His actions sickened me. Coming in contact with the countless faces who were sacrificing their everyday lives and livelihoods to protest in Breonna's honor was bittersweet. It was a blessing to know that so many were on fire and ready to fight against the evil of injustice, but it was sorrowful to know that so much was on the line because some believed in preserving the institution of racism. Although we returned home to New York while awaiting the outcomes, the truth eventually came to the light. In a not so shocking discovery, an officer by the name of Kelly Goodlett made the decision to come forward.

When we first arrived in Louisville in May 2020, the community voices were loud and clear about the real story of what happened to Breonna Taylor. One of the resounding messages was that there were contrasting reports in the media. Moreover, no suspicious packages were arriving at Breonna Taylor's house. This was significant because the police had been using this story to make the case that she was involved in an illegal drug operation. She wasn't. A postal inspector, Tony Gooden, confirmed the same after being asked to investigate. When his investigation concluded, he determined there were no suspicious packages being delivered to her home. Even if the world at large did not know the truth, there were many in the local community who did the whole entire time.

The lies from the police department were proof of its corruption. A massive cover-up was at play, and it was proven that the officers involved lied about everything that happened. Without their suspicious package story, there would have been no way to obtain a warrant. It is also documented that the initial warrant was changed to a knock warrant, meaning the officers were legally required to knock and loudly announce themselves. Despite this fact, the officers did not make themselves known upon showing up at Breonna's apartment the night they took her life. The other neighbors in the building did not report hearing the officers announce their presence, only loud bangs.

The public outcry for the real story spanned the course of three years and the truth did not materialize until long after we were back in New York. Even so, location had no bearing on the blood, sweat, and tireless efforts that we continued long after returning home to inform the world about the story of Breonna Taylor. Those who called us crazy now knew we were not and those who stood and worked alongside us realized some sense of accomplishment because of the new development.

We were not in Louisville, Kentucky, in search of fame or fortune. Our presence had nothing to do with celebrity appearances or influence. We were there with a burning desire for justice.

As they say, the truth shall set you free. Officer Goodlett recognized the feds were getting closer to unraveling all of the failed attempts made by the state of Kentucky to hide their hands washed in blood, lies, and deceit. In fact, they had already confirmed the warrant to invade Breonna's home was illegal because it was obtained with false information. Officer Goodlett was also pregnant at the time of her admission and was likely considering what her future may have been as a confirmed participant in the cover-up.

An article featured on the Department of Justice's website, titled

"Former Louisville, Kentucky, Police Detective Pleads Guilty to a Federal Crime Related to the Death of Breonna Taylor," documented Goodlett's admission to conspiring with other officers and a former LMPD detective. Their efforts to falsify the affidavit needed to obtain the warrant had failed. These thugs thought they would get away with murdering a young Black woman—they did not. I am proud to be a part of the many voices who said not on our watch.

In May of 2023, *The Nation* ran an article with the headline "The Man Who Called Breonna Taylor's Killing 'Justified' Could Be Kentucky's Next Governor." The article went on to recount both the death of Breonna Taylor in Kentucky and George Floyd in Minnesota, noting that the justice being served (or lack thereof) looked starkly different in each region and drew a direct correlation between the leadership responsible for oversight in each state. Democratic attorney general Keith Ellison was noted to have taken charge of George's killer, Derek Chauvin, who was found guilty of second-degree murder, third-degree murder, and second-degree manslaughter. To the contrary, conservative Republican attorney general Daniel Cameron justified the behavior of Breonna's murders under Kentucky law. Unlike in Minnesota, there were no charges in Kentucky. There was no accountability on Cameron's watch. Therefore justice had not been served—or so we believed. Many felt a sense of hopelessness as Cameron's political campaign and ambitions seemingly gained steam before the 2023 gubernatorial election in Kentucky. It was feared that he would not only dodge accountability for his lack of effort to address Breonna's senseless murder but also be rewarded for it with a new office. That didn't happen. We worked day and night. We canvassed, held events, and organized to ensure he did not get a promotion for disrespecting Breonna and her family. On November 7, 2023, Governor Andy Beshear, a Democrat, was projected to win reelection for a second term in office—and he did just that, defeating Cameron. Beshear's documented 60 percent approval rating was proof that Cameron's antics were not a reflection of the majority. To read the words "Daniel Cameron concedes after losing the Kentucky governor race" was surreal. That night, there was a fire of emotions brewing in my soul. The poem "Invictus" speaks of a head that is "bloody, yet unbowed." For so many of us, the fight had at times been unbearable, but at no point in time had we bowed our heads. We owed Ahmaud

Arbery more. We owed Breonna Taylor more. We owed George Floyd and so many others more.

I could write a book about our time in Kentucky alone. The highs of a people determined not to be broken by an unjust system. The lows of the loss of life and bloodshed—too many to count. In Kentucky, we weathered the torrential storms of injustice. We stood ten toes down in the face of grave adversity. We fought the good fight. With Daniel Cameron no longer in office, the universe was now resetting. The community was vindicated. We were vindicated and preparing to fight another day.

AS TOLD THROUGH ANGELO'S EYES

When you first meet someone, you do not really know them. However, in the movement you can quickly see who a person is.

In our work with the Justice League, I first saw who Tamika was. Particularly in the context of the movement. We were traveling, I believe it was Flint, Michigan, during the water crises. Tamika was taking us to and connecting us with local churches and their congregations. In this moment I saw the critical importance of her leadership. A woman who could connect frontline organizers with community leaders who often had large communities in need. In many ways Tamika is a bridge. A bridge not only connects two separate sides and makes access to both sides easier, but it also protects those who are crossing the bridge from potential danger beneath. Bridges hold people up and protect them from falling. Falling into danger or to their demise.

Tamika was firmly rooted in her leadership, even when she may not have desired it. However, in life, we all have defining moments that transform us. For Tamika, the George Floyd uprisings would not only be a moment that would transform her but that would transform the world.

When the uprisings began, we were doing what we do, being present and providing support. Until Freedom was young and finding its footing and Tamika was the same, she was finding her footing in the next chapter of her work. The literal and figurative fire and pressure of the uprisings was probably a moment made for Tamika. A moment that needed a voice—a raw, unflinching, yet seasoned voice that understood this moment and that could put into words what the people were experiencing and what the world was witnessing.

This moment would not only alter the world, it would catapult Tamika to a larger public scale and, more importantly, into a new arrival of her identity as a leader, in our community, in the movement, and with Until Freedom. It was a new beginning.

—ANGELO PINTO

EPILOGUE

YOU WON'T BREAK MY SOUL

By now, you may be thinking that the life documented on these pages was pretty unpleasant. So much of this book describes the unfortunate moments and the pain—there was lots of it. I declare that pain is not the sum of the life I've lived thus far. Even amidst the process of documenting so many moments of sadness, I rediscovered a well of joy that can never run dry. That well had always been there. It was waiting to be discovered. As the profound gospel classic by Reverend Paul Jones goes—"I've had some good days, I've had some hills to climb, but when I look around and think things over, I won't complain."

My life and my story are a testament, proving that there is always someone somewhere fighting a battle the world knows nothing about. I most certainly had been. Far too often, we hide in the shadows of the trauma, trials, and tribulations as they haunt us and crush our spirits, making even the very act of breathing too much to ask for on the hard days. I am reminded of the piercing smile and joyful dancing of DJ Stephen "tWitch" Boss from *The Ellen DeGeneres Show*. Although I did not have the opportunity to meet him, I, like the rest of the world, took notice of the special moments he commanded in that studio. We were all the better for his presence. The headlines announcing his untimely passing were jarring, leaving us all who knew him to consider how fleeting life can be. I'm sure it pained people close to him that they hadn't noticed the presence of sadness behind his smile. The sentiment of melancholy he likely experienced felt close to home, because I too have visited such dark places. I too have worn two faces—one with a smile in front of the world, and the other buried in burrows of sadness. Telling my story forced me to confront every new difficult moment head on. I was compelled to hold myself accountable for every personal decision I

284 I LIVED TO TELL THE STORY

made, every person I let down, every person I let into my life who did not have my best interest at heart, and every moment when I missed the lesson God was attempting to teach me. Taking ownership of your shortcomings is no easy feat. The process of documenting them proved to be even harder. Baring your soul to the world—a herculean task. People cautioned me about what to write; many of whom warning that my words could be used against me. I also knew that the revelation of my truths could result in the uncovering of pain for others. Every time I sat down to write, I resisted the urge to put my pen down. This was much more challenging than writing my first book, *State of Emergency: How We Win in the Country We Built.* That book was, in fact, my prescription for healing America. This book has been a prescription for healing *me*, and hopefully healing you. This book was a divine assignment, one I can now say I have completed.

In retrospect, God has never left nor forsaken me. He used every encounter to mold and fine-tune me, in preparation for the pursuit of purpose. In this space of enlightenment, I also recognize I am but a vessel, tasked with sharing God's grace and mercy—the two things that kept me. My work husband, the legendary Reverend Mark Thompson, once told me "pain is the price of leadership. This may feel unfair, but is it truly unfair at all?"

Today, I'm still that same little girl running through the house yelling "power to the people." The same sentiment of invincibility that she felt is within me. The same sense of pride she took in being Black runs through my veins. The warrior who stood up for a little boy named Malcolm is the same warrior who has wedged herself between adult men and police without a second thought. It is me who sees that in spite of everything that has happened in my life, and every decision I have made, good, bad, indifferent, I am worthy. I am worthy of life, liberty, and the pursuit of happiness. I am worthy of seeking and experiencing deep, unapologetic joy. Most profoundly, my voice deserves to be heard. It has the power to call people to action and the power to heal.

When it's all said and done, and this life is over, the only questions that will ever matter are: *What did it all mean? Who was it all for?* I don't have all the answers (I don't think I ever will). However, I have learned that every lesson is an invaluable piece to complete the puzzle of our existence. I use the term *our* because we—all of us, regardless of where we come from and what we align with, are interconnected. What happens to one of us also happens to the sum of us. My narrative is our narrative. In spite of these truths, I must acknowledge that I am yet a work in progress. I no longer stress about mastering life. I am not certain we are called to do so. Instead of mastery, my goal is to simply be better, day by day, and to pour every ounce of what I have learned in my lifetime into the world. If one person's life can be positively affected, then it has all been worth it.

Although I am clear about the weight of my assignment, I no longer focus on carrying the load alone. My job is to carry the baton for my short time in the race and to pass it along lighter than when I received it. I understand my assignment with deeper clarity. It was never my job to fix systemic oppression alone. I do not believe this can be done by one individual. My responsibility is to be a soldier who does her part. One who activates more soldiers. It is my responsibility to be a teacher who imparts the knowledge I've gleaned along this journey. Also, my job is to remain healthy and to never question the power of my voice. I recognize that to fulfill a calling of this magnitude, protecting my peace is not an option. It is lifesaving. My success is in equipping every soul with whom I come into contact with the tools to challenge any notion that we as Black people are not equal. Women are not equal. People with disabilities are not equal. Our LGBTQIA+ family members are not equal. We are not only fighting the war on racial discrimination—we are fighting for humanity.

In this new season, I have resolved to take the time and liberty to experience the fullness of my days. I am only concerned with not disappointing the woman I see staring back at me in the mirror. My narrative is now controlled by me and the Most High. I have learned that God is the only source to which I owe answers. This newfound freedom and mind-set have allowed me to exhale for the first time.

With increased vision comes clarity about the neverending quest for perfection. I now know that perfection in human form does not exist. Whether we are striving for this imaginary goal in our outward presentation to the world, in our work, and even in our relationships, it will never happen. The cost of the pursuit of perfection is fatality. I want you to see me fall on my face and get up again. I need you to know that I was wounded deeply, and yet somehow, I am determined to get back up again. I've uncovered my most profound insecurities, uncertainties, and unforgettable moments of defeat. Through it all, I got back up again. This same power lies within you. In my heart, I believe that if I show you some of my darkness, you will discover your light.

I have also been fortunate to discover my own sources of light. Light for me lives in the countless souls who didn't allow me to take this journey alone. My support system was and still is top tier. From my parents and family and friends to the little guy that stole my heart—my son, Tarique. There were so many mistakes I made with him that forced me to pray for redemption, and then one day it arrived in the form of a beautiful granddaughter, Blair. The documentation of my trial-and-error moments are here in this book so she does not have to experience them all herself. It is with the greatest intention of my heart that I endeavor to walk alongside her as she navigates the landscape of her own life. She will be the fruit of my labor—she is my legacy.

––––––

I'm sure you've heard it said before, but this phrase is worth repeating: I don't look like what I've been through. While on the front lines, fighting for justice, I still managed to discover love, and moments of happiness, to dress, fly, while taking tips from my girlfriends Jennifer Williams and Candice Grace on how to put things together. My grandmother always taught us that no matter how awful we felt, it was in our best interest to get dressed up and put on some lipstick before leaving the house, and I've done just that. I have cooked delectable meals and cleaned to my heart's desire (I've driven a few people crazy with how much I love to clean). I took long drives with my hair blowing in the wind. I have traveled the world and received numerous awards—too many to name, all of which I count as a blessing. I've endured moments of bellyaching laughter while being the jokester of the bunch, sandwiched between two families who are known as the definition of a good time. As the kids say—I have *lived my best life*. My plan moving forward is to live even better. I was born fighting for freedom and I will die fighting for freedom—but this time freedom will include me. My story is proof that overcoming is our birthright. There are yet new chapters of my life to be written. What didn't kill me has made me stronger. This book is proof that I lived to tell the story.

ACKNOWLEDGMENTS

In the words of the great philosopher Snoop Dogg . . .

I want to thank me for believing in me. I want to thank me for doing all this hard work. I wanna thank me for having no days off. I wanna thank me for never quitting. I wanna thank me for always being a giver and trying to give more than I receive. I wanna thank me for trying to do more right than wrong. I wanna thank me for being me at all times. *Tamika—you really are that girl.*

And yet, while I am that girl, make no mistake—GOD is greater. He is the Alpha and the Omega of my life, the source of my strength and the heartbeat of everything I do. Nothing in my world moves without His divine hand guiding it all.

To my brother and the person I love to debate the most—Lenard McKelvey, aka Charlamagne—this book is here because of you. You created a space and gave me a life-changing opportunity. I am eternally appreciative.

To the greatest publishing team in the game—Black Privilege Publishing and my entire Simon & Schuster family—thank you for supporting my vision. Nicholas—you truly believed in my story and allowed me to document my truth. Thank you, Libby and Shida and Maudee and Karlyn and Abby and Hannah, for all you've done for me. You all are the real MVPs.

Marc Gerald and Ashley Antoinette—thank you for being the engines behind this project. You saw the impact my story could have even before it materialized on the pages. I couldn't have asked for better book agents as partners in this process.

Ardre—Whew, what a ride! Two years of writing, crying, laughing, and praying together. We didn't just write a book; we birthed a piece of history. I'm so proud of what we've created and even more grateful to call you my friend.

LaToya Bond, my manager and sister—We made it happen *again*! We've set a new standard, and history has been made. Thank you for rocking with me every step of the way.

To my Until Freedom family—I can't imagine a world without you. Mysonne Linen and Angelo Pinto, Esq.,—you have been with me through such crucial moments outlined in this book. We've walked through the fire together, but we also created a space filled with love and support. Linda, we've cried tears no one will ever see, but we've also shared moments when we laughed until we couldn't breathe. That's my favorite part of our sisterhood. We always rise no matter what life throws our way. Monique Idlett, our dedicated board chair and my confidante, Until Freedom started in your living room as a dream. I hope you are proud of us as you watch the organization continue to grow. Jaime Perrington and Julianne Hoffenberg, thank you for holding it down and piecing together the puzzle of our work. Your dedication keeps the wheels turning, and I am beyond grateful for the two of you. I am because WE ARE.

My love and deepest gratitude to my extended family—Breewayy, Justice League NYC, United Justice Coalition, Black Church PAC, Mobilize Justice, Woke Vote, Atlas Group, Faith for Black Lives, Win With Black Women, Glossy Posse, the Black Effect Podcast Network—Dollie Bishop, Shanelle Collins, Taylor Hayes, and Ihaku Ngokwey—and the TMI Podcast team—Cathleen Trigg, Janice Rodriguez, and Latisha Elmes—the memories we created building the podcasts together will forever hold a special place in my heart.

To all the families I have had the honor of serving throughout my career, you all have my heart. Since the summer of 2020, I've been blessed to forge more beautiful, lifelong bonds. Through unspeakable tragedy, the families of Ahmaud Arbery, Breonna Taylor, George Floyd, and Shanquella Robinson have welcomed me with such open arms. I am blessed to be able to stand with you and to fight alongside you. May we continue healing together. May our pursuit of justice never waver.

To all my people—my friends, my mentees—there are too many of you to name. Know that you are cherished and beloved. My glam squad, Alysha and Tatiana, thank you for waking up in the middle of the night or not going to sleep at all sometimes, to make sure I look and feel my best before those 6:00 a.m. flights. ALL OF YOU have been with me through some tough times. The way you show up for me and care about me is everything. You all bring me indescribable joy.

To my cornerstones—Hazel N. Dukes and Cora M. Barry, there are times when I can't see the next minute, let alone the rest of my life. You have greeted me in the wilderness and guided me back toward the light so many times. Thank you for giving me way more than I could ever give back.

To my sisters—Alpha Kappa Alpha Sorority, Inc., especially the Pzi Zeta Omega chapter, in addition to the Metro Manhattan Links—you are my tribe. The bonds that tie us together make me stronger. Thank you for affirming me.

To my family—Not even the phrase "blessed and highly favored" can capture the depth of love you've shown me. You raised me and supported me with unyielding care. You all have held me up with your strength and you have kept me grounded with your honesty. You have been my foundation. Your hands and hugs have healed my soul, and your hearts have made me whole. To my siblings, aunts, uncles, nieces, nephews, cousins, and lifelong family friends—know that you are seen, cherished, and deeply loved.

To Mom and Dad—There is no me without you. The very thought of your steadfast love moves me to tears. I know it must have been painful to relive parts of my story, but I pray you feel proud of where I am today. You gave me your blessing and permission to serve, in an effort to make the world a better place, and yet my world is as good as it can ever be because I was born with both of you in it. Just, THANK YOU!

Tarique, Niyah, and Blair, you are my connections to time and space. You are my sunshine after the rain. My outlook on life is filled with abundance because of you. Your faces are my reminders that I am alive. And every day that I am blessed to open my eyes, I consider you—hope for you—pray for you, with the deepest sincerity of my heart. I take great pride in knowing that should there be a time when I'm not covering you—God is covering all of us. His blessings, mercy, and favor are the ultimate prize. Always remember to keep God and family first.

To everyone out there getting into *good trouble*—To every activist, all the community violence intervention experts, every supporter, every person who argues on my behalf in the comments section, and most important, to every soul who has ever lifted a prayer in my name—I give you my deepest love and gratitude. You are the wind at my back.

And while I know there will come a day when I look back at these pages and remember names I should have included, charge it to my head and not my heart.

If you are reading this, know I thank you from the bottom of my soul.

ABOUT THE AUTHOR

Tamika D. Mallory is a trailblazing social justice leader, movement strategist, globally recognized civil rights activist, co-founder of Until Freedom and the historic Women's March, and author of *I Lived to Tell the Story* and *State of Emergency*. She served as the youngest ever executive director of National Action Network. Her speech in the wake of the murder of George Floyd in Minneapolis, Minnesota—titled "State of Emergency"—was dubbed "the speech of a generation" by ABC News. Mallory is an expert in the areas of gun violence prevention, criminal justice reform, and grassroots organizing.